SOCIOLOGICAL WONDERMENT

The Puzzles Of Social Life

Paul Higgins
University of South Carolina

Roxbury Publishing Company

NOTE TO INSTRUCTORS: A brief Instructor's Resource Guide is available.

Library of Congress Cataloging-in-Publication Data

Higgins, Paul.
  Sociological wonderment: the puzzles of social life/Paul Higgins.
  p. cm.
  Includes bibliography references and index.
  ISBN 0-935732-55-1
  1. Sociology.   I. Title.
  HM51.H54 1994   93-46596
  301—dc20   CIP

SOCIOLOGICAL WONDERMENT:
THE PUZZLES OF SOCIAL LIFE

Publisher and Editor: Claude Teweles
Copy Editors: Anton Diether, Sacha A. Howells,
  and Dawn VanDercreek
Cover Design: Allan Miller & Associates, San Diego,California
Typography: Synergistic Data Systems, Pasadena, California

Printed on acid-free paper in the United States of America

ISBN 0-935732-55-1

ROXBURY PUBLISHING COMPANY
P.O. Box 491044
Los Angeles, California 90049-9044
(213) 653-1068

With love, to Leigh and our children,

Samantha and Cole.

What a joy it is to live and act together with them!

Acknowledgments

Social life is produced through the efforts of people, not just a single individual. So too are books, even for a sole author. I would like to acknowledge and express my appreciation to Claude Teweles of Roxbury Publishing Company for his support of my work; Anton Diether for his editing; Peter Adler, Jeanne Ballentine, Patrick Donnelly, Isaac Eberstein, Conrad Kanagy, Jack Niemonen, Frank Scarpitti, and Richard Wright for their reading and commenting on an earlier version of this book. Thanks.

Students in several introductory sociology classes read partial or entire earlier versions of this book. How they worked with the earlier versions and with the ideas contained within them helped me to improve this work. My thanks to all of you as well.

The Department of Sociology, University of South Carolina, has always supported my work. In particular, the assistance of Fay Gage and Yoriyasu Maeda is highly appreciated. Woody Carlson and Shelley Smith, two of my colleagues in the department, called my attention to and reminded me of some very good sociological ideas. Again, my thanks to all of you.

Without the wonderful work of social scientists, I could not have written this book. I hope the many citations therein reflect my debt to their accomplishments. As a special mention, I would like to acknowledge Randall Collins' delightful work, *Sociological Insight*, for its contribution to Chapter Four. I don't know what Dr. Collins would say about my references to his work, but I found it very insightful.

Finally, Chuck Tucker and Bob Stewart have been my colleagues for more than 15 years. We have encouraged one another in our teaching and research on social life. I know that I would not have been able to write this book without our many discussions. In the past several years, Chuck has enlightened me on the work that he and others in the Control Systems Group, a scholarly association, are doing to explore the seemingly simple but profoundly significant idea that people direct themselves. I have drawn upon his insights and some of the work he has brought to my attention primarily in Chapter Four. He has also read and commented on an earlier version of this book. Thanks, Chuck.

More than any colleague, Bob Stewart has enabled me to see that social life is puzzling. How *do* we live and interact together? Our discussions and his profound work in progress, *Living and Acting Together*, have enabled me to explore and teach more usefully about social life. I have drawn significantly from this work in progress for *Sociological Wonderment*, particularly in Chapters Two and Three. Now and again,

I have even used a variation of that wonderful phrase of his, "living and acting together." I trust that the citations to his work do justice to my debt to it. Yet, the understanding that I have developed out of our discussions on social life for more than 15 years cannot be easily acknowledged by citations. Thanks, Bob.

About the Author

Paul Higgins grew up outside of Washington, D.C., in a family of five children, of which he is a triplet. His parents, both deaf, taught at Gallaudet University, a university for deaf men and women, located in the nation's capital. Before attending graduate school in sociology at Northwestern University, Dr. Higgins taught one year at a state school in Maine that educates deaf children. A professor of sociology at the University of South Carolina, he now lives in Columbia, South Carolina, with his wife Leigh and their two children, Cole and Samantha.

Paul Higgins has primarily researched and written about disability. His most recent work was *Making Disability: Exploring the Social Transformation of Human Variation*. Please send any comments or suggestions about *Sociological Wonderment* to him at the Department of Sociology, University of South Carolina, Columbia, South Carolina 29208.

TABLE OF CONTENTS

Social life is everywhere, so it must be natural...or is it? Does anything guarantee "successful" social life? If not, then how can we make sense of it? Human nature, desires, and personalities—three common explanations—may not be very satisfactory.

We all try to make sense of our lives and worlds. Yet how can we know that what we claim to be is really so? How can we know when we have developed knowledge—and not nonsense? Supernatural, objective, and constructive knowing are three attempts at understanding ourselves.

The world appears familiar to us. But if it is, then how can it be that some people are one of three "sexes," others "change" their race, and still others have many "selves"? How do we create and recreate our world?

Can we, with the right approach, make people do what we want? In a sense, this is a frightening thought—but is it true? If nothing makes people act, then how can we get people to do what we want? And what are the conflicts we create when we attempt to control others?

The world is troubled, perhaps more so than ever before. Or is it? Through social inventions and other means, we have revolutionized the world in the space of a few centuries. Yet in doing so, we have created unprecedented new challenges for ourselves.

We create social life. This is a seemingly simple statement. Yet many people overlook or deny their responsibility for creating social life. *"That's just how it is." "I didn't have the time." "I couldn't do otherwise." "It was just fate or a divine spirit."* Yet we *are* responsible for the wondrous and sometimes horrific social life that we possess.

Prologue

Once the world was mysterious. People were amazed about their world; they approached it with awe. To make sense of what was mysterious, they developed a fantastical understanding of it. Spirits populated their world, transforming from animals to people and back again. Gods moved mountains and hurled thunderbolts. Good and evil battled in the heavens and on earth. People became possessed. *What might happen next?* they wondered.

The world today is becoming humdrum for most of us. Science has offered more satisfactory explanations for the natural and physical worlds. While those worlds are still wondrous to scientists, they are not to many of us. We often take them for granted. We may not understand much about physics, chemistry, or biology, but we do not worry a lot about them. We let scientists discover the world and inventors and engineers supply us with the technology that develops out of those discoveries. *What will they think of next?* we wonder, but just for a moment. Then we quickly return to our everyday lives.

It seems to me that we do not wonder much about social life either. We may worry a great deal about *our* lives, but how curious are we about how we live and act together? We worry about our relationships with families and friends. We become anguished when those we love seem not to return our love. We worry about our grades, our jobs, our future, and much more. But personal worry is not sociological wonder.

Many of us are titillated by the private misery made public on televised talk shows. We may be momentarily intrigued about how those people could do *that*—whatever "that" happens to be on today's program. Then, with a click of the dial, we simply turn off our curiosity.

Have you wondered much about social life, about how people live and interact with one another? Most of us do not live in isolation. We work, play, love, and live in so many ways with each other. From a two-person conversation to the complex interactions in societies of hundreds of millions of people, we live and interact together.

Have you ever considered how we successfully talk with one another and understand each other in a conversation? Are we pleased by the end of it? Many times we don't succeed. Sometimes the results prove tragic.

Have you ever thought about why some groups are effective and others fall apart? In some groups the members work well together on the tasks of their organizations, coordinating their activities and committing their energies to the groups' goals. But in other groups, they just don't "pull together." Some companies succeed, but others go bankrupt. Some student groups grow strong, while others wither away. Some athletic teams become close-knit; others are wracked by dissension.

Have you thought much about how students and professors make a satisfying class, one that comes alive, that intrigues, that challenges—one that you can't wait to get to? Have you ever experienced such a class? I hope you have. But I imagine that you and your professors have also produced classes in which almost none of you wished to participate—and many of you didn't even attend.

In some countries, citizens work and live together satisfactorily. But those in other countries struggle violently with one another. How do you make sense of that? Before answering too quickly, consider how much citizens in your own country have fought with one another. In America during the Civil War, we killed hundreds of thousands of our fellow citizens—and that is only one example of our violent history. Each year we murder tens of thousands of our fellow Americans.

Have you wondered much about intimate relationships? Some soar and others crash miserably. How do people sometimes produce relationships that enrich one another but at other times imprison each other? I believe many of us take social life too much for granted.

By the end of this book, I hope you will wonder more about social life and become more curious about how we live and interact with one another. To use a word that we have made less significant through our slang, social life is *awesome*. I marvel at how we sometimes live and interact gloriously together; yet, I am also seriously concerned about what harms, even what horrors, we produce. In the following pages I invite you to begin to wonder about social life—to find it awesome.

I will not explore all of social life—I don't know enough to do so—but rather five of its fundamental puzzles. By doing so, I hope that you will begin to find social life as puzzling and intriguing as I do. The five puzzles that I will explore are:

1. What is so puzzling about social life?
2. How do we know?
3. How does our world exist?
4. How can we get people to do what we want?
5. In what shape is our social world now and how did it get there?

I hope these five puzzles are already beginning to intrigue you. I will not say too much about them now. To do so would only lessen the enjoyment of wondering about these puzzles.

I believe that you will benefit most from this book if you actively read these pages and wonder about the issues that I explore. Take time to formulate your own ideas. Check them against the ones that I present here. Disagree with my ideas. Discuss them with friends, as do some of the women and men in my classes. And keep wondering.

Consider this, for example. Worldwide, people donate billions of dollars and hours, their own organs, and even give up their lives to help one another. Yet, they also take the lives of hundreds of thousands, perhaps millions, of people each year. How can you and I make sense of that? Would you ever, voluntarily, physically and seriously hurt others because they made mistakes? Those who would must be sadistic, brutal people. You and I would never do that, right? Or would we?

As another example, how do you successfully end a conversation? If your answer is, "I just stop talking," you might want to think again. In Chapter One, I hope you will begin to wonder about what is so puzzling about social life.

When talking with others, how do you know that you have understood them? It's obvious, isn't it? You "just know." But do you? When my two-year-old daughter tells me something with her child-like pronunciation, how do I know that I understood her? Okay, it may be difficult to grasp the words of a little child, but not those of an adult. Really? How do you know that you have fully understood your professors? Have you ever thought you did, only to learn later that you did not?

Have you ever served on a jury? I have, once even as a jury foreman (or foreperson). If you ever get the chance, I urge you to take it. It can be a wonderful—and sometimes profoundly troubling—experience. The two juries on which I served ended as "hung juries." We did not reach a verdict in one case in which a defendant was charged with possession of an illegal drug, nor in another in which a driver was charged with failing to stop for a "blue light" (i.e., a police car's blue flasher that signaled the driver to pull over). How do we, the members of a jury, know whether an accused person is guilty or not? Testimony, even eye-witness testimony, may be faulty, contradicted, or recanted. How do we know if we have reached the right verdict?

Whether we are parents of young children, jury members, citizens, or scholars, how can those of us who try to know our worlds be sure that we know anything about them? How do we know? In Chapter Two, I will try to grapple with that puzzle.

Have you ever eaten a cockroach? In many parts of the world they and other insects are considered good to eat. What makes something food? What "race" are you? I imagine that many of you are "white," some are "black," and a smaller proportion are one of a few other races. But not in Brazil. In Brazil, you could be one of hundreds of different races. How much is sixty seconds? It's one minute, right? Time "adds up." But it doesn't everywhere. What sex are you? Male or female, I bet.

Would you take me up on that bet? Sounds like a "sucker's bet," one that I could never lose. Among some people, an individual can be one of *three* sexes. And almost all of us are *many* selves, which may change from one encounter to another. How can this be? In Chapter Three, I will explore some of these aspects of our mysterious world.

Have you ever said, "That made me mad or happy or sad" or "They made me do it"? If you did, what did you mean? Can anything or anyone make you or anybody do anything? Even with a weapon, can anyone *make* us do anything? If not, then how do we get others to do what we want them to do? Parents, teachers, and employers realize that this is a difficult challenge. But we all face it: lovers, friends, colleagues, even presidents and other national leaders. And how we try to get people to do what we want them to do may create conflict. How we try to control one another may create inequality, intergroup conflict, and crime. In Chapter Four, I will investigate the puzzle of how we get others to do what we want them to do when we cannot "make" them do anything.

Our world is in trouble. Families are falling apart; schools are failing; our economy is awful; and relationships between one another are disastrous. Just look at the distrust among citizens and the fighting within and between countries. Starvation, AIDS, pollution, and other problems threaten us. Our world appears to be in terrible shape. But is it? Compared to what? Do you yearn for a return to the "good old days"? When were they? Though we have revolutionized our world through inventions, are these inventions just technological ones? Even as we dramatically change our world, do we create new challenges for ourselves? Where are we, and how did we get here? I will take that up in Chapter Five.

I believe that a common theme runs through all of these puzzles. In the Epilogue, I will focus on it: that we are all responsible for social life. That may seem obvious, but in so many ways we flee from our responsibility. For example, have you ever said to someone, "I'm sorry, I just don't have the time to do it"? Did you not have the time, or did you not *make* the time? To embrace our responsibility is to begin to recognize that social life is indeed awesome. How can you and I create such glorious social life and, at the other times, such horrific social life?

Are you curious about any of the above? Have you begun to wonder about yourself, about living and interacting with others, about social life? If so, then join me on this sociological journey.

But beware: this journey may not be easy for you. It may even be troubling. You may struggle along and wonder whether it is worth the effort. Does this sociological journey lead anywhere? You may think that you have arrived at your destination, that you have finally understood it. But then with the next step you may become lost and wonder what it all means. You may scream, "This makes no sense!" You may give up, deciding that these sociological ideas and whoever believes them are crazy. You may find yourself travelling too far from familiar territory and grow uneasy about where you are heading. You may wish to abandon the journey.

Don't turn back so easily. Too often, when we are bothered by what we confront, we may simply dismiss it as unimportant, nonsensical, or irrelevant. When we do, we do not grow. We stay the same when we avoid what challenges our present understanding. We only grow and learn when we confront, often with difficulty, what we presently cannot do or understand. We only grow when we confront ourselves. I urge you to grapple with these ideas. Take them as seriously as you can. See if you can develop any use out of them. The journey can be an exciting one.

But take my warning of caution seriously. If you journey with me, then your view of the world may never be the same. After all, ideas can be awesome.

Chapter One

What's So Puzzling?

Social life is all around us. Everywhere you look, people live and interact with one another: in stores and on sidewalks; in huge businesses and small bedrooms; in courtrooms and colleges; in homes and homeless shelters; in maternity wards and in the military; on playgrounds and in prisons; throughout the day and late at night; over the telephone and in person; in families; among friends; with colleagues; between lovers; and even between strangers. Social life is natural, right? After all, people live and interact with one another all the time. What's so puzzling about social life? Perhaps the following will puzzle you.

Millions of people donate their blood, organs, time, money, and possessions for the benefit of others whom they often do not know. Americans recently donated more than 3 billion dollars to just one network of charitable organizations. People tutor, provide free medical care and free legal service, visit those who are lonely, take meals to those not easily able to cook for themselves, build houses, serve on public boards and private committees, volunteer for the local fire department, pitch in to help during natural disasters, and much more. They give of themselves to help others.

Yet, throughout the world we kill, maim, batter, and damage millions of people. Since Columbus sailed to the New World (though people had lived here for tens of thousands of years), we have killed about 140 million people in the almost 600 wars that humans have fought (Sivard, 1991). Just during World War II, people killed as many as 55 million individuals—most of them civilians (Chirot, 1986: 165-167). In the more than 125 wars since World War II, combatants have killed about one half million people and have injured more than one million people on the average *each* year (Sivard, 1989). Today, Protestants and Catholics battle one another in Northern Ireland; Jews and Palestinians do so in Israel; Sikhs and Hindus in the Punjab; Iraqis and Kurds in Iraq; Hutu and Watusi in Burundi; Croats, Serbs, and Muslims in what was once Yugoslavia; Armenians and Azerbaijani in the former U.S.S.R.; and many other ethnic and racial groups struggle murderously against one another. (Harris, 1989: 497)

What do you make of the following?

In the United States the police annually record millions of crimes. Children are shot by stray bullets while they play on sidewalks or sleep in their homes. Robbers hold up motorists who are waiting for traffic lights to change. Multinational companies pollute our environment, endanger the health and safety of their workers, defraud consumers, and bilk the government. Accountants embezzle from their clients, doctors defraud their patients and the government, and religious leaders swindle the faithful. Teenagers shoplift merchandise, then throw it away or never use it. Employees steal from their employers and taxpayers cheat the government. And government officials extort kickbacks, snoop on us, and deceive one another and the American public.

But we run into burning buildings, jump into rain-swollen rivers, chase muggers, search for those who are lost, return lost money and other valuables, help stranded motorists, and in many other ways give of ourselves, even risking and sacrificing our lives, to help strangers.

Are you puzzled by the following?

Scores of musicians in an orchestra coordinate their individual talents and playing to produce music that soars, even enraptures. More than 100,000 people, mostly strangers to one another, assemble at a stadium to watch a football game, then depart without anyone being hurt. Without having previously met or seen a picture of each other, two people who live hundreds of miles away from one another rendezvous at an airport, one picking up the other after waiting only a few minutes. As a hurricane approaches, the hundreds of thousands of citizens in its path evacuate without any serious injuries.

But, a husband and a wife "misunderstand" one another about where to dine and ruin the evening. The husband casually replies okay to his wife's question about the family going out for pizza. Yet, when the wife asks if he really wants to go, he explodes that she needs to make up her mind (Tannen, 1986: 20). A hospital staff inadvertently switch two newborns, and the mistake is discovered only years later. Two pedestrians approach one another, shuffle to move out of each other's way, and end up colliding. A prisoner languishes in prison for months after his or her release date as the paperwork goes unprocessed. A son calls the emergency-service phone number to request assistance for his stepmother, who is having difficulty breathing. However, the dispatcher, trying to determine if an emergency exists, delays sending an ambulance while talking, then arguing, with the son about what is wrong with the mother. The mother dies while the delayed ambulance is finally en route. (Whalen, Zimmerman, and Whalen, 1988)

Are you curious about this?

A political party that is trounced in a hotly contested election peacefully relinquishes control of the government; yet, elsewhere only a revolution enables one group of people to wrestle political control from another.

What do you make of this?

Couples celebrate their golden anniversary—50 years of marriage—while approximately 50 percent of present marriages end in divorce. In some cases, two lovers may turn an argument into a deadly quarrel, even though they have previously reconciled and made love.

Can you make sense of this?

Every day millions of parents entrust their young children to strangers—to teachers and child care workers—without incident. Yet, each year almost all American parents hit their young children, one-third hit their teenagers, and parents abuse as many as 7 million children (Straus and Gelles, 1988). However, it is abuse at day-care centers that grabs national attention.

And what about this?

Thousands of people in different companies located throughout the world work to manufacture automobiles that motorists drive for tens of thousands of miles with hopefully little difficulty. Yet, a customer waits months for some furniture to be delivered, and it finally arrives made of the wrong fabric. Or, after waiting in line for 10 minutes at a fast-food restaurant to order your food, then another 10 minutes for the order to be brought to you, you receive the wrong meal.

Or this?

The Soviet Union, once one of the most militarily powerful countries in the world, a country which has most influenced the development of America's foreign policy and defense capabilities since World War II, dissolves into feuding republics after less than a century of existence.

In the United States, one of the wealthiest countries in the world, hundreds of thousands of people live on the streets, sleep on benches and over heating grates, and scrounge from garbage cans. Yet, many restaurants throw away unserved food and companies discard overstocked or slightly damaged goods instead of donating them to the community.

What do you make of this?

> Workers at some factories help management solve the financial diffi-
> culties of their companies, but workers elsewhere strike and sabotage
> the companies for which they work.
>
> Prisoners live orderly and safely within some prisons, but they are
> more likely to die within other prisons than if they are on the streets.
>
> Children learn well in some schools, but those attending others in the
> same school district do poorly; they learn well in some classes, but not
> in others in the same school; and some learn well in a particular class,
> while others in the same class do not. (Wilson, 1989)

How can we make sense of the above examples? They puzzle me. Do
they puzzle you? *What's so puzzling* about them? In this chapter, I will
examine three possible explanations to answer that question: *human
nature*, *wants*, and *kinds of people*. Perhaps social life happens naturally.
Or, perhaps our wants determine social life. If not nature and wants,
then perhaps the kinds of people we are is crucial for social life. I don't
believe that any of these three common responses are as satisfactory
as the idea that we *construct social life* through what we say and do.

By this point, I hope that you are starting to wonder about social
life. But *why should we bother to wonder about social life?* Even if we
do not fully understand how people live and interact together, people
have done so for hundreds of thousands, even millions, of years, if we
include our distant ancestors. I will explain why we may want to wonder
about social life. I will also discuss the *challenge of wondering about
social life*. It isn't easy to wonder about it, but I hope that you will take
up the challenge.

What's So Puzzling?

How can we make sense of the examples that opened this chapter?
They are perplexing to me, even incongruous. We help one another,
literally giving of ourselves; yet we also harm one another, murdering,
battering, and abusing each other. We commit heinous crimes against
many, but act heroically to save others. We successfully interact together, sometimes coordinating the efforts of hundreds of thousands
of people; but we may also fail disastrously trying to talk to just one
other person. We throw away food and other valuable items, while hundreds of thousands of people go homeless. Strangers take care of our
children, but some parents may be harming their own children.

Are you puzzled or confused? That's okay. I am myself. Before reading
further, consider how you might make sense of all the above examples.

You may have responded in various ways. Perhaps you thought about
the above events, were bewildered by them, then ignored them. More

likely, you may have decided that some people are dangerous, deceitful, and to be avoided whenever possible; while others are caring, concerned, and conscientious. Or that perhaps some people are lucky, and others are unlucky. Did you conclude that some people want to get along with one another, while others do not? Maybe you just shrugged your shoulders and decided, *that's life*. You may not understand it, but it will go on anyway. Nevertheless, I hope you will continue to be puzzled.

I believe that the fundamental puzzle of social life is that it *is* puzzling. Sometimes social life is glorious; other times it is horrific. Sometimes we live and interact with one another successfully, and other times we disastrously fail. I think that social life needs to be explained. But how can we make sense of it?

I will present three common explanations for this puzzle. I think many of us are likely to use them, as they are part of what "everyone knows" and what many of us take for granted. I certainly did until I began to explore sociology. The first emphasizes human nature; the second, wants; and the third, the kinds of people we are. These explanations no longer satisfy me. You decide if they satisfy you.

Naturally, Social Life?

Many of us believe that it is only natural to live and interact together. It is human nature to do so. Some observers claim that we are "born with an innate need for close, supportive, and loving relationships" (Harris, 1985: 194). Without continued sustenance from others, we will not survive. We become who we are in the company of others. We live our lives through one another.

Yet, do the earlier examples indicate that our human nature, that the fundamental features that make us human, guarantee that we will live and interact together successfully? Does our nature determine social life? Does it make us socially act in any way? I don't think so.

If our human nature is the same when we sacrifice ourselves for strangers and when we harm our loved ones, then human nature is not a satisfactory explanation for social life. If our human nature is the same when we successfully organize hundreds of thousands to get out of the way of an approaching hurricane, but we fail to get out of each other's way on a sidewalk, then again human nature is not a sufficient explanation for social life. If we have the same human nature when we properly educate some of our children but fail miserably to educate others, then our nature does not determine whether we have done well or poorly. If our human nature has not changed when we fully understand one another in one conversation but tragically misunderstand each other in another, then our nature is not enough to make sense of such contradictory successes and failures.

If we are making our worlds more successfully today than ever, even though we face many challenges in living and interacting together (as I will explore in Chapter Five), our human nature cannot explain such dramatic changes. Our human nature has not fundamentally changed in the past several hundred years, though our social worlds have. Our human nature does not determine our specific *social* life.

Our human nature and genetic inheritance provide us with a tremendous capacity to act. We can act in many ways, but not in all ways. We can jump, but not fly like a bird. We can swim, but not like a fish. We can digest food, but cannot photosynthesize as plants do. We reproduce by joining male sperms with female eggs, typically through sexual intercourse. But we do not reproduce asexually the way that the "parent" organism of some plants and animals becomes an offspring. For example, amoebas fission into two parts and strawberry plants send out shoots that take root and form new plants. We can think unlike any other animal, but not in any imagined way. (Telepathy is still speculation.) Certainly social life would be very different if our human nature were dramatically different. If we photosynthesized, we would not have hunted, gathered, or developed agriculture, all major activities in the changing creation of social life. Can you even imagine what our lives would be like if we asexually reproduced or if we typically lived to be several hundred years old? Our human makeup provides us with a great, but not unlimited, capacity to act (Gould, 1978).

Our human nature provides us with needs that must be met if we are to survive. We must nourish our bodies, and we must reproduce ourselves. It provides us with orientations. For example, most of us are sexually predisposed toward the opposite sex, but not all of us. Yet, sexual predispositions need not lead to biological avoidances. Such avoidances may be socially produced (Harris, 1989: 236-237). But I don't believe our human nature dictates the social life we make.

Our human nature provides us with the capacity to live and act together. We obviously do so, sometimes quite successfully. Our nature also enables us to create social life. We sometimes create social life that is as breathtakingly beautiful as parents and children playing together, or as effective as a collective enterprise overcoming difficulties to produce a product of which it can be proud. Our nature enables us to produce wonderful social life.

But our human nature also enables us to fail miserably, even drastically, in living and interacting together. It provides us with the capacity to create unsatisfying, even oppressive, social life. Consider all the occasions in which you have been involved, from two people in a conversation to a large, organized operation, that went badly. Our human nature provides us with a tremendous capacity to develop either successfully or disastrously our social worlds and our social lives.

Does our human nature make us act in any social way, live and interact together in any way at all, at any time? I don't think so. We also have the capacity to put aside or override what we consider our most basic "needs" or "drives." These basic features of ourselves do not force us to act at the moment in any particular way. When you are thirsty or hungry, do you always immediately get something to eat or drink? Of course not. When you experience sexual arousal, do you always immediately act upon it? Of course not. Some of us override those basic needs completely, such as those who are celibate or practice fasting (Csikszentmihalyi, 1990: 27-28).

Even when you do act to satisfy those needs or that arousal, does human nature dictate what you drink or eat or what you do to satisfy that arousal? Of course, we do act and create social life in order to satisfy our needs. For example, we create many kinds of arrangements for producing food and other sustenance we need to survive, or for producing and raising children. But human nature does not determine specifically what we do to satisfy those needs or even if we will act to satisfy them.

Yet what about a mother's so-called instinct to nurture her baby? Surely that part of our nature determines what we do. But does it? Throughout time, people around the world have killed their young. In hunting and gathering societies, parents perhaps destroy as many as 50 percent of their newborns (Lenski, Lenski and Nolan, 1991: 99). Today, Americans abort hundreds of fetuses for every 1,000 live births (U.S. Bureau of the Census, 1992: 74). Whatever "natural" basis exists for the bonds between parents and their children, it does not make them nurture their young or even guarantee that they will allow them to live (Harris, 1989: 210-214)!

Doesn't it seem odd to you that we sometimes claim that people act in particular ways or make specific social arrangements because human nature makes it so, but then we go to great effort to ensure what nature supposedly has made inevitable (Connell, 1987:79-80)? For example, we may call it natural for mothers to nurture their children, the so-called maternal instinct. Yet, we heavily promote the *duty* of mothers (and increasingly today, fathers) to nurture them. We also emphasize the satisfaction to be received from doing so. From cautionary tales about unmaternal stepmothers to parenting classes to Mother's Day (and Father's Day) to Parents of the Year awards, we emphasize what we also claim to be natural. I think it is a good idea that we do—since we cannot seem to rely on human nature to do it for us!

Our human nature enables us to act gloriously and despicably; to create satisfying social worlds and disastrous ones; to create ways to protect those who are the least powerful, and to send millions of people to their deaths. But it neither guarantees us success nor dooms us to failure. By itself, human nature does not compel us to act socially in any particular way at any given moment.

By now, would you still believe the claim that our human nature determines social life, or that it guarantees that we will successfully live and interact with one another? If not human nature, then what?[1]

Wanting Social Life?

If human nature does not explain social life satisfactorily, then what does? Perhaps our "wants" do. When we want to work, learn, govern, play, and love together successfully, then we do so. But is that so? Are wants enough to satisfactorily explain social life?

If our wants are the key to successful social life, then we must not want to live and interact together. Recall the millions of people we have killed. Keep in mind the millions of crimes that we Americans commit each year. Don't forget that half of all marriages end in divorce. Consider that America is one of the top spenders on schools, yet our schooling is not as successful compared to that in some other countries (Stevenson and Stigler, 1992: 205).

If we really *wanted* to succeed at social life, then we would. But does that make any sense? Do we *want* to produce poor schools, dangerous prisons, conversational misunderstandings, organizations that function badly, conflicts between different ethnic, racial or religious groups, and family turmoil, along with many other difficulties in living and interacting together? I don't think wants will help us satisfactorily make sense of social life.

Certainly we direct ourselves to act in all kinds of ways. As I will explore in Chapter Four, I believe that it is useful to claim that one of our fundamental features is to direct ourselves. Nothing ever makes us do anything, at least almost nothing, as Chapter Four will explain. But we can direct ourselves to act *without* wanting to do so. How often do we go to work, go to school, take up a task, and much more when we do not want to do so?

Some of you may object to this reasoning. True, people may not want very much to go to school or work or do some other activity. But you might argue that people want *enough* to do so, often for less direct reasons. For example, people do not want to be fired, so they show up for work; "wanting enough" is all that matters. But people could call in sick instead of going to work, or they could take annual leave if they have it. They could look for another job. While people may not want to be unemployed, they could act in many other ways. Going to work is just one way to keep themselves employed.

Even when we really want to interact successfully with others or produce some kind of social life, our wants do not help us to understand *how* we live and interact with others. Perhaps this is the key shortcoming of wants as an explanation for social life.

Consider driving. Most of us want to reach our destinations safely. Do you think that, if we left our traffic behavior and control up to our individual wants, we would be very successful? I don't think so. Instead, over the years we have created all kinds of social arrangements in order to enable us to drive safely. We have created traffic laws, departments of highways and public safety, traffic officers and highway patrols, departments of motor vehicles, driver licensing examinations, high school driving courses and private driving schools, all kinds of traffic signals and signs, and much more. Even so, we sometimes cause horrible accidents, even though we did not *want* to do so. Wants do not satisfactorily help us understand how we interact with one another or how we may do so more successfully.

The same shortcoming applies to "reasons." Learning the reasons for *why* people do what they do is not enough to understand *how* people do what they do. I think too often we only ask "Why do we do what we do?" instead of exploring the question, "How do we produce social life?" To produce social life, we usually develop reasons to explain to ourselves and others what we did and why we did it. We try to make sense of our and others' actions. That can be a very important part, but only one part, of living and acting with one another.

Wanting to have a loving family does not produce one. Wanting to create good schools does not educate children. Wanting to govern well does not make it happen. Wants do not explain *how* to accomplish these goals. Wants don't even tell us how to build a house. They are not useful directions for how to perform any social activity, whether done well or poorly. Neither wanting nor even wanting enough is enough to produce successful social life.

Imagine that you are an authority about social life. Members of a family in disarray, management and labor from a company with strife, officials from a congregation in conflict, coaches and players from a team in turmoil, or politicians from an inept government come to you for advice about their difficulties. They want to know how to live, work, manage, and govern more satisfactorily. But the only advice you can offer is, "Want more and try harder."

How does that advice sound to you? It does not seem very helpful to me. But often that is just how we rationalize the successes and failures of social life: those who succeeded wanted it enough; those who failed didn't.

Wouldn't it be more satisfying to offer them directions or suggestions about *how* to live, work, manage, and govern in ways that enable them to act more successfully than to advise them to "want it enough"? I think so. But developing such directions and such useful knowledge can be a tremendous challenge, something I will explore further in the next chapter.

One of the most important challenges in living and interacting with others is how to manage the very different, even incompatible, wants that people may have. The wants of teachers and students, managers and workers, family members, fellow citizens, elected officials, national leaders, and many others who interact with one another may clash, sometimes violently so. How can we manage those conflicting wants so that social life may succeed? I will partly address that issue in Chapter Four.

Our nature provides us with the capacity to interact with others successfully. Our wants provide us with direction. But neither guarantees successful social life. And neither an emphasis on nature nor a reliance on wants satisfactorily explains social life. What then?

Kinds of People, Perhaps?

Perhaps we should focus on the traits and characteristics of individuals. We know that people possess different personalities and develop different patterns of behavior (Ford, 1987: Chapter 3). They vary in how kind, cruel, aggressive, passive, generous, stingy, cool, warm, outgoing, shy, secure, insecure, selfish, honest, and other ways they are. (But wait until Chapter Three—you may not be so sure anymore.)

Perhaps we can explain social life by the kinds of people who behave one way or another. People with certain personalities act differently than those with other characteristics. If we know what kinds of people certain individuals are, then we can make satisfactory sense of the social life they produce. If we know their personalities, then we can understand how they live and interact with one another. Do you really think so?

Let me ask a question that I often ask the students in one of the courses I teach. What kinds of people knowingly and seriously harm others? Don't read ahead yet. Consider first how you would answer, then read on.

Many of my students respond that those who are insecure, emotionally troubled, aggressive, abused as children, or have other flaws are the kinds of people who may knowingly inflict harm. Flawed personalities produce flawed behavior. Are you satisfied with these responses?

Consider the following well-known research conducted by Stanley Milgram (1974). Milgram advertised for volunteers to come to Yale University to participate in an experiment about memory and learning. They were paid less than five dollars to participate. An associate of Milgram, posing as the researcher, explained to each volunteer and a second volunteer—actually another colleague of Milgram posing as a volunteer—that he was conducting an experiment on the effects of punishment on learning. One volunteer would play the role of a "learner," the other a "teacher." Any time the learner made a mistake, the teacher would administer an electrical shock to the learner. The teacher would increase the intensity of the shocks with each mistake. The shocks ranged from 15 to 450 volts, with increments of 15 volts. Shock levels were designated as "slight," "moderate," and "danger: severe shock." Through a rigged drawing, Milgram's colleague was always selected as the learner and the actual volunteer as the teacher who would administer the shocks. (In reality, the fake volunteer never actually experienced any shocks, though the actual volunteer did not know this at the time.) The researcher showed them the equipment, provided a sample real shock to the actual volunteer, then began the experiment.

During the experiment, whenever the learner made an error, the researcher always prodded or encouraged the teacher to shock the mistaken learner if the teacher hesitated to do so. The researcher would tell the reluctant teacher to "please continue," that the "experiment requires that you continue," and other such statements.

Would you have shocked the learner if the learner made a mistake? Would you have increased the shocks up to 450 volts? What do you think most people would have done?

Milgram asked college students, psychiatrists, and middle-class adults these same questions. Everyone replied that they would never shock the learner up to 450 volts. They would stop well before that level. The great majority believed that they would stop before Level 13, labeled "Very Strong Shock." They also believed that most people would stop well before the highest level of shock. Only a tiny percentage of people, not more than 1 or 2 percent, would continue to the highest level of shock, according to these adults.

But what do you think happened in Milgram's research? Many of the volunteers, in some versions of the experiment almost *everyone*, continued to the highest level of shock!

As Milgram developed his procedures, he was dismayed that most everyone continued to the highest level of shock if the learner did not protest. Mild protests from the learner did not dissuade them either. Milgram eventually strengthened the protests.

He conducted many experiments, each differing in various ways. In one experiment, the learner was placed in a separate room from the teacher, who could not see or hear the learner. The learner's answers flashed on a screen. The learner made no vocal protest. At 300 volts the learner pounded on the wall in protest. After 315 volts, the learner stopped pounding and stopped answering. Almost two thirds of the teachers continued to the highest level of shock in this particular experiment. When Milgram introduced voice complaints—the learner groaning, pleading to be let out, refusing to continue and the like, with each complaint tied to particular shock levels—more than 60 percent of the learners still went to the highest level of shock.

Milgram modified the experiments in many ways. In one experiment the learner was in the same room with the teacher. In another the teacher was required to return the learner's hand to a shock plate if the learner took his hand off it. In another experiment the researcher left the room after giving initial instructions, then by telephone directed and encouraged the teacher to shock the learner. In another setup, an "ordinary person" (actually another colleague of Milgram) urged the teacher to continue to shock the mistaken learner. Milgram conducted one experiment at an office in a nearby town instead of at Yale University. And he developed other variations.

How far these ordinary people were willing to go and what percentage of them went to the highest level of shock varied in these different situations, sometimes greatly. For example, when the researcher left the room and continued the experiment by phone, only 20 percent of the volunteers went to the highest level of shock. Many told the researcher that they were raising the level of shock when actually they were not. When the volunteers were given contradictory instructions by two researchers, one telling them to continue and the other telling them to stop, none of the volunteers went to the highest level of shock.

The point here is that these volunteers were ordinary people, like you and me. They had a wide variety of personalities and came from different backgrounds. Yet, depending on the situation and what Milgram and his colleagues did, the participants created a social world in which ordinary people knowingly caused physical harm to others. They often did so with great anguish, even protesting as they went. But they *did* do so. Yet, equally important, the participants also at times created a social world in which few ordinary people knowingly inflicted physical harm on others.

Can we make any satisfactory sense out of Milgram's research by pointing to the personalities of the people who volunteered to be the teachers? I don't think so. I do not believe that we can satisfactorily explain social life by relying on "kinds-of-people" explanations.

We often make sense of what people do by pointing to their traits, characteristics, or the background experiences out of which their personalities presumably developed. We may claim that those who do poorly in school are not hard-working or do not care. Perhaps they come from unsupportive families. Or we blame their teachers for being uncaring. We believe that spouses who stay together are kind and considerate, while those who split up are immature or mixed up. We argue that those who donate money or themselves to charities or community service are generous. We believe that those who succeed in business are assertive and industrious. We think that those who harm others are emotionally disturbed. We "know" that countries in turmoil are populated by "backward" citizens. And so on.

I do not think it is as useful as many of us believe to try to make sense of our successes and failures in social life by pointing to the personalities, characteristics, or traits of people. I do not believe that, by primarily emphasizing differences in people's personalities, we will be able to produce more successful social life. We do recognize that people differ in their personalities. (Though, as I will explore in Chapter Three, who we are may be far more complicated than you think.) People do come from varying backgrounds and they do produce different patterns or styles of personal behavior. But we all have a great capacity to act in many ways, though we do not all have the same capacity. Perhaps we should focus more on what we do to produce social life than on the personalities of people.

Kinds-of-people explanations individualize social life. Instead of examining our actions, arrangements, practices, and policies with one another, these explanations focus only on traits "inside" of people. They fit very well our strong individualism in America. "Pull yourself up by your bootstraps," "rugged individualism," and the "rights of individuals" are three important maxims that speak to that strong individualism. Individualism stresses that whatever people do and become is due to their own individual efforts. It stresses the significance, even the sacredness, of the person as an individual. As many of the women and men whom I teach tell me, "Each of us is different and unique." Individualism is important. But, as I will explore in Chapter Five, people have not always emphasized individualism. Individualism pays much less attention to social life. It downplays the fact that we live in social worlds with others, not as isolated individuals. These social worlds may provide great opportunities and obstacles for us. Individualism forgets that who we become and what we accomplish is forged out of our interactions with others. It does not address the fundamental truth of human existence: we are nothing without others.

Kinds-of-people explanations are comfortable for many of us, because they fit our sense of strong individualism and they shield us from the disturbing behavior of our fellow humans. "Those" kinds of people commit wrong, bad, inappropriate, despicable acts, but you and I do not. We are not those kind of people. When we make such claims, we separate ourselves from others. We put ourselves above them; we are better than them. And we do not entertain the possibility that we have the capacity to act like "those" people.

Kinds-of-people explanations are conservative. In using such explanations, we focus on the traits of people, even their background experiences. We do not examine our present actions, arrangements, practices, and policies through which we produce social life, nor do we explore what we could do differently that may be more successful. Of course, if we benefit from our present social practices and believe that we are doing just fine because of the "kinds of people" we are and the good traits we possess, we may not be very interested in changing those practices.

For example, to people who believe that children in some neighborhoods do poorly in school primarily because they are lazy, uncaring, and disrespectful, it may make little sense to spend more money on the schools in those neighborhoods or to change how the children are being educated. It may make even less sense because to change the kinds of people those children are would be difficult, if not impossible. Why waste money on "those" kinds of children or disrupt the present educational practices to try something different? Better to give the resources to other kinds of children who can benefit from them (Kozol, 1991).

Consider people who believe that women do not advance in businesses as well as men do because they are less aggressive, independent, logical, and ambitious. To those who hold such beliefs, there may be little reason to modify schooling that may educate men and women differently, adopt new hiring and promotion practices in male-dominated organizations, or change taken-for-granted expectations about family responsibilities to improve child-care policies, and so forth. If they focus only on the kinds of people they believe women to be, then they have little reason to examine how we create our social worlds that may favor men.

We often use kinds-of-people explanations to explain social life. Even when we do not generalize over an entire category of people, we too often focus on the specific traits of particular individuals to make sense of what they do and the social worlds they create. I do not believe that such explanations are as useful as we might wish. But you decide.

I don't believe that we can convincingly argue that only those who are a certain kind of person can participate successfully in this or that social world. For example, people with widely varying personalities participate successfully in the sacred worlds of religious worship and in the fun-loving worlds of high-spirited parties with equal fervor. But when they do so, they act very differently in those two contrasting worlds. We all have the capacity to participate in many kinds of social worlds, even if the kind of person we are may be very different. But perhaps we do more than just participate in social worlds. We may also *construct* them.

Constructing Social Life?

If human nature, wants, and kinds of people are not satisfactory enough for understanding social life, then what is? If nature does not guarantee successful social life, if it does not make us act in any way at any particular moment, if wants are not enough for understanding how social life is produced, if a focus on the traits or personalities of people overlooks their capacity to act in many ways, then how can we explain how people live and interact together?

This book is a small start at exploring how we produce social life and how we can learn about it. The following few paragraphs will introduce you to what will come later.

If you attended a party, a business meeting, a football game, a worship service, a court, or any other gathering of people, what would you notice? If you could fly magically around the world and eavesdrop on people, wherever they may be, what would you observe?

You would find people in action, moving themselves about in all kinds of ways. They would be walking, running, standing, sitting, looking in various directions, extending their arms and hands, picking up and putting down, pushing, pulling, and much, much more. Most importantly, they would be talking (or signing if deaf, as my parents are) to others and to themselves.

Perhaps through *what we do*, we produce our social worlds and our social lives. Perhaps we construct social life moment by moment. Through our actions, we make all of social life, from the minutest detail to the grandest spectacle. We make it, maintain it, challenge it, revise it, remake it, and so much more. Through what we do, we produce the web of diverse relationships that we have with others. Through what we do, we live and interact with one another.

But what is it that we do? What do teachers and students do when they produce classes? What do spouses do when they produce marriages? What do the members of a club do when they produce that club? What do we do when we produce social life? To say that teachers teach and students learn is not very useful. In Chapter Three I will present a small description of what some participants do to produce a gynecological exam.

But this seems so ordinary, so humdrum. There's nothing special about this, you might be saying to yourself. Where is the mystery of life here? This isn't the mystery of genes, quarks, or black holes. This is nothing to get excited about. But isn't it? Maybe through what seems to be ordinary behavior—people acting, talking, thinking—we create the most extraordinary social life and the most terrifying! Through our actions, we created a holocaust in which we killed perhaps 6 million or more people. And through our actions, we can create an intimate communion between two people who support each other. Isn't it mysterious how we produce these and the other dramas of social life? It is to me. Perhaps by now it is becoming so to you.

Do you know how sometimes we create loving families, avoid conversational misunderstandings, manage whole organizations, develop stimulating schools, reduce interracial and interethnic strife, produce cohesive societies instead of societies in turmoil, and handle all the other challenges of social life? How do we produce all that and more, especially when nothing guarantees that we will succeed? To deal with the challenges of social life, we need to know how to act and move ourselves with one another successfully. I certainly don't know how to do all this. Do you?

To turn to what we say and do in order to understand how we construct social life does not make social life any less wondrous. Instead, to turn to what we say and do puts the responsibility for living and interacting together where I believe it belongs—on ourselves. But how we do it, there's the wonder!

Consider once again Milgram's troubling research. It is troubling to me because of the deception he used and because he so dramatically showed that we do indeed have the capacity to act horrifically. What did Milgram, his colleagues, *and* ordinary people who participated in the research say and do that enabled the volunteers to shock others?

Milgram conducted much of his research at Yale University, an institution that commands great respect. The participants drew on that respect. They also drew on the respect for science that we have developed over centuries, especially in Western society. Milgram's experimenters were dressed as scientists, and the volunteers took the research to be serious. The experimenters used props and staging to create a physical location. The researcher asked the volunteers to apply initially "mild" shocks and only gradually increase them. As mentioned above, the researcher reminded the volunteers of the necessity of continuing to administer the shocks and prodded them to do so. Some volunteers asked if the learner would permanently suffer from the shocks. The researcher assured them that the learner would suffer no "permanent tissue damage." Others asked who would take responsibility for the experiment. The researcher replied that he would. Some volunteers reasoned that the learners must be stubborn or in some other way have brought the shocks upon themselves. They provided reasons for or interpretations of what they did. This is an important part of producing social life, as I mentioned earlier.

Milgram, his associates, and the volunteers created a dynamic social world, one in which many ordinary people shocked others. But at times it also became a social world in which some ordinary people did not shock others (Miller, 1986).

I hope you have begun to wonder about how to make sense of this troubling research. You might care to read Milgram's account or Dan Miller's analysis (1986). Chapters Three and Four might also be helpful. While I do not take up Milgram's research in those chapters, some of the ideas I will explore may help you continue to wonder about how Milgram and the other participants produced a "shocking" social world.

Why Bother to Wonder About Social Life?

Are you wondering more now how we produce social life, how we live and interact with one another? Perhaps your head is aching. Maybe you are not so comfortably sure about social life anymore.

Why should we bother to wonder at all about social life? It will be difficult to do so, even troubling to some people. Is it really necessary? After all, people have succeeded in living and interacting together for hundreds of thousands of years, several million if we date back to our earliest ancestors. During almost all that time, people were unable to explain very well how they did so. Yet, they did and somehow will continue to make social life. We do not need to know how people do so; luckily, they just do. Does this reasoning satisfy you?

Of course, we do produce some kind of social life. But do we produce social life that we find satisfactory? Do we produce social worlds in which we can all meaningfully participate? Do we live and interact together in ways that enhance us and do not demean us?

If you believe that we cannot improve how we live and interact together, then don't wonder about social life. You will be wasting your time. But if you believe that we might improve it, even a little, even for just a moment between a few people, then continue to wonder with me how we produce it. Out of our wondering, we may produce more satisfying social life.

Consider the natural world. For much of human history, people have had relatively little useful understanding of it—at least according to our present pool of knowledge. However, the natural world continued in spite of our ancestors' ignorance. And our ancestors more or less made their way through it. But not always. All kinds of difficulties and disasters befell them—volcanoes, hurricanes, tornadoes, droughts, famines, diseases, plagues, illnesses, and the like. People often perished. For example, the Black Death in Europe from 1350 to 1450 killed about one fourth of the population—20 million people (McEvedy and Jones, 1978, 1979: 25). Today, with more useful information, we have more ably made our way in the natural world, even though we continue to grapple with diseases, hurricanes, tornadoes, droughts, and other natural phenomena. I think we can reason similarly about the social world.

Throughout history, people have had relatively little explicit understanding about social life, about how they lived and interacted together—at least according to our present knowledge. In spite of their ignorance, our ancestors still managed social life. They banned together to sustain themselves, communicated with one another, raised children, governed themselves, managed relations with outsiders, and much more. However, they often did so with great difficulty and frequent failure. People have long been an endangered species (Stark, 1992: 530), barely able to sustain a small band of from two to four dozen persons in any one group. Today, people are more successful—they create groups of millions and billions of people (see Chapter Five).

But, as the opening examples indicate, people still experience tremendous difficulty in creating and sustaining social life. We continue to endanger ourselves. We war with one another, harm one another, tragically misunderstand one another, abuse one another, unsatisfactorily teach one another, misgovern ourselves, poorly organize ourselves, and on and on. But not always. Sometimes we gloriously succeed. But how do we succeed? If you believe we can create more satisfying social life, then continue to explore its puzzles with me.

The Challenge of Wondering

Wondering about social life can be a challenging experience. That is so for many reasons. As many of us have grown up, adults have tried to drum wonderment out of us. To wonder about social life may pose a challenge to others who tell us what is so. To wonder also makes us uncertain about ourselves and question our world, which can be uncomfortable, even threatening. To wonder about social life requires that we make the familiar strange.

As children we always wondered about the world. We continually asked our parents and others, "Why?" But in the process of becoming competent adult members of our world, many of us simply ceased to wonder. We were also educated out of our wonderment. We were told what, who, when, where, why, and how. We were told what to think, what was so. We were often told "no."

How often are you asked to question how we educate ourselves, govern ourselves, provide justice for ourselves, minister to ourselves, nurture ourselves in families, or live and interact together in other social realms? How often are you asked to question how we create our social worlds and social life? How often are you required to respond in prearranged, set ways, merely repeating what you were told? We must regain the capacity to wonder. To do so may challenge others' attempts to tell us what is so and what must be so. To wonder will challenge the objective, taken-for-granted social world that we create for ourselves (which I will explore in Chapter Three).

Sociological wondering is challenging. To wonder sociologically is to humble ourselves and make ourselves unsure. Most of us realize that we know little about the natural world—about biological life, about the heavens, about atomic and subatomic matter. But so often we consider ourselves very knowledgeable about people and social life. After all, we participate with many people in many activities. Indeed, we are the stars of social life, and we take it for granted that we know a great deal about it. But how often do we question that knowledge?

To sociologically wonder is fundamentally to question ourselves and our understandings about our world. To do so can be quite threatening. We may lose what we took to be familiar, to be obvious. With what understanding will we replace what we now question?

To wonder is to make the familiar strange. That can be very difficult when the familiar seems so obvious.

A classic example of this is Horace Miner's (1956) description of body rituals among the Nacirema. Miner has described the Nacirema's great emphasis on the body and their concern with its appearance. They spend much of their resources and time on the body, trying to enhance it and keep it from deteriorating. The Nacirema have shrines within their homes, where through ritual and ceremony they attempt to ward off the degeneration of the body. The more powerful members may have half a dozen shrines. After children are initiated into these rituals, the rituals are carried out in secret. The focal point of the shrine is a "charm box" on the wall within which are various mysterious potions that the Nacirema use to ward off the many maladies that afflict the body.

Beneath this box is a font where "each day every member of the family, in succession, enters the shrine room, bows his (or her) head before the charm box, mingles different sorts of holy water in the font, and proceeds with a brief rite of ablution." The Nacirema have an "almost pathological horror of and fascination with the mouth, the condition of which is believed to have a supernatural influence on all social relationships." They believe that the quality of one's mouth is related to one's moral quality. Without the many mouth rituals practiced by the Nacirema, they believe that friends would leave them and their loved ones would reject them (Miner, 1956: 504).

The Nacirema have many other strange beliefs and practices concerning their bodies. For example, they believe that parents, particularly mothers, can bewitch their children. If people become bewitched, they can visit a special witch-doctor, a "listener" who listens as the cursed individuals tell all their troubles and fears. The Nacirema are embarrassed when they talk about sexual intercourse, which is often scheduled by couples. They seem to be fixated on the size of the female's mammary glands. Some females with large mammary glands make money by traveling from village to village where the villagers pay to stare at them.

Are you curious about who these Nacirema are? The word spelled backwards is "American." That's right, Americans! Miner has momentarily made these and other familiar practices of Americans strange (Miner, 1956). He has charmingly and disarmingly encouraged us to stand outside our taken-for-granted way of life and wonder about it. But by doing so, he may have also threatened our comfortable social world.

Consider this depiction of a common event with which most of us are familiar. Each year as the fall harvest approaches, thousands of people assemble weekly at large temples for sacred, yet orgiastic ceremonies. To prepare for the ceremonies, many of them imbibe large amounts of potent brew that is forbidden within the temples. During the ceremonies, the worshippers holler, curse, chant, clap their hands together, slap the hands of nearby participants, and sometimes moan until they slump to the ground in exhaustion or ecstasy. Chant-leaders raise the assembled masses' emotions to a feverish crescendo. The focus of the worshippers' attention is young, male warriors who knock one another about as they move a sacred object about the floor of the temple. Some of the warriors collide so violently with one another that they break each other's bones. The warriors' elders rant and rave throughout the ceremony.

Do these events that surround college football begin to seem a little like an odd tribal ritual? Miner's charming piece and my less accomplished example encourage us to wonder about the ordinary, the commonplace. I sometimes ask the men and women in one of my classes to try to create their own Miner-like description of some social activity with which they are familiar. It can be hard to do. Some write about eating meals, working out at a health spa, playing a sport, driving, watching television with others, and other social activities. Why don't you try it? If you do, you may begin to develop a very different, perhaps uncomfortable, view of your social world.

Nothing but Talk

Consider conversations. They're certainly ordinary enough. We all converse, usually successfully, but not always. But most of us cannot explain very well what we do to converse successfully. For example, to have a conversation we need to start one. How do we do that? Merely starting to talk in the presence of others is not the easiest way to begin a conversation. Try it yourself. While in people's presence begin to talk about some matter. For example, you might start with "I saw an interesting movie the other day . . . " Instead of smoothly beginning the conversation, you have likely created some uncertainty about what you are doing and to whom. That confusion will need to be straightened out before any conversation can proceed. Instead, we need to summon whomever we want to talk to and draw the person's attention. But how do we do that? Addressing them by name is one way, but not the only way. Getting people's attention can be quite difficult, as the homeless know too well. So do parents, teachers, reporters at presidential news conferences, and many others. To get people's attention we must interrupt whatever they are doing. That can be very risky and tricky. And that is just the beginning (Schlegoff, 1968; Wardhaugh, 1985).

How about ending a conversation? Do we just stop talking? Try that next time you are talking with someone. Stop talking after a few minutes of a conversation, even in the middle of a sentence, and leave. How successful do you think you will be at ending the conversation? Of course, that is absurd. To just stop talking in the middle of a sentence will not work. Instead, try to stop talking at the end of a sentence, or better yet at the end of a thought, and leave. That will not work too well either. Try saying "good-bye," too. That too will not work very well. Normally, this is not all we do to end conversations satisfactorily. We may not only end a conversation, we may jeopardize a friendship.

Actually, neither party to a two-person conversation satisfactorily ends it by himself or herself. Both parties "converse to a close" when they care not to offend each other. They stop an activity that both have mutually committed themselves to doing. The challenge is to end the joint activity so that neither person feels slighted. That is not easy to do, something that social scientists have begun to explore (Schlegoff and Sacks, 1973; Wardhaugh, 1985). You might read what they have written.

This last point may be surprising because we common-sensically think that one party ends a conversation. But if we consider the idea of social life and of living and interacting *together* seriously, then it should not surprise us. Social life is accomplished through *our* actions, not merely yours or mine.

Conversations, which seem so simple, are quite complex. But why should we worry about how we talk? Even if we cannot explain well how we converse, most of the time we do so successfully. But many times we fail. Parents and children miscommunicate. So do doctors and patients, teachers and students, lovers, friends, even enemies, and many others. Sometimes the failure is tragic, as happens when doctors, who control conversations with patients by their questioning practices, interruptions, and management of topics, misdiagnose serious illnesses (Paget, 1990). Remember the son who called for an ambulance because his mother had difficulty breathing? While the son and the dispatcher argued about whether an ambulance should be sent, the mother died. How could such a tragedy occur?

When police and fire departments are called, dispatchers screen calls to determine if assistance is warranted and, if so, what kind. The mere request for service, as if it were for the delivery of a pizza, is not grounds enough for providing emergency service. Unfortunately, the son who called because his mother had difficulty breathing seemed to assume that his request for an ambulance was sufficient reason for dispatching the ambulance. When the emergency service operator and then a nurse-dispatcher asked him about the condition of his mother, the son understandably became exasperated. He knew that his mother's difficulty in breathing was an emergency, and the questioning was simply delaying the dispatch of the ambulance. However, the nurse-dispatcher did not know what was happening. The son's impatient cursing and "uncooperative" responses to questions (such as replying, when asked what the problem was, that if he knew what the problem was he would not have needed to call) became the focus of the conversation instead of his request for an ambulance. Through that difficulty and others, the son, the nurse-dispatcher, and other officials involved in the conversation created a tragedy (Whalen, Zimmerman, and Whalen, 1988).

However, they created a tragedy not because they did not *want* to understand one another. To the contrary, they wanted desperately to understand one another. Instead, they failed to pull off the very complex social activity of conversation. We all fail at times to do so, though most of our failures are not so tragic.

Non-obvious Wonderment

When we begin to wonder about social life, we may need to turn our typical view upside down. Too often we take ordinary, satisfactory social life for granted, then wonder why it fails. Perhaps we need to wonder about our ordinary successes, too (Boswell, 1980: 48-49).

For example, many of us might briefly wonder why people commit crimes. Certainly many social scientists have wondered long about that. (Though, as I will briefly explore in Chapter Four, most of our standard explanations may not very useful.) I would wonder *how* people move themselves into crime, not just why. Yet it may be just as useful, perhaps more so, to wonder: how is it that people *don't* commit crimes? To wonder why people commit crimes is to assume that it is natural not to commit crimes and to be law-abiding. But is that so? Observe young children. In their own way they regularly rob and assault each other. Law-abiding behavior is a tremendous social accomplishment. We need to explain it as much as we need to explain unlawful behavior. People "pull both off." They don't just happen. Going even farther, we might want to explore how some behaviors become crimes and others do not. After all, are such behaviors naturally criminal?

We can wonder in a non-obvious way about all aspects of social life. For example, instead of just wondering why people divorce, we might also explore how people remain married. Instead of wondering why students drop out of school, we can also wonder how they continue. Instead of focusing only on why nations war with one another, perhaps we should explore how they produce peace with each other. Instead of examining strife between workers and management, we might wonder how any harmony is created. Instead of asking why some experience difficulty making friends, we might question how anyone makes and keeps friends. Instead of investigating why people produce misunderstandings, we might study how people come to understand one another.

Instead of trying to analyze disruptions in social life, we need to explore the production of social life. What are people doing when they produce social life, whatever it is they are producing, however well or poorly they are producing it?

If you are still puzzled about social life by the time you finish this book, then you and I have succeeded. If you are confident and certain about how we live and interact together, then I at least have failed. To embrace uncertainty is an enormous challenge. Almost all of us flee from it. But by fleeing from uncertainty, we imprison ourselves in our present arrangements. We do not wonder about how we do what we do. We do not wonder whether we could do otherwise. Wondering is the first step toward understanding—and possibly even toward creating—more satisfying social life.

Conclusion

Social life is indeed puzzling. Sometimes we succeed gloriously in living and interacting with one another. Other times we fail disastrously. Common explanations for social life do not satisfy me. Perhaps, by now, they do not satisfy you either.

Human nature provides people with a great capacity to act in many ways. But human nature does not compel people to socially act in any particular way at any given moment. Human nature does not guarantee that people will live and interact together successfully.

People pursue many wants. Those wants are important. But their wants do not explain *how* they produce social life. Even when they want to produce satisfying social life, they may fail to do so. Thus, asking people to try harder may not be very useful advice.

Finally, people may have different personalities. They develop different "styles" of acting. But no matter what their personalities, most people have the capacity to participate in a wide variety of social worlds, where they act in different ways in each world. Thus, our individual traits do not satisfactorily explain social life.

Instead, you and I produce social life. Through what we do, we create social life that either soars triumphantly or crashes tragically. But whether social life soars, crashes, or just hums along, how are we producing it?

I encourage you to start wondering about your social life. What are you and others doing (how are you acting, what are you saying, what sense are you making, etc.) to produce whatever relationships you have with one another, whether in your families, among friends, in your dorms, or elsewhere? What do you and other participants do to create the classrooms and courses in which you spend hours each week? What do you do on your job? With whom? How? What could you and others do differently?

And wonder about the larger worlds—the organizations, the community, society, and this era—in which you live. At times these worlds seem beyond us. They seem so remote, so impervious to what we could do to affect them. But these larger social worlds are made, maintained, challenged, and even changed by ordinary people like you and me. And we can always act differently within them, even if we cannot much change them.

The sociological ideas that I have presented in this chapter and throughout this book may challenge many people's common understandings. How can we know that these ideas are so? How can you know that you have understood these ideas? I think they are difficult. How do those who try to make sense of their worlds know that they have produced knowledge and not nonsense? How can we know? In Chapter Two I will explore this puzzle.

Endnotes

1. Some scholars claim that specific human genes control particular *social* behavior; for example, altruistic behavior or the division of labor by sexes. However, no credible evidence exists (Gould, 1978). Scholars also investigate and debate over human universals: what they are, whether they exist, what kinds do exist, and how to explain them. For example, all people breathe. But if people act *socially* in certain universal ways, then can human nature satisfactorily explain those universals (Brown, 1991)?

Chapter Two

How Do We Know?

We all try to make sense of our worlds. For example, children try to figure out what their parents expect of them. Executives worry about what's wrong with their slumping businesses. Coaches ponder over why their teams are doing better than they expected. Parents wonder how to raise their children. Community officials investigate how other cities are developing economically so that they can better develop their own community. These children, executives, coaches, parents, and community officials are all trying to know their worlds.

Scientists and scholars try to do likewise. They try to produce knowledge about what concerns them. They make claims about black holes, quarks, cell biology, human physiology, personality development, the behavior of rats and college students, past events, the meaning of poetry and prose, social life, and so forth.

I believe that knowing the world can be very difficult. How can children, executives, coaches, parents, community officials, scientists, and scholars be sure that what they know is so? How can they be sure that what they claim to know is true knowledge and not nonsense? This is the puzzle of social life that I will explore in this chapter.

Let me put the puzzle another way. Imagine that you have been challenged about what you know. Many of us have been. "How do you know?" the skeptic asks you. How do you respond to that challenge? How do you try to convince someone that what you know is so?

I would imagine that you might respond in many ways: someone else told you; you read it someplace; you learned it in school; "everyone knows that"; you "just know it"; you were there; or perhaps some other reasons for how you know what you know. I have used those reasons, too.

But should we be satisfied with these explanations? I don't think so, at least not by themselves. How does the person who told us know? How does the author of what we read know? How do our teachers know?

I am not encouraging you to disbelieve what others tell you, but to wonder how they could know what they know. To claim that "everyone knows it" or that we "just know it" too easily skirts the challenge rather than addresses it. Even the response that we were there does not completely satisfy me. Haven't you at times been in a situation where you did not understand what was happening or disagreed with others about what happened? How can we convincingly prove that we know?

My concern in this chapter is *not* how to produce knowledge or how to research social life or any matter that concerns us. How to create knowledge is a tremendously difficult task, for which scientists and scholars have developed many techniques. Instead, my concern is the concept of knowing itself. What *is* knowing?

In the following pages I will explore some puzzling but helpful ideas about how we know. First, I will illustrate the challenge of knowing by discussing *censuses, courts,* and *conversations.* Knowing is an important and difficult part of each of those social worlds. I will then explore three ways of knowing: *supernatural, objective,* and *constructive.* Many people use all three of them, though each is very different from the other. Finally, I will re-examine the topics of censuses, courts, and conversations with a constructive way of knowing the answers to: *how many people are in a country, did the accused do it,* and *what was said?* To try to know constructively can be very useful, but you will need to decide that for yourself.

Censuses

What is the population of the United States? On April 1, 1990, it was 249,632,692. How do I know? The Census Bureau told me so. How does the Census Bureau know? The Bureau counted. What could be easier than counting? We all learn to count when we are young. But to count the population of a country is an enormous task. It took hundreds of thousands of people, millions of maps, years of preparation, and more than 2 billion dollars to count the population of this country.

The Census Bureau began preparing for the 1990 census in the early 1980s. In 1988, it held a "dress rehearsal"—a full-scale mini-census in several locations representing different types of areas that the Census Bureau would encounter in 1990. The Bureau conducted a massive public service campaign to inform the American people of the 1990 census and to enlist their cooperation.

To enumerate the population, the Census Bureau delivered census questionnaires to approximately 100 million addresses, followed by reminder cards to many of these households. Approximately 200,000 enumerators went into the field visiting more than 30 million households. On the evening of March 20 and the early morning hours of March 21,

1990, enumerators counted the homeless people staying in shelters or on the streets. The Bureau also provided some 40,000 local government jurisdictions the opportunity to review preliminary figures and document any discrepancies that might lead to more follow-up visits. After all that effort, the Census Bureau must have been right. Right?

Wrong. Nobody "in the know" believes that the population of the United States on April 1, 1990 was 249,632,692—not even the Census Bureau itself! The Bureau estimates that it may have missed as many as 6.3 million people, some groups more frequently than others. For example, it believes that it undercounted blacks and Latinos more than it undercounted whites, and that the racial difference in its undercount has increased. As undercounts vary by geographical area, the Bureau undercounted cities, especially those with large percentages of minority groups and immigrants, more often than suburbs. New York City officials have claimed that the Bureau missed almost one million New Yorkers.

The Census Bureau's count is politically important. It can affect the reapportionment of seats in the House of Representatives and the redistricting of states. Billions of federal dollars are distributed based on population. Officials base public policy on the Bureau's counts and other information it provides. Therefore, the census can be a politically charged arena.

Thousands of localities challenged the preliminary figures of the Bureau. More than 50 lawsuits challenged the 1990 figures, and the city of New York filed suit against the Bureau even before the 1990 census was conducted. In other lawsuits, local and state government officials demanded that the Bureau release adjusted figures based on its estimates rather than maintain its original count (Anderson, 1988; Robey, 1989; Passel, 1991; Feeney, 1992). Counting is not as simple as first imagined, is it?

So, what *is* the population of the United States? You may now be tempted to answer, "Nobody really knows!" I would be tempted to agree with you, but I will not. Instead . . . well, let me postpone my own response until the end of this chapter.

Courts

A few years ago, a nominee for the United States Supreme Court was accused by a former employee of sexually harassing her. Later that year, the nephew of a U.S. senator and member of a famous political family stood trial accused of sexually assaulting a woman. Several months later, a former heavyweight boxing champion also went to trial accused of the same thing. Did they do it?

During the hearing and the trials, Americans discussed and argued over the accusations, the accused, and the accusers. They tried to decide who was telling the truth and who was not, wondering what really happened. They speculated about why the women had made the accusations and whether the men had or had not committed the sexual offenses. They made assumptions about truth-telling and how to decide when people are telling the truth.

For example, people used different assumptions about truth in deciding whether the Supreme Court nominee or his accuser was telling the truth. Some believed that, since the former employee was raising charges against the nominee years after the alleged incidents of harassment, she was not telling the truth; and that her accusations were politically motivated. Others believed that, because a black man from impoverished roots was about to hold a high position, these accusations were designed to keep him in particular, and black people in general, "in their place." Still others believed that, because many of the nominee's former employees never complained of any kind of inappropriate behavior on his part (to the contrary, they claimed that he always expected people to act in the most professional manner), the accuser must have been mistaken or lying. On the other hand, many others believed that, because the accuser came from a small-town, religious family, told several people of the nominee's sexual advances years before the hearings, and was a "caring" person, she was telling the truth. Finally, after a nationally televised hearing, the United States Senate voted to confirm the nominee.

In similar fashion, Americans everywhere speculated over who was telling the truth in the other well-publicized cases. After a sensationally publicized trial that was televised throughout the country, the jury found the senator's nephew not guilty. After another heavily publicized trial, the jury found the former boxing champion guilty. But did any of them really do it?

Many Americans concluded that no one will ever know what "really" happened in those sensational cases, except the participants. I find that conclusion appealing, but it is not my sociological conclusion. Again, let me hold off my response until the end of this chapter.

Conversations

When we converse with others or just listen to them speak, how do we know that we have understood them? When my two-year-old daughter says something, how do I know that I have understood her? You may respond that, while understanding young children can be difficult, understanding adults is not. But is that really so? How do you know if you have understood your professors when they discuss quadratic equations, genetics, chemical reactions, the meaning of a particular poem, or other matters? How do you know that you have understood what I have written? You might reply that sometimes it is difficult to know whether one has understood another, but most of the time it is not. I agree. The majority of the time we understand quite well, or we understand well enough. What the other said seems so obvious to us.

But how do we *know* that we understand? If I ask you how you could be sure that you understood what another person said, how would you respond?

Some of you might reply that from *experience* you know what the person has said. I agree that we draw upon our experiences to enable us to understand others, but emphasizing experiences alone is not enough. After all, we do misunderstand even those with whom we have shared the most intimate, prolonged experiences. My wife and I misunderstand each other at times.

Others of you might say that, if we can repeat what the other said, then that is proof enough that we understood. But is it? Repeating doesn't guarantee understanding, though too often that is all we may be expected to do in our education. What words a person speaks and what the person means by them are not necessarily the same. "I could eat a horse" does not mean that I can or will eat a horse. Therefore, repeating spoken words would not be satisfactory evidence of understanding them.

I would imagine that you could provide other arguments for how you know that you have understood another person. I will not explore these any further, but I hope you will begin to wonder how you know that you *do* know what another said.

Conversations are very complicated. You may not realize all the skill and effort it takes to produce a successful conversation. Thankfully, we need not be able to explain all that we do in order to do it, though at times we don't do it very well; the tragic emergency phone call mentioned in the previous chapter is just one example. Nor do we need to understand precisely what others meant in order to converse successfully most of the time.

I believe that we can provide a strong argument to convince others that we have understood what another person has said. We can do so by applying the same argument and evidence that we can and sometimes do use to decide when we know and when we are ignorant. This is a way of knowing that we might wish to use more often. It is *constructive* knowing. We know when we can do. *Knowing is doing.* But what does that mean?

Before I explore constructive knowing, I will examine two other ways of knowing. People have developed many ways of knowing, but here I will explore only three. While I believe that constructive knowing is

useful for social life, you must decide for yourself. Which way of knowing is the "right" way? And how will you know?

Three Ways of Knowing

How do we know? We may know by supplicating divine spirits or by
attempting to enlighten ourselves objectively through observation.
These are two major ways that we know. But we may not be satisfied
with either of these dominant approaches and instead decide that we
can never know what the world "really" is. However, we can develop
useful ways of understanding that address our concerns. The first I will
call *supernatural* knowing; the second, *objective* knowing; and the third,
constructive knowing (Stewart, forthcoming).

Supernatural, objective, and constructive knowing differ greatly
from one another and even conflict with each other. Nevertheless, people often try to know in all three ways. We are not necessarily consistent
in how we know.

Supernatural Knowing

Throughout history, most people have believed that they could not
learn much about how the world worked. Instead, the world was mysterious, awesome, and disorderly. Supernatural forces—spirits and
gods—that existed in their own realm invaded the world of humans
and determined all that happened. If the crops flourished, the spirits
made them do so. If a person caught many fish, then the hook had been
imbued with great supernatural force. If a member of a tribe acted bizar-
rely, then he or she had been afflicted by spirits. When much needed
rain came, the spirits had smiled benignly. People could not know; only
the supernatural spirits could know. To imagine that one could understand was the ultimate act of hubris (Stewart, forthcoming).

People could try to appease the spirits and gods, to seek their favor,
and to avoid their wrath. Through offerings and sacrifices, through
prayer and devotion, they could submit to the them; and the gods and
spirits might reveal their will back to them. However, people did not
always submit to supernatural forces and sometimes even reproached,
threatened, lied to, or tried to outwit the spirits (Harris, 1988: 453).
Such profoundly disrespectful behavior could often bring down the
wrath of the gods.

For example, Eskimo hunters knew that their success was never certain. Though highly skilled and equipped with many ingenious weapons, they believed that unseen spirits could create disaster for them.
Therefore,

> [p]art of each hunter's equipment was his hunting song, a combination
> of chant, prayer, and magic formula that he inherited from his father or

father's brothers or purchased from some famous hunter or shaman. This he would sing under his breath as he prepared himself for the day's activities. Around his neck he wore a little bag filled with tiny animal carvings, bits of claws and fur, pebbles, insects, and other items, each corresponding to some Spirit Helper with whom he maintained a special relationship. In return for protection and hunting success given by his Spirit Helpers, the hunter had to observe certain taboos, refrain from hunting or eating certain species, or avoid trespassing in a particular locale. (Harris, 1988: 455)

People who live in such sophisticated societies as America do not take the supernatural very seriously. A belief in the supernatural is only for those who do not know any better. But is that really so?

On the contrary, supernatural knowing remains strong in America. While Americans may not apply it to as wide a realm as did people who lived hundreds and thousands of years ago, or do those who live today in less technologically sophisticated societies, they still rely on the supernatural. The superstitions used by athletes to stay on the winning side; the general acceptance of good and bad luck; the use of rabbits' feet or the act of knocking on wood; "lucky" items of clothing; and the popular concern over Friday the Thirteenth are everyday examples of appeals to the supernatural. Once on such a Friday, I recall my older daughter teasing me that our family should stay out of the way of our black cat.

Americans believe in a wide variety of supernatural forces. A Gallup poll showed that 11 percent of us believe in ghosts, 10 percent in witches, 29 percent in astrology, 39 percent in devils, and 54 percent in angels (Gallup, 1978). The wife of a recent U.S. President consulted astrologers to plan her husband's schedule, as do many Latin American leaders who rely on seers and psychics (Oppenheimer, 1993). Many Americans consult the stars in making personal and business decisions.

And, far more profoundly, Americans consult their god. Compared to those from other technologically sophisticated societies, Americans are quite religious, despite the complaints of some over the lack of official support for school prayer, the supposed moral decay that suggests this is a godless country, and the like.

More than 1,500 denominations exist in America. Almost two thirds of Americans are official members of a local congregation (Stark, 1992: 418). Nearly 40 percent of Americans report that they attend religious services every week, compared to one in ten in Great Britain, France, and Germany (Caplow, 1991: 66).[1] Almost 90 percent of Americans claim that religion is important to them. More than half have been aware of or influenced by a presence or power outside of their everyday self. Nearly two thirds believe that religion can answer all or most of today's problems (Gallup, 1991). Indeed, a great majority of Americans believe in God.

I don't mean to disparage such religious faith by linking it with the supernatural. Yet, by definition a faith in God is a faith in a power beyond the natural world.

Many Americans claim to know once they understand what their god wishes of them. Their prayers, devotions, and other religious practices are means for learning and submitting to God's will. Almost two thirds of Americans believe that it is essential to follow God's will (Gallup, 1983: 27). To most of them, the Bible is God's direct or inspired revelation (Gallup, 1981: 186). When they consult the scriptures, they are seeking otherworldly wisdom. When they claim that some tragedy is God's will or that some joyous occasion is a blessing from God, they give testimony to their supernatural understanding. When some claim that AIDS is divine retribution for offending God, their judgment attests to the strength of the supernatural in their lives. Cultural clashes in America over prayer in schools, abortion, homosexuality, family values, creationism, and other issues reflect at least partially the abiding belief of many Americans in divine power and unquestionable, sacred truth (Hunter, 1991). Many Americans have faith in supernatural knowing.

Objective Knowing

Nowadays, objective knowing competes with supernatural knowing and, for many people, surpasses it. Starting with Newton, Locke, and other Enlightenment thinkers of the late 1600s and the 1700s and continuing today with the advance of science, people believe that they can objectively know the world—how it "really" is. While in the Enlightenment thinkers' time that idea was considered revolutionary, today many take it for granted.

Objective knowing assumes that the world is an object, independent of us. It is "there," operating as it does, whether we are aware of it or not. The world is orderly. It is neither chaotic, nor inherently mysterious, nor subject to supernatural forces, and certainly not revealed divinely. The world operates according to natural laws. Even what seems to be chaotic—hurricanes, tornadoes, and other mass disturbances—operates according to natural principles. With careful, systematic observation and reasoning, we can discover these natural principles and predict what will happen next (Stewart, forthcoming).

Many of us are aware of some of these natural principles. For example, Newton's law of inertia states: every body continues in its state of rest, or in uniform motion in a straight line, unless it is compelled to change that state by forces impressed upon it (Hewitt, 1985: 45). The first law of thermodynamics, the study of heat and its change to mechanical energy, states: whenever heat is added to a system, it transforms to an equal amount of some other form of energy (Hewitt, 1985: 265). Einstein's famous equation $E = MC^2$ means that energy equals mass times the square of the velocity of light (Hewitt, 1985: 569).

To objective knowers, the world operates according to these and other natural principles. These principles are often expressed in very elaborate mathematical equations, which many of us do find mysterious. Ironically, science can be as mysterious to most of us as the supernatural has been for all of us. But objective knowers believe that their understanding can enable people to live more successfully, in two very different ways:

First, people should not interfere (much) with nature, because to do will upset the natural regularity and working order of nature. Instead, they should try to be in harmony with it or avoid its destructive path. For example, if we can learn to predict the occurrences of storms, then we can better prepare for them. If we know the functions of the body and the composition of plants, animals, and other objects, then we can avoid eating objects that will harm us.

Second, objective knowledge enables people to use the principles of nature to improve their world. For example, with an objective knowledge of plant science, scientists can improve the growth of crops and even develop crops not found in nature. With an objective knowledge of human physiology, biochemistry, genetics, and other areas, scientists can develop medicines and other procedures to assist the body in restoring its health. Objective knowledge empowers people (Stewart, forthcoming).

Many of those concerned with the social world, including the Enlightenment thinkers, also believe that objective knowing is the goal to understanding the affairs of people and social life itself. In the view of objective social knowers, social life is an object that operates and develops according to natural, social principles.

> Sociology is a science, and thus, like other sciences, it assumes natural law. Human beings are part of nature, and they are subject to regularities than can be isolated, understood, and predicted. (Charon, 1992: 21)

Sociology, therefore, is the pursuit of objective knowledge. It is designed "to determine that what we say we have observed actually 'is there' and is not just what we want to see" (Charon, 1991: 18). Many sociologists have heavily emphasized objective knowing. They have tried to follow what they understood to be the stance of the natural sciences in their efforts to achieve success and respect for their work (Douglas, 1976: 2).

However, they admit that trying to develop objective knowledge about social life may be more difficult than doing the same for the natural world. Sociologists are members of their social worlds, their abilities to observe carefully and reason clearly are limited by their involvements with people, by their passions and preconceptions, and by their cultural perceptions.

For example, many Americans in the late 1880s and early 1900s were concerned by the large number of people immigrating to America, as they still are today. Many of these new immigrants came from Southern and Eastern Europe, rather than from England and Northern and Western Europe as had the predecessors of many Americans at that time. They spoke languages different from earlier immigrants and often practiced a different religion, such as Catholicism as opposed to Protestantism. They settled in America's developing cities, boisterous metropolises that seemed to threaten the small-town, rural way of life experienced by most Americans. A prominent sociologist wrote:

> It is fair to say that the blood now being injected into the veins of our people is "subcommon." (Many of these new kinds of immigrants) are hirsute, low-browed, big-faced persons of obviously low mentality. . . . Clearly they belong in skins, in wattled huts at the close of the Great Ice Age.
>
> That the mediterranean peoples are morally below the races of northern Europe is as certain as any social fact. Even when they were dirty, ferocious barbarians, these blonds (northern Europeans) were truthtellers.
>
> The Northerners seem to surpass southern Europeans in innate ethical endowment . . . but they will lose these traits in proportion as they absorb excitable mercurial blood from southern Europe. (Ross, 1914 quoted in Stark, 1992: 307)

Social scientists can be misled by the people about whom they are trying to develop objective knowledge. Their subjects may deceive them by talking and acting in their presence as they believe the scientists want them to, covering up their actions, providing superficial responses, and otherwise distorting their typical behavior when unobserved.

To combat these dangers to objective knowledge, social scientists have developed scientific methods.

> Strict rules tell scientists how to create good theory, how to sample, how to accurately observe, how to control the study so that it focuses only on what they want to study, how to carefully interpret the data, and how to refine theory on the basis of the evidence. Strict guidelines tell scientists how to report to other researchers the way in which an idea was formed, how a test was developed, what was observed, and how the results were interpreted. (Charon, 1992: 19)

For example, when sociologists contact people from a community to interview them, they often try to select a random sample. Through random sampling, every member of the community has an equal chance of being selected. (One way to create a random sample would be to place everyone's name in a hopper, mix them up, then draw ballots.) A random sample of people is more likely to be representative of the entire community from which the sample was drawn. Objective knowers would not want to interview an unrepresentative sample, reflecting only a segment of the populace, if they are to learn anything about the entire community. Doing so could distort their findings. For example, interviewing primarily engineering and pre-med students to learn how much time college students spent on their studies may provide unrepresentative information. Only by carefully following scientific procedures can social scientists try to develop an objective knowledge of social life.

Objective knowers of the social world attempt to develop theories that explain human social behavior, which become the natural principles and laws of social life. They apply to all times and all places, so long as the appropriate conditions for their operation exist. Yet, there are patterns of social behavior that social scientists have discovered but that their powerful theories have not yet explained.

Using the scientific method, objective knowers test their explanations against their observations. Based on their theories, they predict how the world should be. They make observations of the world to check their predictions. When their observations fit their predictions, then they are confident that their theories are appropriate depictions of the world, at least for the present.

Knowing that the social world is complex, objective knowers realize that their theories never completely depict the world. Explanations that seem so promising at one time may later be abandoned as flawed. With perseverance, however, social scientists strive to develop increasingly accurate explanations of the social world.

Sociologists can not now state the patterns, principles, and laws of the social world as precisely as those of scientists about the natural world. Nor do sociologists agree with one another about the adequacy of their theories on human behavior as well as do scientists about their theories on the natural world. The following are a *few* of the patterns and principles that objective sociologists have put forth about the social world:

1. People who are similar to one another according to age, sex, education, and other social characteristics are more likely to interact than those who are dissimilar. This has been called the homophily principle (McPherson, Popielarz, and Drobnic, 1992).

2. The larger is the ratio of the rewards of non-crime to the rewards of crime, the weaker the tendency will be to commit crimes (Wilson and Herrnstein, 1985: 61).

3. When people work together on a task or a job, individuals "perceived as having higher status or ability participate more and are more influential when disagreements occur" (Berger et al., 1992: 843).

4. Religious individuals are less likely than the non-religious to violate norms, but only in communities where the majority of people are actively religious (Stark, 1992: 97).

5. The characteristics of technologically advanced societies have increasingly come to be the characteristics of the world at large (Lenski, Lenski, and Nolan, 1991: 64).

6. Downward law is greater than upward law. That is, legal social control directed by those with higher status toward those with lower status is more likely to occur and to be successfully applied than legal social control directed by those lower in status toward those higher in status. For example, the criminal justice system will punish an offender more severely when the victim is of higher status than the offender than it will when the victim is of lower status than the offender. (Black, 1976: 21).

7. The fortunes (personal and material well-being) and fertility of people proceed according to a self-generating process in which a small generation of people that is relatively prosperous is followed by a large generation that is not so fortunate, which in turn is followed once again by a small generation that prospers. At least this seems to be the case in America since World War II (Easterlin, 1987).

Sociologists have put forth many other principles and patterns of social life, some of which have been expressed in mathematical equations.

Objective knowledge of social life may enable people to live more successfully, claim objective knowers. Yet, some remain cautious. They believe that people should not try too much to intervene in the natural workings of society. Objective knowledge can enable people to refrain from disrupting social life.

Others believe that people can use an objective knowledge of human behavior to improve how the social world works, such as to address poverty, intergroup conflict, deviance, and other social problems (Stewart and Reynolds, 1985; Stewart, forthcoming; Sowell, 1987).

To reduce crime, for example, officials could use an objective knowledge of the principle that the larger the ratio of the rewards of non-crime to the rewards of crime, the weaker the tendency to commit crimes, to increase the rewards for acceptable behavior and increase the costs (i.e., various punishments) for unacceptable behavior.

Those who embrace supernatural knowing, however, often resist attempts to objectively know human behavior and social life, because such attempts seem to make people less special. Instead of being the handiwork of the divine, they argue, people become the inevitable result of just so many human forces and factors.

A student once told me that he believed everyone's life was predetermined, not spiritually, but by all the forces and factors that have influenced our lives up to the present. He's not alone in that belief.

Objective knowers have often dreamed of some "grand formula" that would fully explain the entire world (Lincoln and Guba, 1985: 112-113). If that is how social life works, if it is completely the result of the operation of basic principles, then people are not very special after all. They also do not have much, if any, responsibility for what they do (Kohn, 1993). Does that make sense to you?

Constructive Knowing

Some people try to constructively know the world. They try to create useful statements that enable them and others to manage their concerns more satisfactorily than they were able to do before creating those statements. Constructive knowers concerned about the social world try to create ideas that enable people to live and interact together more satisfactorily than in the past. When we can do what we were unable to do before, then we know constructively. Constructive knowers try to create their knowledge in order to create their worlds more satisfactorily. In that double sense, knowledge is constructive.

To constructive knowers, knowing is *doing*. No matter how hard people have tried to create intriguing or fascinating new ideas, if those ideas do not enable people to act in a way they could not satisfactorily do before, then they have not created knowledge. What they have created may be valuable for academic or other reasons, but it is not knowledge.

Constructive knowing was one response to the failures of objective knowing, particularly those of Enlightenment thinking. Based on objective knowing, people tried to recreate their societies. The French Revolution was perhaps the most dramatic example of one such attempt that ultimately failed. Its original intention was to usher in a natural state of freedom, harmony, and order. Instead, a dark era of tyranny, despair, and disorder reigned for decades. What went wrong?

Some concluded that objective knowing was not possible. How could ordinary citizens imagine that they could understand the world and govern themselves? How could they have the utter gall to usurp both the divine and the divine will of kings? Others concluded that objective knowing was indeed a possible goal to improve society, but the Revolution was premature. Out of a need for more careful, systematic study in order to achieve enlightenment, objective sociology developed.

A third response arose from a group of artists and writers now known as the Romantics. Their response ultimately led to constructive knowing. No matter how hard they tried, they could not know the world independent of themselves or of how they tried to make sense of it in their painting, writing, or composing. Regardless of their efforts to "capture" nature as it "really" was "out there," they could not do so. Out of these disappointments, however, some thinkers developed constructive knowing (Stewart, forthcoming).

Constructive knowers argue that objective knowledge is impossible. No matter what we may do, we cannot understand the world independent of how we experience it and make sense of our experiences. We cannot describe or explain the world as it "really" is, as it exists or operates separate from us. We can never escape our experiences. This is so for both the natural and social worlds, both the world of atoms and the world of people.

When we look, hear, touch, taste, and smell, we typically have sensations. But our sensations are *not* the world "out there." When we look at a star or a person, our looking is not that star or that person. When we listen to a bird chirping or to people talking, our listening is not the sound of the bird or the people—it is our *experience* of them.

We can make some sense of our experiences. We can classify them, count and measure them, manipulate them in various ways, and do much more to them. We can give meaning to our experiences and express that meaning in sophisticated ways, such as the mathematical formulations of physicists and chemists, the scholarly statements of historians, or the everyday conclusions of citizens. Scientists and people do this all the time. But we can never check those experiences or the sense we have made of them against the world as it "really" is, separate from us.

We can compare our experiences with the experiences of others. For example, I could assemble a team of people to observe a class. One of the members could observe from the back of the room, while another could interview the students and the teacher. Yet another could distribute a survey for the students and teachers to fill out. Still another could videotape a class session and watch it many times. And on and on. Through each of these means, the team could develop experiences about the class. Each member of the team could compare her or his experiences against the experiences of the other members. But none of them could check those experiences against the class as it "really" was, independent of their or anyone's experiences.

More importantly to constructive knowers, the team could decide if they have created any statements that would enable them or the members of the class to meet their concerns a little bit better than before. If the team members have done so, then they have constructed knowledge.

For example, imagine that we observe two groups of people in conflict with one another, and we wish to lessen that conflict. Through our observations and our thinking, we decide that groups often create conflict between themselves when they compete against one another for desired goals. Therefore, we develop activities and arrangements through which the groups can cooperate to achieve common goals. If our ideas and actions enable us to reduce that conflict, then we have produced constructive knowledge that has enabled us to create our world a little more satisfactorily.

As it happens, many concerned people have used the idea that competition for goals creates conflict in their attempts to reduce conflict between people of different races, ethnicities, religions, and other social characteristics. For example, educators have used this idea to enable them to educate together students of different races, ethnicities, and other social characteristics, as well as students with and without disabilities (Higgins, 1990: 118). It is a great challenge to teach together children who often live apart, but it can be done.

Constructive knowers do not worry over whether or not the "competition creates conflict" idea is a basic principle of social life or if that is how social life "really" operates. It is enough for them to be able to use it to manage their concerns about intergroup conflict.

Constructive knowers argue similarly about the natural, physical world (see Lincoln and Guba, 1985: Chapter 2). Scientists cannot check their experiences and knowledge against the physical world as it "really" is. However, if the ideas that scientists have created about energy, motion, cells, quarks, black holes, and still more enable them and others to meet their concerns, then that is constructive knowledge. For example, if a law of physics enables scientists to launch rockets to their destinations, then they have produced constructive knowledge from that law.

People have created ideas that are more useful than what others had created in the past. Scientists have created ideas today about the human body that are more useful than the ideas of medieval physiologists who "knew" that the balance of the four humors—blood, phlegm, black bile, and yellow bile—determined people's health and temperament (Conrad and Schneider, 1980). But scientists cannot in any satisfactory way show that their ideas are closer to how the body "really" is than those of medieval physiologists—only how more useful they are.

A Potential Misunderstanding
About 'Experiences'

Whenever I explain constructive knowing to my students, many of them have difficulty understanding it. That is okay. It can be difficult. I continue to grapple with it myself. One of their misunderstandings concerns the emphasis on experiences.

Constructive knowers believe it is useful to assume that a world of rocks, mountains, oceans, stars, people, families, universities, weddings, parties, meetings, contests, and other objects is "there," independent of their experiences of it. It is useful to assume that the world is "there" whether people are looking at it or not, or whether people are even around to look. It is even useful to assume that people's experiences are in some way connected to the world around them that exists independent of them. *But people cannot possibly check those assumptions.*

Constructive knowers claim that people are dependent on their experiences. However, they may create their experiences in very sophisticated ways, develop them with others, tell others about them, train others to create experiences in similar ways, and evaluate how useful is the sense that has been made of the experiences.

Constructive knowers do not need to be directly, personally involved in order to create experiences about what concerns them. For example, it is obvious that one need not be a whale to research whales or to create experiences of whales. Similarly, social scientists do not need to personally participate in the social life that concerns them. They do not need to be a machine operator in a factory to research the factory. They do not need to commit crimes to research criminals. They may personally participate in the social world that concerns them, and some social scientists urge their colleagues to do so, but they do not *need* to do so (Douglas, 1976).

Constructive knowers can create their experiences in many ways: through the use of space telescopes, electron microscopes, particle accelerators, carefully developed surveys, experiments, conversations, and observations. Research is a formal, often very technical and sophisticated way of creating experiences which are typically called "data." It may takes years to learn how to research. Science is a social activity of creating collective experiences. Scientists work together and sometimes in competition with one another to create experiences that are similar for many of them.

Though people are always dependent on their experiences, this does not mean that their experiences are merely their own, confined to each individual. Nor does it mean that their experiences are produced haphazardly or that each person's experiences and what he or she has made of them are equally useful. As many of my students are fond of saying,

"We can each have our own opinion." Certainly we can. But our beliefs, our "opinions," need not be knowledge. We often hold beliefs that create difficulties rather than solve them. But however people produce their experiences, they cannot check those experiences against the world as it "really" is. Of course, they can decide, though at times with great difficulty, if what sense they have made of their experiences is useful.

Critiquing Objective Knowing

Constructive knowing is difficult to understand. To make it clearer, I will now critique objective knowing from the stance of *constructive knowing*. Remember, constructive knowers believe that the aim of objective knowing is not possible. It is not possible to discover the principles that "really" govern social life as those principles supposedly operate outside the realm of people's attempts to make sense of their experiences. To critique objective knowing, I will consider a principle about deviance that some objective knowers believe they have discovered.

Consider the principle that the more socially integrated a community is, the lower its rate of intentional deviance will be. Social integration is the strength of ties that bind together the members of the community. Intentional deviance is objectionable behavior that an offender has planned and calculated, such as burglary (Stark, 1992: 192-197). If social behavior operates according to the above principle, then communities with strong social integration will have lower rates of burglary and other forms of intentional deviance.

But objective knowers did not *discover* this principle as it "really" operates in social life, independent of researchers' attempts to make sense of their experiences. Constructive knowers would argue that *only* social scientists produced that "principle." The key issue is whether the idea is useful, not whether the world "really" operates according to it.

Social scientists created the concepts of social integration and intentional deviance. These concepts do not exist apart from the people who develop and use them. Social scientists could develop them differently or not use them at all, but the world as it "really" is did not tell them what to do. They decided how to observe, measure, and classify communities as having more or less integration, higher or lower rates of intentional deviance. Social life did not. For example, they may decide to use police records for measuring the amount of intentional deviance in communities or to survey residents who report their criminal activity. You may think this latter approach cannot work, but it can be *useful*. The social scientists decided if the information they collected fit their predictions, but social life did not. These scientists produced that principle, but they did not discover it.

Objective knowers who realize they do all of this may reply that they are creating models of how they believe the social world operates, ones that best fit their observations. While they cannot describe the social world as it "really" is, that is the goal that guides their work. Yet, if they concede to this limitation, then they completely undermine their goal.

If objective knowers can no longer describe and explain the world as it "really" is, then how do they decide which observations become the standard against which to check their explanations and models? What makes one set of observations more appropriate than another? Objective knowers may claim to have followed scientific procedures, carefully and completely laying down the correct steps for producing scientifically acceptable results. (Does this seem to you a bit like scientific rituals, not much different from such supernatural ones as the Eskimo's hunting ritual used to appease the spirits?) But what makes those procedures scientifically acceptable? Can objective knowers check those procedures against the world as it "really" is in order to verify them?

No. Instead, they can only reason carefully about their procedures, check them against their experiences, and decide if they are useful. If the procedures enable objective knowers to create useful information—constructive knowledge—then they would be wise to continue to use them. For example, if random samples are more useful than selective samples, then use random samples.

Constructive knowers do not necessarily discard what objective knowers have produced. While they do not believe objective knowledge is possible, they may find some of what it has produced *useful* for meeting their and others' concerns.

For example, if by using the ideas of social integration people can reduce burglary and other deviance without creating more difficulties than are presently experienced, then those ideas are useful. They are constructive knowledge. If by using them, social scientists can make better sense of their research observations concerning deviance, then those ideas are once again constructive knowledge. For example, ideas about social integration and intentional deviance enable social scientists to make some sense of research that indicates that cities with high population turnover (and therefore possibly low social integration) have high rates of known burglary or larceny but not necessarily high rates of homicide, which is not as likely as burglary or larceny to be planned or calculated (Stark, 1992: 192-197).

The most important problems in social life concern how people can live and interact together satisfactorily. However, social scientists may work on problems that do not immediately concern that challenge, such as how to make sense of differing, puzzling, or conflicting research experiences. Addressing such research problems may eventually enable them to handle the more important problems of living and interacting together satisfactorily.

Let's now return to my earlier examples concerning censuses, courts and conversations. How do you think constructive knowers would handle these three problems of knowing? How many people live in the United States? Did the accused do it? What did the other person say? How can we know?

How Many People?

How many people "really" live in the United States? Constructive knowers believe that the question makes little sense. The Census Bureau cannot discover a "real" number that is waiting to be found. Instead, the Bureau *produces* the population figure of the United States by how it counts.[2]

The U.S. Constitution requires a periodic enumeration of the population of the United States in order for the nation to govern itself. From this enumeration come political representation, the distribution of federal money, and perhaps greater or lesser attention to particular populaces and places.

The concerns of politicians, business leaders, community officials, scholars, and others have shaped the course of "population politics" and the production of population figures (Anderson, 1988: 3). Representatives of rural and urban areas, minority groups, and other demographic concerns have often pressured the Congress and the Census Bureau to count more accurately "their" people. Court challenges and court decisions have helped to produce this population count. For example, a U.S. District Court decision, while not addressing the substantive issue of whether illegal aliens should be counted, upheld the Bureau's practice of doing so on procedural grounds.

We cannot ever know the population of the United States apart from what we do to know it. And when we change what we do to know it, we may change what we know the population to be.

In 1790, for example, U.S. marshals with the assistance of approximately 650 appointed assistants traveled to citizens' homes to count the population; hence, America's first census. Today, the Bureau primarily mails census questionnaires to people, uses massive advertising campaigns to increase citizen awareness and willingness to participate, holds "dress rehearsals" in several cities, prints the forms in multiple languages, uses hundreds of thousands of field enumerators to complement the mailings, and does much more to count the population of the United States (Anderson, 1988).

The problem faced in this endeavor is to produce a figure that a diverse range of people and institutions will *accept*. Local and state government officials, community and business leaders, census experts, Congress, the President, representatives from all segments of the country, and the courts—with often differing concerns—must accept the figures. If they do not accept them and cannot address their concerns, then the reports created by the Census Bureau are not constructive. To those who cannot proceed with the population figures, the figures are not knowledge at all. They are nonsense!

This is an enormous challenge, to which the 2 billion-dollar 1990 attempt attests to. It was one that was not met in 1920. As part of a larger controversy about our changing country, Congress did not reapportion itself after the 1920 census. One of the concerns was that the Census Bureau undercounted the rural population. Critics charged that, by conducting the census in January instead of the spring, the Bureau missed rural households due to bad weather. Counting during a post-World War I winter "temporarily inflated" population figures for the city. Consequently, Congress did not pass a new reapportionment bill until 1929 (Anderson, 1988: Chapter 6).

Has the Census Bureau succeeded constructively in producing population figures for the United States in 1990? Not completely. As of this writing, local governments are still challenging these latest figures in court. If they lose and decide to accept the federal figures so they can proceed with their concerns, then the population figures are constructive, at least to them.

No doubt, out of these court challenges and other efforts, the Census Bureau will count differently in the year 2000. Some have already suggested that it use sample surveys or a phone census, rather than a household-to-household count (Anderson, 1988: 239).

So, what is the population of the United States? It was 249,632,692, as of April 1, 1990. The Census Bureau has produced a figure that is useful (for most concerned parties, though not for all), and helps to meet the challenges people encounter in the process of governing themselves.

Not so fast, protest those skeptics of constructive knowing. Surely we can objectively know the number of people in a small town, they might argue. If not a small town, then certainly a neighborhood. To know the population of smaller groups is not as difficult as counting the population of an entire country.

I agree, to a point. We can often count more satisfactorily the population of a small town or neighborhood than that of the whole country. But our counting does not uncover an objective number of people in that small town or neighborhood, nor does it uncover a number that exists separate from our counting and against which we can check our particular count. Through our counting we have produced a population figure for that small town or neighborhood. That number may be useful, but it is not objective, existing separate from us. After all, numbers are our own invention. They do not exist "out there."

Did They Do It?

Reconsider the Supreme Court nominee (now an Associate Justice) accused of sexual harassment and the two prominent men accused of rape. Did they do it? What "really" happened?

Constructive knowers again insist that it makes little sense to ask the second question. People cannot ever know what "really" happened independent of what they do to produce their knowledge. They never *discover* what happened. They *only produce* what happened by how they make sense of their experiences.

Rape and sexual harassment are fundamentally defined by people. Behaviors by themselves are nothing until people legally or otherwise define them as something. Defining a class of behavior as rape or sexual harassment does not by itself tell us whether *this* particular incident was rape or harassment. People must decide that, going through all kinds of procedures, using all kinds of principles as guidelines for what to do and not to do in making their decision. One principle in the American court system is "guilt beyond a reasonable doubt." Another is the rejection of coerced testimony. The complex interactions between participants in the criminal justice system also produce a judgment about what happened. The investigation of detectives, the questioning by lawyers, the testimony offered by witnesses, the decisions to prosecute vigorously or not, and the difficult deliberations by juries produce what officially is known.

Some of you who are not ready to give up objective knowledge may grant parts of what I am saying here, agreeing that people do decide what kinds of behaviors make up the categories of rape and sexual harassment. But once those categories have been decided, then some acts are objectively rape or sexual harassment. It does not matter what people say, though it does matter that they do not have complete information about what happened. If they did, then they would know what "really" happened.

Many people may wish for such certainty. Yet, does it make sense to say that some actions are objectively rape or harassment? Does it make sense to say that some actions are rape or harassment independent of how people gather, assess, and interpret that information in light of what they understand rape or harassment to be? I and other constructive knowers don't think so. Even when most people agree about a particular case, they have not uncovered what happened. They have produced what happened through the way they tried to know. Agreement among knowers may be useful and is required in many trials. But even that agreement was produced by people trying to know. People produce what happened, possibly doing so in ways that meet the challenges they face.

What was the challenge faced by the Senate Judiciary Committee in reviewing the nomination for Associate Justice of the Supreme Court and, in particular, the charge of sexual harassment? The challenge was not to "find the truth," but to pass judgment on a nominee under highly charged political circumstances, with conflicting interests everywhere. The challenge was to conduct an inquiry that would not disastrously undermine the credibility of the confirmation process. The Senate Judiciary Committee did so in a way that the American people accepted, if just barely. No one stormed the U.S. Senate or the Supreme Court after the nominee become an Associate Justice. No one took to the streets to overthrow the government. No blood was shed. This may seem farfetched, but look at the turmoil in many countries.

Nevertheless, did the nominee for the Supreme Court in fact harass an employee? The Judiciary Committee and the Senate were not charged with reaching a decision about the accusation of sexual harassment. For their practical purposes, the nominee did not harass his former employee. The Senate confirmed the nominee, and the American public accepted that confirmation even if some disagreed with it.

In the two cases of rape, consider the challenge that the juries faced. It was not to discover the "truth," nor to decide what "really" happened. If truth was genuinely sought, then the courts would admit all kinds of evidence that they presently do not. They would encourage the police to pursue practices that are presently prohibited. Even then, they could not know what "really" happened.

Instead, the challenge was to produce justice, one that the American people could abide by. The challenge was to conduct a trial in which the rights people created for the accused are protected from the powers created by the state, and thus justice would be "served." With all the shortcomings of the American system of justice, most Americans still abide by it, though many others are greatly distressed by it and are no longer much committed to it.

When the verdicts in the two rape cases were announced, again people did not spill blood in the streets or use force to undo the verdicts. That was in itself a great achievement. But it is not always achieved.

In the case of the four Los Angeles police officers accused of beating a motorist, it was not achieved at all. After the jury's verdicts of not guilty were announced, thousands of people, primarily in Los Angeles but also elsewhere, did take to the streets, burning, looting, assaulting, even killing. (Some, though, gallantly tried to help victims and protect property, and others tried to calm angry citizens.) What people know does not need to be popular. But when what people know, in this case a decision reached by a jury, leads to less faith in justice and to death and destruction, obviously people did not know constructively. What the jury "knew" was overwhelmed by what many citizens "knew," as fueled by the media's persistent broadcasting of a videotape of a small segment of the incident.

A more satisfying, constructive knowing would have recognized what the public knew and accommodated it. It would not necessarily have conceded to what the public knew, but it would have prepared it for an alternative understanding of "what happened." A constructive knowing may have had to involve such changes as how the knowers (i.e., the jury members) were selected and from where, how the media portrayed the process of knowing (i.e., the trial), how the media displayed and commented on the videotape segment that was repeatedly aired, and more.

People produce what they know within their complex, often conflicting world. Even with the best of intentions, they may not succeed in constructively knowing.

The second, federal trial of the four police officers for civil rights violations was held a year after the first trial and its destructive aftermath. That second trial produced constructive knowing, *not* because two of the officers were found guilty and two were found not guilty, but because it produced a decision that the citizens could accept and with which they could live.

What Was Said?

Let's reconsider conversations. How do we know that we understood what the other said? Once again, constructive knowers do not believe that we can ever know what the other person "really" meant, as the meaning exists separately from our attempts to know. But what can we do to know that we understood? There's the clue: *what we do*. We know that we have understood one another when we can act satisfactorily. We know well enough what the other said when we can meet our concerns, which of course may also concern the other person.

When I ask my two-year-old daughter what she wants and I am able to respond in a way that satisfies her, if that happens to be my concern, then I constructively understood what she said. Whether she "really" said that she wants the cookie I gave her is not the issue. If she is satisfied when I give her one, which is my concern, then I constructively understood.

When a student earns a grade on a test that satisfies her or him, that student understood constructively what the teacher explained—at least so far as the student's concern with a grade goes. (Of course, the student may have many other concerns than a grade.) Did the student fully understand the teacher? That would not be a useful question.

If a medical intern satisfactorily performs a medical procedure explained by a senior physician, then that intern constructively knew what the doctor meant. Again, the question "Did the medical intern 'really' understand the physician?" is not useful.

Constructive knowing is satisfactory doing. It may vary greatly from one conversation to another. In some conversations, a shrug of the shoulders or even silence may be good enough for people's purposes, even when they are uncertain what was said. Simply continuing the conversation met their concern. In other conversations, only very complex, sophisticated action will meet people's concerns. For example, only the precise adherence to a chemical procedure will meet an assistant's concern to know safely what the chemist told her or him. In all conversations, people constructively understand when they can act satisfactorily.

Conclusion

So, how do we know? We know in at least three major ways: supernatural, objective, and constructive. Supernatural knowers find the world mysterious, so they know only that supernatural powers beyond them are to be supplicated or appeased and cannot be deceived without risking the terrible wrath of those powers.

Objective knowers search for the natural principles by which the world works. Through careful procedures and clear reasoning, objective knowers try to discover how the world "really" is.

Constructive knowers create their understanding to meet their concerns and challenges. Knowing is satisfactory *doing*. When people can live and interact together more satisfyingly than before, if only just a little, then they have produced constructive social knowledge. By tomorrow, of course, continuing challenges will press upon people, new challenges will need to be tackled, and constructive knowledge will become inadequate. People will have to produce new constructive social knowledge in order to reconstruct their social life.

To construct social knowledge is even more challenging than I have discussed here. Social knowledge enables us to meet our concerns in living and interacting together better than before, but exactly *whose* concerns? Mine, yours, or theirs? Are people's concerns similar, compatible, or conflicting? Imposing one's will on others is certainly not constructive. Creating knowledge that enables *everyone's* concerns to be met is the greatest challenge. And people may not know for years whether what they believe to be constructive knowledge has actually met their concerns. There are no quick fixes for the serious challenges of social life.

For example, how might we handle the conflicting concerns of those who call themselves "pro-life" and those who style themselves as "pro-choice"? Can we develop knowledge that will enable us to meet both sets of concerns and transcend the conflict? If we could develop medical and social knowledge and the practices such that women conceived only when they wished to have children, would that begin to transcend the conflict? Perhaps, but I don't know. Let's keep wondering.

I have not explored how we can produce useful ideas, nor discussed how sociologists research the social world. They do so in many different ways. If you are interested, I would encourage you to explore further into sociology.

How will you know if you have understood what I have written? You will know if you can act more satisfactorily than before. And that is the measure you should use to judge the ideas in this book. After reading it, can you act more satisfactorily, even if only to a small degree? If so, then this book has merit for you.

Is the world becoming a little more puzzling to you? I hope it is. But surely some things are certain. After all, we know that, when we see a bug in our homes and if we are not too squeamish about it, we will most likely squash it. But look again. That bug may not be a pest—it may be something good to eat! How can that be? Turn to Chapter Three and find out.

Endnotes

1. A recent study questions this commonly reported 40-percent figure. It may be that only half as many people attend church services each week as typically reported. When surveyed, people may overreport their church attendance, perhaps because they know it is socially desirable to attend church. They know that their society looks favorably on church attendance. Or they may overreport because it is personally desirable to do so, due to satisfying previous experiences in church, as well personal expectations that they indeed go to church regularly (Hadaway, Marler and Chaves, 1993). If Americans overreport their church attendance, then I wonder if Europeans do so, too. If so, then Americans would still attend church more regularly than Europeans. This recent research points to the challenge of how we know that what people claim to be is necessarily so. How do we know that we have produced knowledge and not nonsense?

2. Incidentally, sometimes census takers do not always follow procedures. For example, they occasionally make up numbers and fill in forms without having contacted those to be counted. Don't be too horrified by this. Workers of all kinds often do not go "by the book." They may not be clear about or agree upon what the "book" is, but they know that they may not get their work done if they try to go by it. They also may not do what they are asked to do. I will take up this last, extremely important issue in Chapter Four. Regardless, even if census takers did what they were supposed to do, they would still be producing a population figure rather than uncovering the "real" population number (Altheide and Johnson, 1980).

Chapter Three

What in the World?

Our world is all around us. All you need to do is look to see what is so obviously there. But look again. Our world may not be what you think it is.

Consider race. Americans know their fellow citizens to be primarily white, black, Latino, or Asian, along with a few other races. If one parent is black and the other is white, then their child is considered black (Harris, 1989). A while ago in Louisiana, if a person had at least one thirty-second "Negro blood," then that person was black. The white-skinned descendant of a black female slave and a white planter challenged Louisiana's practice and lost in court (*Columbia Record*, 1982, 1983).

In any event, there are only a handful of primary races in America. But in Brazil, there may be *300 to 400* racial types (Harris, 1989: 107). How can that be?

Several years ago, a black, former council member in the predominantly black and Latino district of a California city charged that the current councilman, who presented himself as black, was actually white. The councilman in question, who had blue eyes, tan skin, and kinky reddish-brown hair, was the only black member of his family. His grandparents, parents, siblings, and children of a previous marriage were white. Though he was raised as white, he did not realize that he was black until his early twenties when he moved to the city where he later became a council member at the time of the controversy (*Newsweek*, 1984). What is going on here?

Before the South African government began to dismantle its system of apartheid, South Africans regularly altered their colors or races, as many as 400 people each year. During one 12-month period, almost 1,000 people changed their colors or races: 3 white people became "Cape colored" (a mixed-race designation); 722 Cape colored became white; 109 black people became Cape colored; 11 Cape colored became blacks; 15 whites became Chinese; 7 Chinese became whites; 4 Malay became white; 1 white became Malay; 1 Indian became white; 1 white became

Indian; 1 black became Indian; 3 blacks became "other Asian"; and more than 100 other people changed their race or color. However, whites never became black and blacks never became white—at least not officially. That was "too extreme," according to government officials (Tyson, 1983). What is happening here?

Consider sex. Although people's sexual behavior may vary widely, their sex is straightforward. They are either male or female. Males have an XY chromosome pattern for their sex, and females have an XX pattern. What could be clearer than that? But is sex that straightforward?

Officials at the Olympic Games have been concerned that some female athletes are actually males in disguise. For nearly 30 years, female athletes were required to appear unclothed before a panel to verify their sex. Officials have since replaced that degrading procedure with a genetic test that requires only a sample of saliva. However, about one female athlete in every 500 is found to have a Y chromosome. Is she a male? Sex may not be merely a matter of X and Y chromosomes.

A variety of birth conditions can cause a discrepancy between the sex and chromosome composition of some people. Some women have a Y chromosome; some men do not. The test used by the Olympic officials may only cause injustices rather than fairness. Other sports associations do not use genetic testing. The *Journal of the American Medical Association* (1992) has urged an end to all sex testing as cruel and discriminatory (*The Washington Post National Weekly Edition*, 1992).

In America and most parts of the world, people are either male or female. But in some societies, men who engage in homosexual behavior may be regarded as an "in-between, third sex, or not-man-not-woman." Fellow citizens do not ridicule people of this third sex. Rather, they value them for their supernatural powers or other services. For example, participants in Afro-Brazilian spirit-possession cults often consult a not-man-not-woman leader "for help in finding lost valuables, missing persons, the causes of misfortune, and cures for illnesses." Among some North American Indian tribes, not-men-not-women (the *berdache*) "bestowed new names on young men and women at puberty, marriage, and other life crises," organized ritual dances, or "performed special functions at funerals." In India, these not-men-not-women (*hijras*) "undergo castration . . . dress like women, wear their hair long, pluck rather than shave their facial hair, take women's names, sit in places reserved for 'ladies only' on public conveyances, and have been agitating for the right to be counted as women in the national census." They traditionally earn most of their living by performing various rituals. During ceremonies for newborn males, the hijra "picks the infant up, holds it in his/her arms, and goes into a dance during which he/she inspects its genitals and thereby confers fertility, prosperity, and health on the infant and the family" (Harris, 1989: 243, 244).

Recently, a person in the Philippines, a hermaphrodite (someone with the reproductive organs of both sexes) but legally a male, became pregnant (*Newsweek*, June 15, 1992: 17). How do we make sense of all this?

When you see a cockroach, how do you react? Do you flee in terror? Do you squash it? Or do you *eat* it? Do you savor its delicacy? Have you just become nauseous thinking about this?

Throughout the world, people eat insects with great gusto. They consume grasshoppers, ants, termites, locusts, and the larvae and pupae of butterflies, beetles, and large moths. But in Europe and America insects are usually considered disgusting. Many Americans squash them, spray them, and flee from them in terror. They are certainly not food. Most Americans would prefer beef or pork. But Hindus are revolted by beef, and many Jews and Moslems cannot stomach pork. Americans and the English do not generally consume horsemeat, but many Europeans thoroughly enjoy it (Harris, 1985).

Throughout most of recorded history, numerous gods and spirits inhabited the world. Today in most areas of the world, only one god exists. What happened to the rest of them?

Most American adults today worry about young people, particularly adolescents. My oldest daughter will soon be a teenager. Perhaps I should be worried, too. Americans are concerned about adolescents' education, sexual behavior, drug use, moral development, future, and much more. They believe that these youth will find it more difficult to get jobs and that their quality of life is worse now than ever (Gallup, 1991).

Before the nineteenth century, however, nobody ever *became* an adolescent as adolescence exists today. In past eras and in other places, children became adults as they grew older—but never adolescents (Skolnick, 1991: 39-40 156-161, 206-212).

Once born, we are considered human, aren't we? In many societies, newborns are not human until they undergo a ritual, such as being baptized or facing the moon. Where infanticide is tolerated or encouraged, societies define newborns as non-persons and do not perform such rituals on those that they kill (Harris, 1989: 210-214). In other societies, a newborn without a brain but with activity in the brain stem is a still living person until that activity ceases. Yet, under the Constitution of the United States, a fetus with a fully functioning brain is *not* a person. When and where in the world are humans persons?

What's your favorite color? Might it be purple? Blue? How about green? To Liberians who speak Bassa, purple, blue, and green are all one color: *hui* (Brown, 1965: 315-316).

Do you like rice? The Hanunoo of the Philippine Islands prepare 92 kinds of rice (Brown, 1965: 317). I only know of white and brown, as do most Americans.

The annual national debt of the U.S. government is hundreds of billions of dollars. Yet, some tribes have no specific number beyond five (Harris, 1989: 72-73).

Western time adds up: 60 seconds equal one minute, 60 minutes equal one hour, and so on. But among the Thonga in Africa, time does not add up. A medicine man who had memorized a 70-year chronology noted that this period was also an "era" of 4 months and *800 years* (Hall, 1959: 39).

We homo sapiens appeared on earth perhaps 100,000 to 250,000 years ago (Harris, 1989: 92-93, 102). Our distant ancestors broke off from the ancestors of the modern chimpanzees and gorillas about 5 million years ago (Harris, 1989: 14-19). But for others, humans appeared in their present form only within the past 10,000 years. Those others are Americans! Almost half of all Americans know that humans only recently appeared on earth (Nicholson, 1992). For these Americans, humanity has not existed as long as it has for others.

What in the world is happening? What should be so obvious may now seem rather perplexing. What exists for some people does not exist for others. What exists at one time does not exist at another time. In an instant a natural feature changes its nature (e.g., a person who is white becomes Chinese). Objects vanish over time or across space. They are here and then gone. What puzzles me is, *how do the world and its objects exist for us?*

Before I directly explore this puzzle, I will briefly discuss two common ways of making sense of the previous examples. One is the *absolute* view; the other, the *relative* view (Hunter, 1991). Neither one satisfies me in making sense of the question, *what could the world be?* I then argue that people *make the world* by the way they mark and manage their experiences. If you can take this idea as seriously as possible, then you will begin to see the enormous responsibility for social life that you and I have.

What Could the World Be?

People may make sense of the previous examples from an absolute or a relative view; some mix the two views together. To some people, only one absolute world exists. The world is what it is and always has been, and its objects are what they are naturally meant to be. Though we may view the natural world imperfectly, there is only one world. People who in past eras believed that the earth was a stationary disk were proven to be mistaken. Today's understanding that our planet is a rotating, slightly flattened sphere may in the future be proven incomplete or even wrong. But that does not mean that the world has become any different. To know the one absolute world is difficult.

To some, the social world is also absolute. Life is meant to be one way only. Either a divine authority has decreed it so or nature has made it so (Stewart and Reynolds, 1985; Goode, 1994: 12-13). Any other way is sacrilegious or unnatural. To many people, homosexuality is absolutely unnatural and sinful; men and women are designed to pair off and procreate. Families are naturally composed of a father who works, a mother who raises the children and keeps the house, and children who are dutiful to their parents. People should be with their own kind, and any or too much "mixing" is unnatural. That is just how the world is meant to be.

To others, the world is also absolute, but it is naturally meant to be something else. For example, there are those who believe that men are naturally meant to have more than one wife. That is just how the world is meant to be. So the absolute worlds of different people are bound to clash. Whose absolute world is the "real" one?

To others, the world is relative. This primarily affects the social world. Some take their way of life for granted. They are accustomed to it. It works for them. But when they look around, they see that other people take different ways of life for granted. These other ways of life may appear strange, intriguing, even enticing. To those for whom the world is relative, these other ways of life are not unnatural. They are simply different.

In India, for example, people are not spiritually equal. Instead, the gods have established four levels of being, or *varnas*. People cannot change their level of being during their lifetime. Each varna has its appropriate "path of duty," its *dharma*. Upon the death of the body, one's soul will transmigrate into a higher or lower being, depending on how one has followed one's dharma (Harris, 1988: 418). To you, is this way of life unnatural or different? Is your world absolute or relative?

I do not believe that those two views of the world, either the absolute or the relative, are adequate for understanding our social world. Though the relative view is more useful, it does not satisfy me. Do either of these views satisfy you in making sense of the unusual world described by the opening examples?

I and other sociologists believe that people make their worlds and everything in them (Stewart, forthcoming). They can even make their worlds to be absolute or relative or whatever they succeed in producing. Now, what in the world . . . ?

Making the World

You and I make the world. Through *marking and managing* our experiences, we produce our worlds and *all the objects* in them. Though we can do this in countless ways, only some ways become *workable*. Worldmaking is not the activity of isolated individuals, but one that takes place through interpersonal, organizational, and societal practices. We *socially* make our worlds. Our most powerful tool is the seemingly flimsiest of means—sounds in the air and scratches on paper: *language*. Our most important product, above all, is one another. We make *people*, too.

If you and I make the world, then it may be useful to understand social life as *social drama*. We become the playwrights, actors, producers, choreographers, stagehands, and even the audience of social life. What talents we have that we did not realize!

Although it may be useful to claim that the world is the product of our handiwork, we make it appear as if it were not. We make the world as a phenomenon existing independent of us. We make the world to be *objective*, this available-to-all, that's-just-how-it-is thing that most of us take for granted.

When we make the world objective, it is not one that equally suits all of us. Some members of society *monopolize* the making of the world, and whatever suits those in control is assumed to be natural for all people. What suits the monopolizers may become the often unrecognized standard that straightjackets the rest of us. I will now take up in order each of the above issues about worldmaking.

Marking and Managing Experiences

I would imagine that most of us believe that the objects of our world come neatly bounded and separated from all other objects. They come prepackaged, labeled, and with directions for what to do with them. I certainly believed that when I was growing up. But examples such as those presented earlier concerning how people produce different races, sexes, colors, diets, and other things have long since shaken that belief.

We make our world through marking and managing our experiences. (See Stewart, forthcoming, for the foundation of this discussion.) As I explained in the previous chapter, it can be very useful to claim that a world exists independent of us, but we can never check. Instead, we are left with what we see, hear, taste, smell, feel, and experience. So how we mark and manage our experiences *becomes* our world.[1]

We *mark* our experiences by pointing to, drawing a line around, tagging, touching, and in other ways designating our experiences. Haven't you ever pointed to something, perhaps in the sky, on the ground, nearby, or in the distance, directing someone's attention toward a particular thing? "No, not there, a little higher, a little to the right," you tell them. You are marking an experience for yourself and trying to do the same for them. Most importantly, we name our experiences or provide symbols with which to identify them. By marking these experiences, we bound and separate them from other experiences. We turn them into something toward which we can act.

People may mark their experiences in very different ways. Some of the earlier examples attest to the diversity by which we mark our experiences. Consider some more examples:

Members of many preliterate societies mark between 500 and 1,000 species of plants. Most urban Americans can mark only one tenth as many. While Americans and others mark numbers into the trillions and beyond, other people have no specific marking beyond the number five. In certain tropical societies, preliterate people do not separately mark hand from arm or leg from foot (Harris, 1989: 72-73). Students at the Massachusetts Institute of Technology at one time marked more than 90 kinds of engineering (Brown, 1965: 317). How many do you mark?

We have a great capacity to mark our experiences in innumerable ways. However, I do not believe that we have a similar *social* capacity to do so. The worlds we make and in which we live do not necessarily enable us to mark what people in other worlds designate. Medieval peasants could never mark atomic and subatomic particles, though their biological capacity to do so is no different than ours. Likewise, we cannot mark the spirits that animate the plants, animals, and other objects of some tribes, unless we became members of their worlds. The world-making of every group channels the capacity of its members to mark their experiences.

We also *manage* what we mark by acting toward the objects we have designated. We put the marked object into various relations with other marked experiences. By doing so, we make the objects what we know them to be.

Consider simple balls. We manage them as balls by swinging at, kicking, throwing, catching, and acting in other ways toward them. But some people even worship them. Can you guess who? If not, I will tell you at the end of this section.

Many Easterners manage insects by ingesting them into their stomachs, while Westerners crush them under their feet. Americans and others slaughter cows and dine on their meat; but Hindus revere them like gods. Many Westerners insert little pieces of metal through their ears; while others pierce them through their noses, lips, and elsewhere.

At one time, Americans typically put men "above" women and children, poor people "down," and black people at the "back." Nowadays Americans are putting men, women, children, poor people, and black people in different relations to one another. They are making people more equal, which I think is an improvement. What do you think?

Americans put "justice," "trial by one's peers," and "effective legal representation" all together, though they have not always done so for all people. Many people put "homosexuality" and "unnatural" together and try to put the former as far from themselves as possible, though not everyone does that. Today, politicians, military officials, judges, and others are grappling with how to manage people marked as "gay." For example, in what way, if at all, should those who are gay serve in the military?

Some women who are beaten and otherwise physically assaulted by their husbands, lovers, or boyfriends do not manage such experiences as "abuse." Only later, often much later, through continuing experiences of these assaults and making sense of them, do these women mark them as "abuse" and act to escape them (Ferraro and Johnson, 1983). Increasingly now, our communities are marking and managing such forceful acts as abuse. Through marking and managing our experiences, we make our world.

By the way, have you decided what people worships balls? Americans do, of course. They treat them like "sacred" objects, ritualistically collecting them, lovingly handling them, having them autographed, proudly displaying them at home, and even enshrining them.

Which Comes First, the Object or the Marking and Managing?

Do we manage objects in particular ways because that is what the objects "are"? Or by managing objects in particular ways, have we made them what we know them to be? For example, what makes something food? Do we eat some object because it *is* food? Or have we *made* it food because we have eaten it successfully? Do we laugh at a joke because it *is* funny, or by laughing at the joke do we *make* it funny? Do we build with rock because it *is* good building material, or by building with rock successfully have we *made* it good building material? Do we honor someone because that person *is* a hero, or do we *make* that person a hero by honoring her or him? Which comes first, the object or our marking and managing of experiences?

By marking and managing our experiences in particular ways, we initially create the objects of our world. Having previously made the objects, we now "know" what they "are" once we encounter examples of them. We know what their characteristics are and how we can and should act toward them.

For example, most Americans think of bugs in the home as nasty pests and often destroy them at first sight. Having thought of them as such—and not something good to eat—we know what they are and what to do with them when we next encounter them.

In the social world, many adults mark children as irresponsible humans by allowing them little opportunity to be responsible or to make decisions. They manage them into being more irresponsible by scolding or punishing them when they do not like what they have done. When they next encounter children, "knowing" them as irresponsible, they try to make their decisions for them. By the way, do adults ever "ground" themselves for staying out too late?

Workable Making?

Although we make our world through marking and managing our experiences, nothing forces us to act in any particular way toward the experiences that we mark. Instead, we can mark and manage them in innumerable ways. Yet, not every way will work.

Did you ever play a game where you had to put a familiar object, perhaps a box or a cup, to as many uses as you could imagine. Some of us had difficulty with that. We could not imagine that a box could be anything other than a storage place or a cup anything more than a drinking container. But others of us, if only for a moment, realized that they could be anything that we could successfully make of them.

Christina, a "deaf-blind Rubella" child who resided in a state hospital, was once befriended and observed by a social scientist. Clinically, Christina was profoundly retarded and without any verbal language. However, she could "ambulate, grasp, and eat normally" (Goode, 1984: 242). The following is the social scientist's account of a videotape of Christina managing a rattle. As we "know," a rattle is a certain kind of object which is "naturally" shaken. That *is* what a rattle is. But is that always so?

Chris brings the rattle—this particular instrument has a corrugated wooden handle, smooth spherical container and tiny metal cymbals—to her right eye (Chris can see far more acutely in this eye). She has it close to her eye, perhaps two inches away, and is apparently inspecting its features. She begins to turn the rattle this way and that in order to reflect the florescent light overhead. She grasps all the different surfaces, tilting them and moving them closer and further from her eye, trying to see what she can visually produce with the rattle. After a minute of this she begins a whole series of usages in and around the mouth. Different parts of the rattle are used as tongue thumper, lip stimulator, teeth banger, and pushed against the cheek. The bumps of the handle are rubbed rapidly across the front teeth, the neck, then the breast. It appears to descend further to the genital area. (I cannot be sure from the tape but

I have seen her do this commonly when presented with new objects.)
(Goode, 1986: 97)

The social scientist counted more than twenty distinct ways
Christina acted toward the rattle in the approximately eight minutes
she was allowed to have it without others showing her what to do with
it (i.e., showing her what rattles really "are" and how they are used
"naturally").

Because Christina was known as retarded, she was allowed greater
license to manage her experiences than those who are known as "normal." People would not usually allow a normal person to act toward a
rattle in such an "inappropriate" and possibly "unnatural" way. After
having learned what rattles are, normal people would not permit themselves to misuse one. But isn't it those who imagine new ways of acting
toward their experiences, creating something new from something previously marked, whom we call inventive and sometimes even geniuses?

We can make the world in more ways than we have tried or have yet
to imagine. But we cannot make our world in any way we choose, since
not every way of marking and managing our experiences will necessarily work. After all, Edison tried thousands of different materials before
he satisfactorily made a filament for his light bulb.

Not just any way will satisfactorily meet the challenges of living and
interacting together. Not just any way will work *and* uphold the values
we hold for ourselves. For example, we may be able to get ahead by
pushing others out of our way, but for many of us that is not an acceptable way to act. We can create schools in which students from poor
districts receive poorly funded education. But is this something of
which we can be proud? We can make a world in which one group of
people, e.g., women or those who are disabled, are made subservient
to men or the able-bodied. But to me and others, such a world would
lessen us all. How about to you?

I believe that, under the best of circumstances, we can appropriately
construct our world within the moral standards that we set for ourselves. *Our success in accordance with these standards marks the value
of our makings.*

While we can mark and manage our experiences in innumerable
ways, not all these ways constructively meet our challenges and concerns. I will offer some examples, from the apparently absurd to the
serious.

Eating what we have marked as bananas works better for most of us
than eating cigarettes, though some people do so as part of a trick or
as a result of abuse (Taylor, 1987). Drilling holes in one's skull to enable
evil spirits to escape can be done, but it does not work as well as taking
certain chemicals known as medicines. We can act inhumanely toward
people of different pigmentation, but doing so creates considerable

problems and can be morally repugnant. Educating disabled children with normal children can work well in particular situations, but just sticking them in a class with non-disabled children could fail badly (Biklen et al., 1985; Higgins, 1990). Giving workers the responsibility to organize their work can produce successful results, while close supervision over repetitive tasks may not work as well (as I will explore in the next two chapters).

Some people can mark and manage humans as three sexes and hundreds of races, which works for those people; while marking people as the traditional two sexes can at times cause trouble when a distinction has to be made in assigning people to one or the other sex. We may have even greater trouble in managing the two sexes that we have marked. How will we act toward those we categorize as female or male?

We make our world, but not any making will necessarily work. Consequently, we should question ourselves. How are we making our world? What are the consequences of our present making? Are we ignoring our values in what we make for the sake of expedience? Are we satisfied with the values that we have made for ourselves? Can we make our world more satisfactory? More satisfactory to whom?

Making all Objects

We make all objects of every kind in our world. We make those objects commonly recognized as manufactured, such as automobiles. We make the natural world, from the stars in the heavens to the smallest subatomic particles. We also make the social world—the ways we live and act together—and the world of ideas such as right and wrong, which have no corporeal existence. We make what troubles our society, all the social problems that beset us. And we make them all in the same fundamental way, through marking and managing our experiences, acting toward that which we have designated.

Consider manufactured objects. Some are still made by "hand." We conceive them, then fashion them out of other materials that we produce. Through how we act toward what we manufacture, we give them even more properties.

For example, in the process of making automobiles a useful means of transportation, we made many other parts of our world—highways, gasoline, traffic signals, traffic officers, driving laws and customs, and much more. More than just transportation, Americans have made cars an integral feature of their country. Love blooms in cars, and families are conceived in cars. Some people's identities are harnessed to the horsepower and appearance of their cars. Cars are stolen for joyriding and for stripping. People shoot each other over cars. Many Americans revere their cars in auto shows, museums, and advertisements. Ameri-

cans have built much of their economy on cars and view foreign competition as a threat to their national well-being (Halberstam, 1986). In
all these ways and more Americans "make" cars.[2]

Consider the social world. Perhaps you are now willing to grant that
people make objects, such as schools and all that goes on in the name
of education, systems of justice, the political process, the economy,
health care, the family, and countless other social arrangements. You
may wish to explore more in order to learn how people make those
social worlds.

People also evaluate what they and others make and do, praising and
condemning. But aren't some behaviors inherently wrong? Isn't taking
someone's life, forcing oneself sexually on another, or engaging in sexual
activities with someone of the same sex absolutely wrong? Their very
nature makes them wrong, don't they? Some believe that such behaviors
violate how the world must be, or they break the commandments of a
supreme, divine authority. It does not matter what people say or do.
These behaviors are just plain wrong (Hunter, 1991; Goode, 1994: 12-
13).

Are you satisfied with that absolute view? I am not. The claim that
some behaviors are inherently wrong cannot exist on its own. Even an
appeal to divine or supernatural powers is *made* by people. According
to this absolute view, certain behaviors are abominable, not because
people say so but because *it* must be so. That is the nature of the world.
Who would dare to interfere with nature or the divine?

This absolute view ignores people's handiwork. People make some
behaviors acceptable and others unacceptable. No people can live and
interact together successfully if they let "anything go." But perhaps people should recognize their responsibility for what they make acceptable
and unacceptable. What are the consequences of their prohibitions?
Do such prohibitions work? Do they responsibly meet their concerns?
These and other difficult questions must be addressed, even though
many people may wish to surrender their responsibility to nature or
the divine.

Making Homosexuality

Most Americans disapprove of homosexuality (Gallup, 1993: 100)
and many "know" it to be unnatural. And yet most societies in the world,
almost two thirds according to one survey, accept or even encourage
some forms of homosexual conduct. Warriors in many societies engage
in homosexual behavior, often with junior apprentices. When they grow
older and acquire enough wealth to marry a woman and have children,
they leave the military camps and their junior apprentices. As they age,
the junior apprentices themselves become the bachelor warriors and

take on their own apprentices. In ancient Greece, almost all the classical philosophers engaged in homosexual behavior. They as well as ordinary men were expected to be bisexual. Incidentally, we know less about females who are gay (Harris, 1989: 236-245).

Christianity has not always condemned homosexuality. It was tolerated in the first several centuries A.D. and again between the eleventh and fourteenth centuries, during which some monks, archbishops, and saints were gay. With the decline of political stability in Europe in the thirteenth and fourteenth centuries, the Church reintroduced its earlier condemnation of homosexuality, which has continued to the present day (Boswell, 1980).

While some people still appeal to divine authority in decrying homosexuality, I believe that most of us have to look to ourselves. Whether homosexuality is wrong or unnatural, we have made it so. Nowadays, Americans are making homosexuality more a part of the diversity of people. Some communities extend legal protection to gay men and women, some companies provide employment benefits to gay partners as they do to spouses, and some elected officials are openly gay. A New Jersey court has allowed a woman who is gay to adopt her partner's daughter. Even the conflict over gays serving openly in the military indicates that Americans can now publicly discuss what was once strictly taboo. Hawaii's State Supreme Court has recently ruled that a ban on marriages between couples of the same sex may violate Hawaii's constitutional prohibition against sex discrimination. Could gay marriages become legally sanctioned, as they are in such countries as Denmark (*The State*, May 7, 1993: 3A; August 11, 1993: 3A)? With continuing conflict, Americans today are remaking homosexuality. I do not know what we will make it tomorrow.

Warring Against Drugs

Turn your attention to social problems. Some behaviors and conditions, such as drugs, greatly trouble America. But what do you think makes drugs a social problem? I think the typical answer is not as helpful as we believe. Drugs or our physiological reactions to them do not make them a social problem—we do! We make the very social problems that bedevil us (Spector and Kitsuse, 1987; Best, 1989; Reinarman, 1994).

The growing, manufacturing, processing, transportation, selling, and use of drugs are not a social problem by themselves. We make them a social problem through how we manage them. Today, we conduct a "war on drugs," the metaphor itself worthy of careful consideration. We spend billions of dollars to interdict, eradicate, investigate, prosecute, imprison, and rehabilitate those involved in drug production and consumption. Through this war we make drugs a troublesome phenomenon.

But we battle only some drugs, primarily cocaine, heroin, and to a lesser extent marijuana and other street drugs. We do not war against tobacco and alcohol (though we inconsistently campaign against them and regulate them)—even though hundreds of thousands of people die each year from using those two drugs alone, while only a couple of thousand people die annually from the use of street drugs. Prior to 1914 and the Harrison Act, no such war against heroin and the like existed. Citizens could go into a drugstore and buy medicines that contained heroin and other opiates. For a short time, even Coca-Cola contained an extract of coca, the plant from which cocaine is obtained (Troyer and Markle, 1983; Reiman, 1990; Inciardi, 1992).

When I say that we make certain drug production and consumption a social problem, I mean that we manage them as something that greatly troubles us. We mark and manage those drugs as a menace; as the cause of crime, urban decay, child mortalities, and other ills. We run thousands of media stories about the dangers of these drugs. We hold hearings, legislate, develop public service campaigns, and allocate billions of dollars to prevent or rehabilitate drug use. Some object to what is proposed and done in this war on drugs, but their objections may be ignored or countered. Through these kinds of acts, people make drugs the social problem they now "know" them to be.

Again, I do not mean that America's "war on drugs" makes matters worse, leads people to take drugs, or produces crime and turmoil, as some people have argued. That is not my point here. Nor am I saying that, without America's war, people would not die from overdoses, families would not be torn apart, or certain neighborhoods would not be damaged. They may be. I am not claiming that America should or should not make particular drugs a social problem. I am merely encouraging you to understand that, if some drugs are a social problem, then it is Americans who gave them more significance over others. America does not turn all drugs into social problems, not even all those that many of us recognize as harmful.

How did America make some drugs a social problem but not others? Is America satisfied with its handiwork? Critics and proponents of America's present policies strongly debate that issue (Reiman, 1990; Inciardi, 1992; Zimring and Hawkins, 1992). No doubt, Americans will in the future continue to "make" and "know" drugs in some way, either as social problems or some other phenomena.

Making the Natural World

People also make the natural world. Through satellite telescopes, electron microscopes, particle accelerators, and an endless array of experiments and very sophisticated, esoteric techniques, people mark and manage their experiences of the natural world. Long ago, they produced a world of alchemy, turning lead into gold. Today, they produce a world of black holes, DNA, and quarks. Tomorrow, they may produce a different world—in ways that I hope will help us to live more satisfactorily.

The histories of physics, chemistry, biology, astronomy, and geology entail stories of the making and remaking of the physical and natural world, none of which came easily. According to some observers, these sciences developed through revolutions (Kuhn, 1970). Science textbooks give us at best a glimpse of that contentious, embattled world of discovery, too often presenting science as a well-agreed-upon set of ideas and findings. They do not tell the story of scientists working with and against each other to make sense of their experiences, sometimes trying to thwart their competitors and other times resorting to fraud to support their ideas.

But it is not just scientists who make the natural world. We all do. Wherever and however we mark and manage our experiences that we connect to the world of nature, we are making the natural world. Some of the thousand plants marked by those preliterate societies and used as medicines are currently being investigated by Western pharmaceutical companies. People throughout the world may know and treat illnesses very differently. Infections, spirits, witches, violations of taboos, and other "agents" cause sickness. People try to cure themselves through bloodletting, dancing ceremonies, chantings, acupuncture, ingesting endless herbs and chemicals, and in still other ways (Murdock, 1980; Honigmann, 1959: Chapter 37). They may also mark and manage the heavens very differently. For example, some people know that eclipses of the moon or sun occur when those bodies are attacked by an evil being. One people of northeast Siberia drives off that evil attacker by making noise and throwing weapons toward the sky (Honigmann, 1959: 604). The natural world is certainly not the same the world over.

Social Worldmaking

Worldmaking is a collective enterprise. While we create reality through marking and managing our experiences, we do not do so as isolated individuals. After all, we are born into worlds made by others, taught by others how to make our worlds, and provided the opportunity through others to develop a fundamental tool in worldmaking—language. We make our worlds as we live and interact with one another, whether individually, interpersonally, organizationally, societally, or even internationally.

Consider schools. We have all experienced them. As students, teachers, principals, parents, and other participants, we mark and manage our individual experiences. We transform them into "a good day," "boredom," "a waste of time," "just a job," "I can't take it any more," "they give us no respect," "you handle it, that's what you're paid for," "I wouldn't do anything else," "I'm pretty good at this," and much more. To transform those experiences, we act: we study, goof off, pay attention, talk with enthusiasm, cut classes, try harder, stay late, work on the weekends, quit, and so on. But we typically do this with and to others.

Interpersonally, we interact, talk, listen, argue, teach, ignore, punish, complain, work with, become upset with, help out, laugh together, and much more in order to make our schools. Organizationally, we hold meetings, debate issues, set policies and procedures, provide funding, hire and fire personnel, evaluate performance, and so forth. Societally, officials, educators, business leaders and members of the community, the state, and the nation debate educational concerns over, create support for, develop opposition to, legislate, and provide funds for creating schools. In the process, they respond to concerns such as the economy, politics, and international relations. While those in a classroom may experience their school primarily on an individual and interpersonal level, the worldmaking activities of those at other levels of organizations and society create a framework and a set of resources and constraints within which our more local worldmaking takes place. We make our worlds within the possibilities produced by others.

Contrast a turbulent inner-city school with a relatively peaceful, supportive suburban school. But do not imagine that inner-city schools are necessarily turbulent and suburban schools peaceful. The youth and adults within those schools make their individual worlds within the opportunities and obstacles they encounter. In the inner-city school that may include: not enough textbooks, broken desks and broken dreams, gun play inside and outside of the school, the suspicion that many students cannot learn well, authoritarian discipline, and other obstacles. In the suburban school there may be more opportunity: computer labs, a half-dozen offered foreign languages, well-equipped science labs, high expectations for students, and parents who help at school, among many others (Kozol, 1991). Once again, we make our worlds as we live and interact with one another.

Language—The 'Flimsiest' of Worldmaking Means

Who do you consider to be important in your society? What kind of career do you want? I believe that many of us would probably consider the President, heads of state, high-level government officials and politicians, lawyers, doctors, business executives, judges, scientists, engineers, military leaders, religious leaders, well-known media people, and others to be important. Some of us may be offended by the question, arguing that we are all important. But the above positions are ranked highly by people throughout the world. (Stark, 1992: 466-467).

What do you notice about these positions? Their power, their prestige, or their monetary rewards? I am struck by the fact that people in these highly regarded positions do not literally or physically make anything. Yet, they are important for how we create our world. They do it through language, typically through talking and writing. They create the world through the seemingly flimsiest of means: sounds in the air, marks on paper, or cursors on a computer screen. (See Stewart, forthcoming, for his insightful discussion on this topic.)

Language is our most powerful means for creating the world. Would a people's world exist for you if you did not know their language? Not very much. Even children do not live in our adult world until they know our language. Do "freedom," "honor," "love," "government," or almost anything in our world exist for a toddler? No.

In football, do "bite down," "blitz" "I-formation," "pancake," and "rip" exist for most Americans, let alone most people in the world? Two spectators, one using this esoteric language, the other a novice, do not see the same game as they sit side by side at the stadium. By the way, the above football objects are: the act of a cornerback running up to a wide receiver; the action of defensive players other than linemen rushing the quarterback; the action of running backs aligned behind one another and the quarterback; a smashing block that flattens a defensive player; and the act of running through a blocker (Sakamoto, 1990). Through learning and language, we make our own worlds and enter others' worlds.

Consider all the things that you and I can do with this wonderful, 30,000-year-old invention (Harris, 1989: 93, 96). We primarily mark our experiences by naming them. And by naming them this or that, we begin to manage them.

Imagine that the following occurred at a shopping mall. You observe an adult beckoning a child. The child does not budge. The adult calls again. After the child refuses to obey a second time, the adult swiftly moves a hand that comes into contact with the child's body. The child shakes and cries. The adult repeats the hand movement several more times. What is happening here?

You do not know what happened until you mark your experiences, probably with a few choice words. I doubt that, even after having just read about this scenario, you would reply that what happened was an adult swiftly moving a hand that came into contact with a child. That seems stilted, uninformative. Instead, you may mark your experiences: the adult "disciplined" the child, "abused" the child, or did something else to the child. Through language, you have turned what was only an experience of people acting into an object that you can now act toward. But if bystanders turn such an experience into "abuse" or "unacceptable behavior" and decide to intervene, they might become an unwelcome intrusion to the adult who "struck" the child (Davis, 1991).

When we create a new word to mark an experience that we had not marked before or not in quite the same way, we have the beginning of a new object. "Sexual harassment" is such an object. Only in the past decade has it come to widely exist. The action that is now increasingly marked as sexual harassment has existed perhaps forever, but the concept of sexual harassment has not. Previously, neither people nor the courts marked crude sexual remarks and actions as harassment. Today, many do.

We manage our experiences through language. We place what we mark in relation to other experiences that we have marked. We talk about the world: "That movie was wonderful, awful, boring, etc." "The criminal deserves to be sentenced to prison, to be executed, to be given another chance, etc." "Women should remain at home, let their husbands make the decisions, take care of the children, go to college if they wish, work as they choose, have equal opportunities, etc." The examples of objective principles presented in the previous chapter are fairly precise ways of using language to put marked experiences into various relations with one another.

Through language we can transcend our present sensations. We can magically bring before us objects that exist elsewhere, from other times and places. Historians, authors, trials, and the news media primarily perform such magic. Or we can create objects that have no corporeal existence: love, justice, honor, and truth, for example. We can imagine possibilities not yet realized, perhaps never realized.

Through language we make our experiences available to others—and to ourselves. We tell others and ourselves how we felt, thought, and experienced. "That meal was delicious, darling." "I felt like crying." "We did a good job." And so on.

Through language we direct people to mark and manage their experiences, and to act: "You must have been angry when they said that." "This report is urgently needed." "That country is threatening us, so prepare for war." "Your dancing is really improving." "It's natural, so don't interfere." We can even send these directions throughout the world.

We can direct people *without* language. Yet to do so is much more difficult, as those who have tried to talk to small children or foreign-speaking persons know too well. Try this: without using any language, make an ordinary request of someone. For example, have the person bring a particular object from another location to you. Good luck.

Through language we can prepare for what others are going to do before they have already done it and it is too late to adjust ourselves: "The professor is giving a test on Thursday, so I better study for it. Nah!" "Taxes are due in three weeks." "My spouse will be home at 5:30 for dinner." "The meeting will be held Tuesday at 7 p.m." And so on.

We can keep our ways of worldmaking for future uses with the help of language. In books, on tape, in computers, and through other means of communication we can store our linguistic worldmaking for future reference.

Through language we perform awesome feats. We can move mountains by redrawing boundaries. We can make the most horrendous actions palatable, even honorable. "We had to drop the bomb on Japan to end the war sooner!" "The baby was so deformed that we did what was best by letting it die." "We had to enslave those people because they were not human." Isn't this what some of the ordinary people who volunteered for Milgram's research did?

By the way, did you notice my powerful linguistic worldmaking in the above paragraph, by referring to the actions as "horrendous"? By using "horrendous" to describe bombing people, letting infants die, and enslaving people, I directed you how to mark and manage those actions. For that matter, this entire book, relying solely on language, is an attempt to encourage you to wonder about your world and possibly to make it differently.

No wonder that social life really flourished when humans developed the tool of language (Harris, 1989: 66-69, 96-99). No wonder that the powerful in this world primarily talk and write (Berger and Luckmann, 1966; Stewart, forthcoming). Many of these people have spent much time learning how to do so, often in esoteric ways. No wonder we often "war over words." Children on playgrounds demand to know what another said about them. Supreme Court decisions revolve around the wording of the Constitution and of other laws. Negotiators endlessly debate how international treaties will be written and how they are to be interpreted.

Don't misunderstand me. I am not trying to belittle those who manufacture, build, move, transport, and the like; or those who work on assembly lines, erect structures, saw, hammer, wire, plumb, operate machinery, and prepare food. They, too, use language in their work. But they also produce, often with great ingenuity and stamina, the physical and "natural" objects of our everyday world. Their worldmaking is vitally needed by us all. But their worldmaking typically occurs within the worlds created by those who talk and write powerfully.

I urge you to read and listen carefully to what others say and write. You may believe that what they say or write is merely a neutral, objective reflection of how the world "really" is. But how could it ever be? By speaking and writing, are we making and maintaining the world at that very moment? Do we talk *about* the world, or through talk do we begin to bring a world into *existence*? Is it a world in which you wish to participate? Or can you stand against it and try to remake it?

For example, when commanders-in-chief state that they have taken military action to "liberate" another country, try to imagine if the word "invade" or some other worldmaking term might be used instead. When we call someone else's view "extreme," particularly someone from a "foreign" group, have we made it easier for ourselves to dismiss that person or group? When we tell someone that a "spanking" (i.e., a beating) was for a child's own good, have we fashioned some objectionable action into something praiseworthy? When we call the loss of thousands of people's lives in a mudslide a "natural disaster," have we deflected our attention from the fact that poor people live precariously on the side of an arid, unyielding mountain while others live safely on flat, fertile land? What is "natural" about that disaster and what have we produced (Apple, 1993: 104)? Through language we do not merely reflect our worlds—we *make* them.

In deciding how you will use your time, you might consider the power of language. Might it be useful to harness the power of language for yourself?

Making People

Have you ever experienced the following? You and friends are talking about another person not present at a gathering. That person may be a well-known individual, another friend, or a casual acquaintance. Each of you presents a different picture of that person. The person could be "really nice," a "jerk," "friendly but shy," "conceited," "competent," "stupid," "honorable," a "liar," or whatever. Suddenly you become puzzled about what the others are saying, and they are puzzled by your remarks. You all not only disagree but become angry at one another for what each has said about this person. You wonder how your friends could be so wrong about the person, and they wonder likewise about you.

Was Adolf Hitler an evil tyrant or a great leader? Most of us would say that he was evil, but not everyone. There are some (too many for me) who "know" him to have been a great leader with a strong, just vision for his country. How could that be?

Remember Christina, the clinically retarded, deaf-blind child without language? In the state hospital where she lived, she was "three different people," though all negatively valued.

> One 'version' of Chris was produced by custodial personnel on the ward, who talked about her in terms of her abilities (or lack thereof) to perform those tasks which they required of her during eating, bathing, dressing, pottying, playing, etc. Another identity was afforded Chris by clinical staff at the hospital who were charged with examination, diagnosis and remediation of her condition and health in general. These staff employed a mechanistic-model (in which Chris . . . was construed in a deeply pejorative way) coupled with a people work identity (in which Chris was described as difficult to examine, diagnose or cure). Finally, Chris's teachers described her somewhat differently, although in equally negative terms—as unable to be taught, lazy, stubborn, without an attention span, etc. (Goode, 1984: 242-243)

To the social scientist who wrote the above passage and who worked with her for several years, Christina was a different and much more competent person. She and the others who resided in the hospital were

> excellent hospital residents. They were 'institutionalized' which meant (for better or worse) that they understood something of the hospital's routines and rules. . . . One very common scenario involved 'pushing.' The children would typically wait to be taken from one activity to the next. They might be lying on the floor lost in some autostimulatory behavior when a staff member would come up and fairly abruptly pick up a child and push her to her 'next' in the ward's routine. If it was 11:30 a.m. and lunch was approaching, a child would be picked up and pushed toward the bathroom (they were always taken to the bathroom before lunch). The typical reaction, and the child had a wide range of possible things she could do after being pushed, was to understand 'the push' (as I came to call it) as the communication it was intended to be. The child would wander to the bathroom, find a toilet, do her business, stick her hands in the running faucet after she was done, and walk to the (locked) door to the dining area.
>
> To me these actions were clear indications of active intelligence at work. . . . Even stereotyped rocking and repetitive actions without any apparent instrumental value may be interpreted as institutionally adaptive behavior. . . . During a thirty-six hour observation period . . . I realized just how much time she (Chris) was left alone to her own devices to occupy her time. The *vast* majority of the day this was her situation and she did not have external distractions of our culture such as television. She loved the radio (Chris had good sound reception but did not process the sound in a normal way) and whenever one was available she did her

best to get close enough to it to listen. She loved to rock to the music and built some fantastic constructions from available furniture to climb up to a small radio kept, for obvious reasons, on a high shelf away from the hands of the children. But in most places there was no radio and she was left alone to provide herself amusement. She rocked, played with her sight and sound reception, masturbated and so on, *not* because of her organic deficits but because she was bored and these were things she could do by herself and from which she received pleasure, reduction of anxiety or other gratification. . . . She literally waited for everything and I developed a healthy respect for her abilities to entertain herself in solitary pursuits. (Goode, 1986: 94-95)

Who is Christina? Is she the "defective" person that the staff knew her to be, or is she the more competent individual that the social scientist knew her to be (i.e., someone who entertained herself for long periods of time)? Or is she all of these people? Is the social scientist right about Christina because he was more sympathetic? Or was the staff right because they were more realistic? What do you think?

How can we make sense of the above? How can we make sense of the commonplace disagreements between us and our friends about a third person, or of conflicting beliefs about such people as Adolph Hitler? Doesn't each person have a "true" self?

'True' Selves?

Many who read this book know that every individual has a "true" self, which we understand more or less clearly. If a person *appears* differently to each of us, it is simply because we have different knowledge of that person. Or an individual has acted differently with different people, so we each have different experiences of that person. Furthermore, each of us may be more or less competent to know other people; some with little insight, others with keen perception. Therefore, if we disagree about who a person is, we do so because we have different insights into that person. Do these views fit yours? I wonder if these common understandings are as useful as we think.

When we express these common replies, we assume an objective world. Since the world exists apart from us, our goal is to try to discover how it "really" is. However, objective knowers realize that they may never be able to completely succeed in discovering how the world "really" is. Only with careful observation and reflection can they gradually come to know the world. This objective view applies to how we view people as well. I have already discussed in Chapter Two the shortcomings of this common, objective view.

Can we ever know people as they "really" are apart from our own experiences? It may be useful to claim that each of us has or is a "true" self, one that continues to develop over time. But I don't think we can ever really know that self—we can only produce people as we mark and manage our experiences "of" them. People may be our most precious productions!

Producing People

We develop selves for people, as we try to make sense of our experiences of them. We interact with them and are told by others about them. We mark them primarily through names, designating them in all kinds of ways: "lover," "friend," "Ms. Smith," "Jim," "them," "our enemy," "sir," "sweetie," "the Honorable Judge," and in still other ways, with all kinds of epithets that do not bear repeating here. We may also point to people or mark them in other ways.

As we designate people by names, we begin to manage them as well. Names carry a variety of connotations that become part of the person we name. Through naming, we place people close to us or away from us, above us or below us, similar to us or different from us, or in any number of relations to us (Higgins, 1992: 81-86).

Can you imagine personally meeting the President of the United States and addressing him by his first name? Most likely you would call him "Mr. President"—which would automatically elevate him above you. Titles and other formal means of naming people create distance, while first names and nicknames may express equality or intimacy (at least in America). The unequal use of formal and personal names between people may create and express unequal relationships. The boss calls workers by their first names; the workers address the boss formally. If you are a woman, has a co-worker or a supervisor ever called you "honey"? How did you react to that? Are men called "honey" by their co-workers or supervisors? Students may address female professors as "Ms.," "Miss," or "Mrs." rather than "Professor" or "Dr." as they likely would do in addressing male professors. That could be a big mistake. Calling some people with severe disabilities "vegetables" is to make them less than human. Naming is an important way to make people.

Consider how you name others and how they name you. Do you name people similarly? Of course not. Are you similarly named? Obviously not. Do you notice any patterns in the way you name others and are named by them?

We also make people by how we act toward them. Through ignoring, listening to, following, praising, condemning, honoring, laughing at, laughing with, sitting beside, pushing away, promoting, hiring, firing, imprisoning, enslaving, segregating, and on and on, we make others the people we take them to be.

By listening carefully to someone, we make that person a worthy individual. By ignoring an individual, we make him or her insignificant. By not giving children much responsibility, we make them the irresponsible kids we "know" them to be. By laughing at people, we belittle them. By laughing with them, we make them friendly. By not questioning doctors and meekly accepting their sometimes unintelligible medical jargon, we make them the formidable professionals that many of us "know" them to be.

By interning 100,000 Japanese-Americans who lived on the West Coast during World War II, we Americans made them a "yellow peril," as we did with such previous practices as prohibiting Japanese immigrants from owning California land (Stark, 1992: 302). Through our actions, we make people who they are.

As we mark and manage our experiences of others, we attribute personalities, individual characteristics, motivations, and other traits to people. Sometimes we use written personality tests, structured interviews, even palm reading, and other devices to produce these personalities. Most of the time, we just use our reasoning and judgment. But our interpretations are not merely individualistic ones. We develop them out of our community's principles for producing people.

A community of people develop conventional methods to judge individuals and decide who they "really" are. Members learn these conventional ways as they interact with others. For example, have you ever said or heard someone say, "You don't know me, only I know me"? Many people believe that individuals know themselves best, except under unusual circumstances when they are not in control of themselves (e.g., when intoxicated or mentally ill). I believe that view might be best understood as a part of the conventional way that people judge one another and just one of many general principles for making people. We all have a multitude of principles we use for knowing, or making, selves. In earlier times, people claimed that a true self was most evident when persons were in control of themselves or when they were acting within the expectations of their community. Thus, individuals showed their true selves when undergoing great challenges to do right. Nowadays, many are likely to argue that a person's real self is most evident during moments of impulse, when inhibitions are lowered or abandoned (Turner, 1976). People use these and many other conventional assumptions when they attribute personalities to others.

I believe that we create personalities for people in order to make our world more coherent and less uncertain. By doing so, we tell ourselves what to expect in the future. By deciding that someone is honest, we will entrust that person with whatever is valuable to us. By deciding today that someone is generous, we may ask that person tomorrow for help. By deciding that someone is cruel, we will keep a safe distance.

When we decide that someone is unreliable, we will not depend on that person in the future. We summarize our experiences with others by attributing personalities to them. We assume that their personalities, who they are, "drive" what they do. If we know who they are, then we can better foresee what they will do. We decide who people are for *our* sake, not theirs. Of course, we may later decide that we made a mistake.

We also create selves for ourselves as we make sense of our experiences of *us*. We reflect upon what we have said and done, as well as what others tell us about ourselves through their words and actions. We act toward ourselves—praising, scolding, feeling happy or sad, worthy or unworthy, giving ourselves a pep talk. We attribute personality traits to ourselves and use those traits as guides for what to do. If we "know" ourselves to be shy, then we often refrain from exposing ourselves to new situations. If we know ourselves to be funny, then we crack jokes. If we know ourselves to be studious, then we make time to study and berate ourselves for not studying enough. We make ourselves as we make others—marking and managing our experiences.

But as many of us know, much of our experience of ourselves derive from others. Through praising, criticizing, defending, condemning, granting, denying, talking to or turning away, giving or withholding responsibility, financially supporting, laughing at, and giving a chance to, others provide the materials with which we can make ourselves. What we make becomes our responsibility, and what materials others provide for us is theirs.

However, we should not be too surprised if those of us who are provided a wealth of materials make more satisfying selves than those of us who are given meager resources. It is difficult to make satisfying selves without social support.

What is a Person?

Not only do we make particular people, we also make the notion of a "person" in general. Societies do that in different ways. Other societies' notions of what comprises a person may seem odd to us, but then ours might seem strange to them. Persons

> may be conceived to dart about nervously at night shaped like fireflies. Essential elements of their psyches, like hatred, may be thought to be lodged in granular black bodies within their livers, discoverable upon autopsy. They may share their fates with *doppelganger* beasts, so that when the beast sickens or dies they sicken or die too. . . . The Western conception of the person as a bounded, unique, more or less integrated motivational and cognitive universe, a dynamic center of awareness, emotion, judgment, and action organized into a distinctive whole and set contrastively both against other such wholes and against its social

and natural background, is, however incorrigible it may seem to us, a rather peculiar idea within the context of the world's cultures. (Geertz, 1983: 59)

For example, the Javanese understand themselves as a bifurcated self: an inner self of experience and emotion; an outer self of external actions, movements, postures, and speech. They know that inner and outer selves are the same in their essence for all people, and they understand these two realms of self as independent of each other, each to be placed in its proper order. Through religious discipline, the Javanese try to thin out their emotional life to a "constant hum." Through etiquette, they "shield" that life from "external disruptions" and make their outer behavior "predictable, undisturbable, elegant, and [a] rather vacant set of choreographed motions and settled forms of speech" (Geertz, 1983: 60, 61).

An inner world of stilled emotion and an outer world of shaped behavior confront one another as sharply distinguished realms unto themselves, any particular person being but the momentary locus, so to speak, of that confrontation, a passing expression of their permanent existence, their permanent separation, and their permanent need to be kept in their own order. Only when you have seen, as I have, a young man whose wife—a woman he in fact raised from childhood and who had been the center of his life—has suddenly and inexplicably died, greeting everyone with a set smile and formal apologies for his wife's absence and trying, by mystical techniques, to flatten out, as he himself put it, the hills and valleys of his emotion into an even, level plain ("That is what you have to do," he said to me, "be smooth inside and out") can you come, in the face of our own notions of intrinsic honesty of deep feeling and the moral importance of personal sincerity, to take the possibility of such a conception of selfhood seriously and appreciate, however inaccessible it is to you, its own sort of force. (Geertz, 1983: 61)

As the above illustrates, the self is not the same the world over.

Successfully Making People?

We can make people in different ways, just as we can make other parts of our world. As I briefly explored above, we can even make the concept of a person different throughout the world. However, not every way of making people will be equally useful. Not every way will work.

Many of my students believe that we should treat people as individuals. What they mean by that, I would assume though I would often disagree, is that we should recognize each person's "uniqueness."

We make people as we live and interact together. In many encounters with others, however, it is not always useful to make people unique, complex individuals. Doing so might even endanger the encounter. Imagine that you are shopping for shoes. Would it make sense for you to regard the salesperson as a unique, complex person with all kinds of emotions, interests, likes, dislikes, and personal traits? If you did view him or her in that light, what would you do? Would you ask him or her about deeply personal matters and reveal intimate information about yourself on such matters? Absurd, isn't it? To even try to do so would deflect yourself and the salesperson from the task of buying and selling shoes, and could undermine the whole encounter. We usually regard the salesperson as a friendly, competent person to whom we are cordial, but that is as far as we go. Most of the time when we interact with others, we would be foolish to try to make them unique, complex individuals. But then, not always.

Consider twelve-year-old Breta, who is "deaf-blind, alingual, nonambulatory, [and] retarded" and who transfers "massive amounts of saliva to objects before touching them more thoroughly" (Goode, 1984: 238, 239). Breta had no "oral or gestural language," "almost no self-help skills," and "required virtually 24-hour custodial care" when Christina's social scientist first met her (Goode, 1984: 239). What would be your first reaction to Breta?

I would imagine that some of you might make Breta to be almost inhuman. Her sympathetic teacher, who worked with her "fairly effectively," according to the social scientist, called her "slug-like." Yet, Breta's mother knew her daughter to be beautiful and claimed that Breta communicated with her "completely" (Goode, 1984: 239). The social scientist could not initially imagine what Breta's mother meant by that. After months of observation in Breta's home, however, he was able to imagine and finally document that communication. For example, once when he was having difficulty giving Breta her milk, her mother told him that he was using the wrong cup and that was why Breta was fussing. After using the correct cup, Breta drank her milk without problems (Goode, 1984: 241).

Surely, how Breta's mother made her was much more useful to Breta and to her mother than how her caretakers made her. Her mother made Breta a much more competent person, one who could successfully express her desires. Her mother provided her child more opportunities and fewer obstacles for developing her capabilities than did the caretakers. In turn, Breta's mother enjoyed a more satisfying relationship with her daughter.

I do not believe, however, that can we make people in any way we wish and succeed. Consider Breta once more. Can we make her a person competent enough to drive a car? Not very likely, and yet her mother made her competent enough to understand what she wanted, which provided a richer life for them both. Not every making will succeed, but I would imagine that we can make people in more enriching ways than we often do.

By creating identities for others, we shape our interactions with them; and by interacting with others, we create identities for them. Identities and interactions are intertwined. But are we creating identities that enable us to manage our interactions more satisfactorily?

Enriching or Dehumanizing People?

When we make people, we do not merely reflect the reality of who people are. We help to create it. When we do so, do we enrich or debase one another?

When we identify children as "slow learners" and place them in separate classes for slow learners, haven't we made them slow learners? They may learn in a way that differs from others, but our act of segregation makes them less worthy children. When police officers stop and frisk young, minority males, because a particular young, minority male has recently committed a crime in the neighborhood, aren't those officers making these youth untrustworthy people to us? When we fire someone who is "difficult," we may have merely excused our own practices that do not enable us to work with a great diversity of people.

When college professors complain to one another that their students "just don't have it," are their complaints a useful assessment of their students? Or are they the justification for creating classes that disrespect students, that neither challenge them nor provide them the opportunity to master the material, or that try to bribe or threaten them with grades, extra credit, or penalties? Do such college professors (working within larger educational arrangements that they did not completely make or may be able only partially to remake) help to create the kinds of students about which they complain?

Making people is our most awesome responsibility, I believe, sometimes even a matter of life or death. Consider Phillip Becker, a teenager with Down syndrome who became the focus of national attention some years ago. His parents institutionalized him on the advice of doctors but refused medical treatment of his congenital heart defect. The Heaths, a volunteer couple who befriended him, eventually began legal proceedings to declare themselves Phillip's guardian and to obtain court authorization for surgery. In his decision to grant guardianship to the Heaths and permit them to authorize the operation, the judge compared the

conceptions each couple held of Phillip and his quality of life. According to the court, the Beckers regarded Phillip as an unskilled, devalued person, incapable of loving others; this was the conception they had acquired when Phillip was born, based on the assessment offered by the doctors at that time. The Heaths, in contrast, pictured Phillip as an educable and valuable person, capable of love. The court treated these comparative assessments as central evidence concerning both who would make the medical treatment decision and whether the heart surgery should go forward. The Heath's conception was more persuasive, reasoned the judge, and offered the least detrimental alternative for Phillip: a life worth living. (Minow, 1990: 344-345)

Haven't we dehumanized millions of people—African Americans, Native Americans, those with disabilities, elderly people, poor people, and so many others? Haven't we made such people less human, even less than human? Haven't others throughout the world done likewise? Having decided that their lives were not worth living, we have done much worse: we have enslaved them, massacred them, gassed them in concentration camps, drove them from their homes, neglected them in nursing facilities, left them to die as newborns, and left them to starve on the streets. But like the Heaths, Breta's mother, and many others did, we can do better. We can enrich the selves we make for people.

Just so you do not misunderstand, my discussion here does not mean that we merely judge people. Making people is much more serious business than that. Certainly we do judge others. But making people is not merely in our minds. The live-or-death situation mentioned above should indicate to you that making people is not just a matter of our opinions.

Socially Making Individuals

We make selves for all the individuals we encounter, but not completely on our own. Person-making is a social process, not an individual enterprise. Together we mark and manage one another. As I noted earlier, we typically learn the conventions of our community for attributing personality traits to others. As the Javanese example demonstrates, conceptions of what is a person may differ greatly between societies. Furthermore, family, friends, teachers, religious leaders, politicians, media people, and others tell us how to make sense of those we encounter. We are told what classmates, colleagues, neighbors, celebrities, and others are "really like," or how to make sense of and often stereotype entire categories of people.

For example, much of political campaigning is and has always been an attempt to portray opponents as unworthy, disreputable people. Sometimes such "negative campaigning" succeeds; sometimes it does not.

Officials in schools, social service departments, criminal justice agencies, mental health facilities, rehabilitation organizations, and other agencies that "process" people typically develop routine procedures for classifying the people they handle. Through formal evaluations and such informal procedures as testing the motivation of "clients," and by reasoning about the behavior of such clients, officials *identify* the people they manage (Higgins, 1985; 1992: Chapter 6). They create identities for them. How they handle them depends in part on the identities they have created for them.

For example, police officers may assume that those who are intoxicated, "high," homeless, live in run-down housing, speak a foreign language, and/or have "unusual" family patterns may be "low lifes," "scum," or "these kind of people." Patrolmen in one southwestern city refer to Mexicans, Native Americans, gay men, and those who live in the "projects" in such terms. When they are called to a scene of domestic violence, they assume that arresting such "low lifes" would not make any difference in their abusive behavior. Therefore, they are less likely to arrest these alleged offenders (Ferraro, 1989: 67).

We also make people through broad, governmental, or social practices. For example, when the U.S. government limited immigration in the early 1920s, prohibiting Asians from entry and severely reducing southern and eastern Europeans, in order to "preserve the American way of life from the 'pollution' and 'degradation' of racial mongrelization," it made entire races of people unworthy (Anderson, 1988: 143). Are we doing the same today with some of our present immigration policies? When we detain or return refugee Haitians but accept fleeing Cubans, what do our seemingly inconsistent immigration policies make of Haitians and Cubans? Through "separate but equal" practices that were not at all equal, voting policies that denied certain people's right to vote, or criminal justice practices that handle less advantaged offenders more harshly (Reiman, 1990), America has made and still makes some people less worthy than others. Governments throughout the world give preferential treatment to some citizens over others, and, even when they try to "right previous wrongs," such preferential treatment may be the focus of great conflict (Sowell, 1990). Producing people is perhaps our most awesome responsibility, but we do not manage it as isolated individuals.

Presenting Selves

Unlike inanimate objects and most animate ones, people can tell others what "object" they are. They can tell others who they are and how others should make them, something that rocks, tomatoes, black holes, and flowers cannot do. While that may seem obvious, it has enormous consequences for social life.

I will not explore these consequences here, except to say that our capacity to tell others who we are complicates social life. For example, if people can tell others who they are, couldn't they also be deceiving them? If they can tell others who they are, how can they do so persuasively? And how can they convince others to make of them what they make of themselves? They may create "character contests" in which they assert selves that others do not accept. Teachers and students sometimes embroil themselves in such contests; e.g., one believes that the other is not showing them the respect that they deserve. Sometimes these contests turn deadly (Luckenbill, 1977).

As we encounter others, we display ourselves to one another. Whether wittingly or not, we provide information about ourselves. We tell people who we are not only through what we say, but through our actions, appearance, clothing, demeanor, associates, props, and locations, to mention but a few (Goffman, 1959; Gross and Stone, 1964). We may work hard at preparing and presenting ourselves. How much time do you spend getting yourself ready, "making your self," when you are going to or hosting some important activity, then even "remaking" yourself during the activity?

If you think the presentation of self is not important, consider your initial reactions when encountering someone for the first time. Before even speaking to him or her, you have begun to make a tentative self for them and thereby plan your action. "I'd like to get to know that person better," you decide, or "I don't want much to do with that person." Later you may revise the self you made of another, but all you are going on is what you have noticed: the person's appearance, demeanor, and even their possessions, such as the car he or she drives.

For example, have you ever heard the saying that the clothes make the person? Some of you might be offended by that saying, claiming that people are more than skin deep or, in this case, "clothes deep." Yet, clothes do make people in the important sense of telling others who they are. Clothes even tell the people wearing them who they are! Take uniforms, for example. Within the social world in which the uniforms operate, such as the military, the police, and hospital staff, participants can quickly identify one another.

Even when clothing is not so standardized, we still tell people who we are by what we wear. And others treat us accordingly (Steffensmeir and Terry, 1973). Try going into an upscale clothes boutique in thrift-shop attire. You may get some attention but not the kind of service you wish.

Because what we wear is important for telling others who we are, people have tried to control who can wear what. Royalty is an obvious example. Sumptuary laws related to the consumption of goods were used from the 1500s to the 1700s as a means of preserving the distinction between social classes. The upper classes did not want the lower classes to imitate them in their material consumption. For example, during the reign of Elizabeth I, only those of higher nobility could wear cloth of gold, silver, or purple silk (Baldwin, 1926; Matalene, 1984; Brinkerhoff and White, 1988).

Presenting Selves on the Street

Consider people who are homeless. We might believe that, with so few resources on hand to construct their selves, their efforts would be meager. Do people without homes create a self of dignity and respect? They may try by using *language*, our most powerful means of making the world.

By *distancing* themselves from others, *embracing* particular roles and identities, and through *fictive storytelling*, those who are homeless use language to try to create acceptable selves. When they claim to be better than others who are homeless, or that the "Sally" (i.e., Salvation Army) treats them like animals, they are distancing themselves from others they know to be stigmatized. They are saying that they are not like but better than the common person without a home, better than the self created by the Sally.

By embracing particular identities and roles, street people take on a particular self. Using a street name like "Shotgun," calling oneself a "tramp," or claiming to be a "Christian" or "spirit guide" are ways of embracing an identity and giving meaning to one's self.

Finally, by telling stories about one's past, present, or future, from minor embellishments to full-blown fantasies, one fashions a more satisfying self. The audience for fictive storytelling may not be able to easily challenge the author because they know little about him or her. Or they may graciously allow such tall tales to be told, knowing that they too may require the acquiescence of others in order to develop more satisfying selves. Those who challenge the fiction may render the drama of self more problematic for the fictive storyteller and ultimately for themselves (Snow and Anderson, 1987).

It is not only homeless and street people who create and present selves through talking—we all do. Listen to others as they make claims about who they are. Listen to yourself, too. In an important way, don't we all talk ourselves into being?

Social Life as Drama

Have you ever been involved in the production of a stage play? In a sense, we all have. We produce and participate in the dramas of social life—in the worlds of classes, courtroom trials, news conferences, parties, business meetings, shopping encounters, dining out or at home, passing people on the street, and more. Through constantly marking and managing our experiences with one another, we produce the worlds in which we live. We are the playwrights, the actors, the directors, the stagehands, even the audience. And in experiencing our own spectacles, we come to decide what our plays are about. You didn't know how talented you are, did you?

For example, we may think of our health system as a large, impersonal phenomenon. But it may be useful to understand the health system as a continuing drama of human interactions: examinations in a doctor's office, nurses talking in a hospital ward, visitors at a sick loved one's bedside, government officials holding hearings about health care, scientists researching a potential new medicine, executives of a health insurance company deliberating over a new policy.

People may speak of the social world as distant and imposing. But I don't think that is how we make social life. We make it with one another. Out of all the little scenes of our lives, we create the larger dramas of our world.

Gynecological Examinations as Drama

Consider nudity. Americans seem to be ambivalent about it. We lust after it, sell it, exploit it, snicker about it, are ashamed of it, ban it, jail people for it, tantalize people with the promise of it, and more. Many of us assume that, if men and women are together and one or both are nude, then sexual behavior is the natural outcome (Weinberg, 1965). How then do we make nudity less problematic than it might be? Doctors and other medical personnel do it all the time—with our help.

Gynecological examinations are potentially threatening, even overwhelming, experiences. Unclothed women "expose" themselves in private settings to men (or sometimes women) who are not their spouses or lovers. Given the great taboo in America about exposing oneself, the personal strain and potential disruption has to be enormous. Yet, gynecologists and women manage these encounters every day without collapsing into nervous breakdowns. How do they do so?

Gynecologists, women, and nurses create a social encounter in which the nude women and their genitals are viewed as asexual. Through conversation, action, staging, props, and coaching, the participants transform a potentially sexually charged encounter into a professional examination. Through a series of "scenes," the doctors, nurses, and women transform the women into patients, then into asexual pelvises, and finally back again to patients and women. Though it may differ from one exam to another, the transformation may look like the following:

When women enter their doctors' offices and wait to be seen, they transform from complex individuals to ordinary patients. They know that they will be treated in terms of their medical needs. When doctors talk to them, they accommodate those needs. Small talk soon gives way to serious medical inquiry, and the doctor-patient relationship begins.

Once doctors decide that pelvic examinations are to be done, they further transform the patients into asexual pelvises. "Pelvic in Room 3," they may call out to their nurses. Nurses then help patients transform themselves into bodily objects. They direct patients to disrobe, tell them where and how to lie, and arrange such props as gloves, a specula for the vaginal examinations, and drape sheets. These sheets cover women's chests down to their legs as they lie on the examination table, but they completely expose the women's pubic areas. The placement of the sheets sets the women's pubic area apart from the rest of their bodies, allowing doctors to view it as a totally separate object. When the doctors return, the nurses chaperone the doctors' examinations of the desexualized vaginas. Their examination gloves not only provide hygiene, but they also separate their naked hands from their touch, further desexualizing the encounter.

By focusing on the exposed pubic regions, their view of the patients obstructed by the drape sheets, doctors can treat them as if they were not present. They are probing body parts, not people. Through side conversations with the nurses, perhaps about some mundane event, they further depersonalize the women. The patients collaborate by playing the role of a passive object. They rarely talk, nor do they make eye contact with the doctors or nurses.

After the examinations are finished, the doctors leave, allowing the women to become patients and eventually people again. As the patients dress, they talk with nurses about their medical conditions, their weight, their pregnancies, or possibly non-medical matters. Through that conversation, the women re-establish themselves as patients, then more richly complex individuals, not merely pelvises.

The re-transformation of the women progresses during a discussion of the examination results with the doctors and perhaps a casual chat about personal things. As the women leave, their transformation to individuals becomes more firmly established. And every day the doctors and nurses transform themselves into their characters.

Through a great deal of effort, doctors, nurses, and women create shifting social dramas that enable them to manage potentially problematic encounters (Henslin and Biggs, 1988). The same transformations usually occur when men disrobe to undergo medical exams. Treating people impersonally may be a successful means of handling what we take to be so personal.

Could such social worlds in any way be undermined? Would minor changes in the procedure jeopardize these delicate social dramas? What would happen if the nurses were called away during the examinations, the doctors inadvertently walked in while the women were disrobing, or the doctors and the women made eye contact during the vaginal exams? Nothing guarantees that every production of the social dramas of our lives will go well. Plays flop and social worlds stop.

Under such circumstances, we may develop means for repairing the damages we create. Think about the times your social dramas became disrupted. Did the play collapse, or did you and other participants make amends and manage to continue? Perhaps you repaired the damage in ways to which you did not then give much thought. Through constantly marking and managing our experiences, we create the social dramas of our lives. If our play falters, we do not typically close the curtain. Instead the show often goes on.

College Classes as Drama

Consider the social dramas that you put on in the college classroom. What issue do you and your fellow actors manage? What props, scenery, and staging do you use? How do you transform yourselves from one character to another? Do you pull off the drama through different scenes, like the participants in a gynecological exam?

In the classroom, for example, don't the participants transform themselves and one another from richly complex individuals into much narrower characters: students and professors? Does the transformation start before people walk into the classroom? What props and scenery do they use? For example, how can textbooks be used as props in this social drama? Around what dramatic tension do these classroom plays revolve?

I wonder if one of the social issues that the participants must manage is the maintenance of potentially shaky social objects—their selves. Do students and professors confront the challenge of exploring ideas in which their selves could be damaged or openly exposed to all (Karp and Yoels, 1976)? They all could be "made" to look stupid, unprepared, or incompetent. Could that be one dramatic tension that they have to manage in their next classroom play? And how would they do so? This is something for you to explore.

Making an Objective World

By now you might be wondering, why does worldmaking seem so "up in the air"? Marking and managing experiences cannot possibly produce a stable, solid world. Yet, as you look around, the world and its objects are all "there," solid and concrete as can be, waiting for people to use and interact with them.

Perhaps one of our most significant accomplishments in life is an objective world. We produce a world that is non-contradictory, settled, and commonly available to all. We make a world that confronts us and appears independent of us. By making that world consistently objective, we can satisfactorily live and interact together. After all, if the world and its objects constantly shifted from moment to moment, if they could be two or more different things at once, if they could be different to different people, how could we accomplish anything? We create and maintain that certainty, that objectivity, in order to proceed.

We create certainty by producing patterns. By repeating what we have done before, instead of developing new ways of acting, we can economically meet our challenges. We may recognize those repeated actions as a pattern: "there I go again" (Berger and Luckmann, 1967: 53). Whenever we face a challenge that seems familiar to us, we can use our previously developed pattern. We don't have to do so, but it is available to us. Two or more people can develop these patterns: "there *we* go again." Groups, communities, and societies create standard means for meeting the challenges of social life: educational systems, banking, military institutions, marriage ceremonies, notions about men and women, language, and so much more. Through developing routine patterns for meeting the challenges we experience, we reduce uncertainty and create order in our world. We create a familiar social world.

However, we often lose sight of our handiwork. We come to understand the world as an object existing independent of us, not as something we produced. "This is what we have done" becomes "this is it." For example, instead of taking responsibility for awarding an A grade to a student, teachers may claim indifferently that an "A" is 93 to 100. They cannot violate the sanctity (i.e., objectivity) of an A by raising the B grade of a student who earned a 92, just short of an A. "Sorry, I can't do it. Only scores of 93 and above are A's." Our handiwork confronts us with a life of its own.

When teaching others about the world, especially the next generation of citizens—our children—we make the world more objective. How do we tell children and other novices about the worlds they are now entering? Do we tell them this is how we and our ancestors have made the world, but we could make it differently? Sometimes. Usually we tell them that this "is" how the world is. We do not normally emphasize the point that we and others made it this way, only that they should listen to what we tell them. "You must mind us, your teachers, and other adults." We tell them how people work, play, and worship; how men and women "are"; how people "really" differ by race, ethnicity, and in other ways; what the meaning of justice "is"; and what all the other objects of their world "are." We also tell children what objects are not.

Rules are not broken, boys do not cry, and teenagers are not to have sex. When they ask why, and surely they will, we often silence them with "That's just how it is" or "That's just how God made it." We invoke the natural or the supernatural to establish that *what is must be*.

Our impressionable, young students accept our teachings as objective: this is how the world is and has always been, unless it naturally changes to what it will be tomorrow. It existed before them and exists beyond them. It waits for them to experience it in one neat package.

When we teach others what the world "is," we also experience in our lessons the objectivity of the world. When we tell children how the world is and must be, we are telling ourselves as well. And the more we tell others, the more we lose sight of our handiwork.

We are all students at one time or another, but none of us have ever experienced our teachers' initial handiwork—we are just told and shown what the fundamental features of the world "are." We were not personally there generations or eons ago when people created those features. Were you alive when Westerners turned bugs into nasty pests? Were you around when humans usefully categorized themselves into two sexes, male and female? Neither was I. No wonder we all typically experience the world as objective.

Eventually, we who have learned what the world "is" may become somewhat doubtful. We may encounter others' worlds that differ from ours. We may experience unfamiliar complexities behind that seemingly obvious objectivity. We begin to imagine other possibilities. Our faith in objectivity may not necessarily be shaken, but our certainty in what things "really" are may very well be (Berger and Luckmann, 1967: 134-136). We may start to search for the "true" way, a way that our parents and other adults never found or have since lost. Our objective world changes and begins to conflict with others' objective world.

Conflicting Accounts and Mundane Reasoning

When we encounter others' worlds that differ from ours, our sense of objectivity may indeed be shaken. But we need not venture to some remote part of the world to find potential threats to our objectivity. We can routinely experience them here in our own world, as we experience *"conflicting" accounts*.

Imagine that you are a manager of a store. A clerk claims that a customer tried to shoplift some merchandise; the customer denies it. Imagine that you are a parent, and your two children are fighting over a toy. One claims to have been playing with it first; the other insists that is a lie. Imagine you are a concerned citizen. One politician tells you that your community has a pollution problem; another contradicts her or him. Imagine that one group claims that homosexuality is unnatural and must be banned; another counters that it is part of the diversity of humanity. Imagine that educators argue that some youth cannot learn complex materials, because it is beyond their capacity to do so; others disagree and claim that nearly all youth can learn them. Imagine that you are a judge in traffic court. An officer testifies that a motorist was speeding; the motorist flatly denies it. What do you make of these examples? Why are the accounts so conflicting, and how do we manage them in order to maintain the objective world?

"Conflicting" accounts of "what really happened" or "what is really so" could be a potential threat to the objective world that we "know" ours to be. If the world is uniformly objective, then how could two people have contradictory accounts of it? How could they have two contrary understandings?

We have developed various patterns of reasoning to handle discrepant accounts, so they do not pose a threat to our objective, coherent world. Our reasoning assumes that people's accounts would be compatible if "all else were equal." We believe that all else is equal when the people who provide the accounts have observed the same scene, are equally capable of experiencing that scene, are motivated to speak the "truth," and speak according to the same shared experiences. But people may not have observed the same event or in the same way; their capacities to experience and make sense of their experiences may differ greatly, some possessing an impaired capacity; they may not give their accounts as literal reports and may be lying, distorting, joking, talking metaphorically, or the like; or they may be using very different frameworks, such as different cultural belief systems, for making sense of their experiences. Our reasoning produces an objective world and protects it from potential harm (Pollner, 1987: especially p. 62).

Consider traffic cases. Drivers and officers frequently give contradictory reports of what "really" happened. But these reports are contradictory only if we assume that the world is the same to all. But drivers, officers, and judges never question the objectivity of the world. Nor do they believe that any contradictory accounts of officers and drivers could be equally true. For example, the police officer cites a motorist for exceeding the speed limit, but the motorist claims otherwise. The officer, the motorist, and the judge would never consider the possibility that the motorist was going two different speeds simultaneously. Instead, the participants may reconcile the contradictory accounts, thus preserving the objective world that they know exists, by claiming that the motorist's speedometer was malfunctioning, the officer's radar was malfunctioning, the motorist was lying, or the officer mistook the wrong car on the highway, and so on (Pollner, 1987: 62-63). Through such reasoning, the traffic court participants produce and preserve the objective world that they know exists.

I am not saying that a motorist can go different speeds at the same moment. It may be possible, but that would be from different frames of reference, something best left to physicists (Hewitt, 1985: Chapter 33). My point is simply that an important part in making our world is to make it objective, uniformly the same for all. We do that through what some social scientists have called "mundane reasoning" (Pollner, 1987).

Mundane reasoning is one way to usefully make our world. Imagine an everyday world in which contradictory accounts of an event—a car turning both left and right, or a person both here and there simultaneously—could be true. It would certainly be a very different world, one that we might find uninhabitable. Mundane reasoning produces a useful objective world, one that is the same for all, and protects it from potential threats.

Motorists, officers, and judges are not the only ones who reason mundanely. We all do, including scientists. Most scientists assume that a natural, objective world exists. As I explored in the previous chapter, they know objectively. Objective procedures and perspective enable them to discover new properties and principles in the world. They know their preferred theories and findings to be "straightforward and unambiguous products of the . . . evidence" (Heritage, 1984: 223). Their knowledge reflects the objective, natural world as such experts can best understand it. Other experts, though, may understand the world differently. Yet this is the same one world which is there for any scientist to plainly see. But many scientists clash with each other about the world. How do they account for such disturbing conflict?

Scientists preserve the objectivity of nature in similar ways as do motorists, officers, and judges. They explain away the discrepancy. Those in "error" do not understand the correct theory. Due to the complexity of the theory, another's disregard for it, personal rivalry, self-preoccupation, or a host of other social and psychological possibilities, those in error do not understand what is so. These accounts of errors assume that the natural world and knowledge about it are objective, and they preserve that objectivity. Scientists bandy these accounts of others' "mistakes" between them, a form of "shop talk," but they rarely go public with them in the scientific literature. If they did, they would undermine the rational, objective nature of science. Science and the natural world "are" objective, because scientists *make* them so (Heritage, 1984: 221-228).

By now, I would imagine that your head is spinning from trying to work through these ideas. They are by no means easy, largely because they are so different from common sense. Yet, so too are some of the most important ideas that people have ever created, such as space-time relativity. So why do I belabor the obvious? After all, a motorist *does* drive at a single speed at any specific time. That you and I consider it so obvious shows how successfully people have made their world objective, uniformly the same for all. To make the world objective, the same for all, can be very useful!

If the world is so objective and the same for all, however, then how is it that three sexes exist in some societies? How is it that Breta can be both "slug-like" and "beautiful"? Is the world "really" objective, or do we often make it so and manage potential threats to the objectivity we have made?

Dismissing Competitors

Mundane reasoning cannot enable us to decide between discrepant accounts. It can only show that the discrepancy does not undermine the objectivity of our world. Then which discrepant account is the "real" one? Is the officer's account or the motorist's account the "real" state of the world? The motorist may be lying, but the officer may be mistaken. Is the theory of one scientist or another the "true" version of the world? The same question can be asked whenever people disagree about how the world "really" is. Whose conflicting claim about the world is correct? Whose conflicting making of the world will *become* the world?

Conflicts may never be resolved. People go their separate ways, at times literally, as people of different societies often do. Even within the same society, people whose way of life differs greatly from the prevailing way of life may segregate themselves from the rest of the world. The Old Order Amish in Pennsylvania and other states, as well as the Hasidic Jews of New York City, have tried in part to do so. However, they have not always been successful in forming their own isolated worlds (Kephart and Zellner, 1994).

One prevailing way to "resolve" people's conflicts is by dismissing competing versions of reality. "No, it cannot be done that way! No, that is not right or natural!" People denounce, punish, ban, dismiss, reindoctrinate, criticize, imprison, segregate, or even exterminate their competitors. They label the competitors mixed up, sadly mistaken, troublemakers, deviant, mentally ill, weird, heretics, traitors, and much else. Reality is far too serious to most people for them to allow too many competing, particularly incompatible versions to be made!

Try the following "thought exercise." Imagine creating alternative, even incompatible objects in one of your worlds. That world might be one that you and your family make, your work group, a clique of friends, or whatever. For example, if people dress a particular way in your group, imagine dressing very differently. If people espouse particular beliefs, imagine expressing a very different view. What do you think would happen? Very likely you would create turmoil in your group's world. The others would be confused initially, but then they would band together to combat the threat—you and your "absurd" behavior.

I don't recommend that you try to carry out this thought experiment in reality. Social scientists have had their students create such foreign objects before, and turmoil has indeed erupted (Garfinkel, 1967). For example, merely asking people to clearly explain such commonplace remarks as the greeting "How are you?" disrupts what otherwise would be a satisfying conversation (Garfinkel, 1967: Chapter 2).

Monopolizing Reality

People make their worlds. They create their reality. But they often do so in conflict with others. The reality that a society or any group creates may suit some members more than others. Yet, the handiwork that suits those members may become the natural, that's-just-how-it-is peghole into which all the others must fit themselves. Some members *monopolize* reality.

Not to oversimplify, but in America and Western society it is usually white, advantaged, able-bodied, heterosexual, adult men who have monopolized reality. They have governed their countries, run the businesses, administered the schools, policed the citizens, controlled the information and entertainment media, and done much more to monopolize reality. Recall again the power of language. Whoever controls what is published and transmitted controls an important means for making the world. White, advantaged, able-bodied, heterosexual, adult men have dominated the making of the Western world.

The individual experiences and concerns of those who have monopolized reality has become the "natural" way of life, rather than one partial set of experiences and concerns among many (Minow, 1990). Take the seemingly trivial example of being "flashy" or "loud." Many of those in the dominant group regard black Americans, gays, and even Jews to be "overly visible." "Those" people are flamboyant, noisy, flashy, loud, pushy, or conspicuous in their consumption (Adam, 1978). That view assumes that one's own behavior is natural and the way all people are supposed to be. Couldn't we turn it around and say that the dominant group is constricted, uptight, and the like?

Consider education. Many Americans are concerned that their country does not properly educate its children. Part of that general concern is that this country does not equally educate America's black youth or anyone who is not white and at least middle-class. All kinds of possible explanations have been offered for these educational shortcomings. One important explanation could be that the way educators instruct children is much more compatible with the family experiences of white, middle-class children and their world than it is with the world of black children and those who are underprivileged.

For example, middle-class teachers (black as well as white) may talk to their students in ways that fit better the experiences of middle-class, white children than lower-class, black children. Middle-class, white parents often ask questions of their children, asking them for information that the children know. Low-income, black parents are more likely to use statements or imperatives with their children. When they do question their children, they may call for comparisons or analogies rather than information. If this is true, then a mismatch exists between the language used in the homes of low-income, black children and the language used in their schools.

Many people have typically explained this mismatch as due to the inadequate language of low-income, black people. But that explanation presupposes that white, middle-class use of language is the natural standard for all. When teachers use language patterns that fit the speech patterns of black communities, black children do better. When teachers use rhyme, repetition, variation in pace, call and response, and other language styles that fit the language patterns of black communities, black children do better.

The same holds true for Native American children and other minorities. When children are instructed in styles that fit the patterns of interaction within their communities, the children's school performance improves (Mehan, 1992: 5-8). If that is the case, shouldn't more varied teaching approaches be adopted?

Finally, imagine that you move about in a wheelchair. Imagine that you cannot hear but communicate through sign language. Imagine that you have difficulty reading or thinking abstractly. Imagine that you are known as disabled, as millions of Americans are and hundreds of millions are worldwide.

Those who are disabled know well that people without disabilities have not built this world to include them, but rather, unthinkingly, to keep them out. Can those who need to wheel themselves into any building, to any floor, or into any restroom stall? Can all understand the spoken dialogue in the movie or the public address announcement at the airport? Why are so few official forms in braille? Couldn't an office job be redesigned so that someone with arthritis need not do heavy physical labor? Must children eager to learn be educated in separate classes and even separate schools just because they are known as mentally retarded? And on it goes (Higgins, 1992).

In so many ways, from the trivial to the profound, people have created a world that better suits only certain members of society. However, we often assume that the world is "natural," that it is how it must be and should be. The partial reality of dominant members has too often become the straightjacket for us all. I urge you to look around, especially from the eyes of those who, in one way or another, are excluded from the dominant group. You may be surprised to learn how much of the world that you have taken for granted so poorly suits many of your fellow citizens.

Today, however, many people are challenging how the world has been and is being made. Women, gay people, children, those who are elderly, those with disabilities, ethnic group members, and others, as well as those in the dominant category, are demanding that we rebuild our world to meet our diversity. And we are beginning to do so. Witness the new civil rights laws for those with disabilities and the countless wheelchair entries, the movement of women into corporations and the military, the greater visibility of gays, the progress that many black Americans and "minority groups" are gradually making, the greater rights of children to make decisions that affect their lives. Not surprisingly, some people who have most benefitted from the dominant way of making the world are resisting these challenges. I do not know how we will manage these conflicts. I hope that we can creatively make our world to include us all.

Conclusion

We make our world what we know it to be through marking and managing our experiences. We make all the objects of our world, the natural, supernatural, and the social, which distinctions become our handiwork as well. We not only give birth to people, we "make" them.

We can mark and manage our experiences in countless ways, but not every way will work. Not every way will help us to satisfactorily meet the challenges of living and interacting with one another. People often make their world in very different ways. Yet many of us believe that only our way is the natural one. We expect others to fit into our worlds, which creates new difficulties. Ask yourself whose interests are served by this worldmaking and whose interests are denied? Can we make a world which includes each and every one of us?

I have argued that we make our worlds, but I have not explored in detail how we make any part of it. I have not examined the tremendous efforts that go into making our world: the developing, proposing, arguing, negotiating, managing, deliberating, securing support, opposing, demonstrating, mobilizing, maintaining, refashioning. To say that worldmaking is hard work is an understatement. That I will leave for you to investigate.

For example, we make people into two kinds of sexes: male and female. That seems useful enough. But we also make males and females different "kinds of people." That may or may not be so useful. But how do we do so? How do we separate humanity into two sexes and create characteristics for each gender? To answer that, I will again leave it for you to discover how we do so in all realms of social life, from athletics to business to education to law to religion to science and onward.

If language is such a powerful tool for making our worlds, then I urge you to consider carefully how we speak, write, and in other ways use language. For example, courtrooms are different from classrooms, and the dialogue that goes on within them may be one major way that differentiates them. We not only talk differently about those two social worlds, we talk differently in them. Through talk, and other means, we make the world.

I hope you have not misunderstood my discussion in this chapter. I have not been exploring people's different "opinions" about the world, but something much more substantial. When one society make two sexes and another make three, opinions do not differ. Worlds do. Put yourself in another world's frame of reference:

Try to imagine yourself chewing and digesting, even savoring, the taste of cockroaches. Try not to see any differences between purple, blue, and green. Try to imagine changing your "race" tomorrow. Consider what your world would be like with three sexes instead of two. Try to imagine a world in which spirits make people sick and die. I would imagine that you cannot do it. We make our own world so powerfully compelling that to imagine radically different worlds becomes almost impossible.

But this raises another question. How do people escape the worlds in which they grew up and now live? I don't believe that any world is so confining that it leaves no room for maneuvering, for imagining and creating other possibilities. Yet, we make compelling worlds that seem to be so obviously what they must be. This is how it *is* and it *cannot* be much different. Or can it? How can we escape our world to envision some other, perhaps radically different, alternative world? How do we create that alternative world in the face of sometimes massive resistance?

Again, you may think that "escaping" one's world is easy. People just "move." They just act differently. After all, teenagers rebel against their parents all the time. Certainly generations disagree and clash with one another, but the "rebellious" teenagers rarely create any startlingly different world. Their rebellion is usually limited to dating, clothes, hair, sex, drugs, music, and other mundane matters. If it is so easy to "escape" our present worlds, then how is it that almost everyone one of us ends up recreating the same world we started with? Yet, sometimes we do escape. But how? I will leave that puzzle for you to explore.

If we make the world, then what an awesome responsibility we have. The most ordinary objects of our world, like food and cars, or the most significant, such as love and honor, or even the ultimate meanings of life become our responsibility. How can we know what is right to do? How can we be certain that we have handled it correctly? I don't believe that any absolute, objective answers are lying around to comfort us. The only certainty we have is that which we have made for the moment. We struggle each day to make our way with one another. And what glories we sometimes create.

We make the world and all that is in it, including what we hold most sacred. To do so, we enlist others. But how do we make them do what we want them to do? What do you think? To consider that puzzle, turn to Chapter Four.

Endnotes

1. Scholars debate how much of our marking and managing is biologically determined. Does our genetic inheritance dictate how we mark and manage the world? Does our genetic inheritance predispose us to mark and manage the world in specific ways? For example, all peoples distinguish between what Americans call "black" and "white," though perhaps not in the same way that Americans do. Some people only make this two-color distinction, putting together all darker hues with "black" and all lighter hues with "white." The order in which people add basic color categories to their language is the same. For example, if a language has only three colors, the third one is "red." Color classification is not completely arbitrary. Neither are other forms of classification, such as botanical and zoological ones (Brown, 1991: 11-14). But are these ways of "carving up the world" biologically dictated or biologically predisposed?

   In an important sense all of our marking and managing is biologically conditioned. Our biological capacities enable us to mark and manage our experiences. Without the capacity to see color, the world would be colorless. Yet, not every marking and managing meshes with our biologies. If we ingest a great deal of lead, we harm ourselves. Our biologies provide potential and limits within which we mark and manage the world.

2. Incidentally, does this seem to resemble in any useful way the reverence of Hindus toward cows? Hindus have made cows an integral part of their way of life. To better understand this, I urge you to read Marvin Harris' (1974) account of Hindus' sacred cows.

Chapter Four

How Do We Get People to Do What We Want Them to Do?

Have you ever tried to get others to do what you wanted them to do? Have you ever tried to get family members, friends, colleagues, teachers, clerks, even bosses and officials, to act? I'm sure you have. We all have. We all create social life, but we don't do it alone. We try to get others to act in order to create social life.

Everywhere you look, people are trying to get others to do what they want done. Parents try to get their children to behave well; to study; to keep their rooms clean; to go to bed at certain times; to eat their food. Children try to get their parents to buy them all kinds of things; to play with them; to take them to movies, malls, and other places; to allow them to go on their own to different places. Teachers want their students to do their best; to pay attention in class; to do their schoolwork thoughtfully; and so on. Many students try to get their teachers to give them good grades and not too much work. But some try to get them to explore challenging, meaningful issues with them. Managers want their employees to come to work on time; to work productively; to follow the regulations of the company; and the like. Doctors want their patients to follow their medical advice. Spouses, friends, and other intimates try to get one another to go with them; do some kind of task for them; to give them things; and do much more. A government expects its citizens to follow the laws. The leaders of one country may demand action from another country. Everywhere people are trying to control one another.

But how do we get others to do what we want done? Many times we don't! At other times we do so only with great difficulty. Children disobey their parents. Parents disappoint their children. Teachers nag their students to no avail. Employees come in late, leave early, and work little.

Patients ignore their doctors' medical advice. Spouses, friends, and
other intimates don't do what is asked of them. Citizens violate laws.
One country refuses to act as another demands. We often fail to get
others to do what we want done.

Nothing in social life guarantees that others will do what we want
them to do. Yet, often we do succeed. But how? That is the puzzle I will
take up in this chapter: how *do* we get people to do what we want them
to do?

Getting others to do what we want them to do is a fundamental challenge of social life. We try various strategies and experience many difficulties in managing that challenge. I will explore only part of the
challenge in this chapter.

My primary concern here is how we get others to perform well—to
act with effort and imagination, to "do their best." I am less concerned
with how we get people *not* to act; e.g., not to "goof off" in school or
not to come to work late. If we are successful in getting people to do
their best, then we will not need to be as concerned about getting them
not to do what we don't want them to do.

To explore this puzzle, let me begin with a very wise retort that my
oldest daughter used to make when I asked her to do something that
she did not wish to do: *"You can't make me do it."* I will next explore
three major approaches for getting others to perform well: *force*, *payoffs*,
and *commitment*. People are likely to use a mix of these strategies. Yet,
none of the three are completely satisfactory, each with shortcomings
that I will discuss. But I believe that commitment best respects the dignity of people. You decide for yourself. I will end the chapter by examining three kinds of conflict: *social inequality*, *intergroup conflict*, and
crime. When people try to control others, they may create conflict.

'You Can't Make Me Do It'

When my oldest daughter told me that I could not make her do what
she did not want to do, I agreed with her. My agreeing with her sometimes "made her mad," as she said. I replied that I could not "make"
her mad. She became madder. This exchange eventually became a routine between us that usually ended in laughter.

People almost never make anyone do anything. We are not capable
of such awesome feats. Nearly always, we make ourselves do what we
do. Only in very limited circumstances, concerning narrow ranges of
activity, do we literally make others do what we want them to do. And
even then, we are often doing *to* them what we want them to do. We
move infants around—pick them up, put them down, change them,
dress them, and the like. Occasionally we do that to older children,
sometimes to adults. Police, correctional officials, and others who man-

age "troublesome" people may make people act. They may literally restrain people, cart them off, or move them about. But very little of social life is accomplished this way. Can you imagine literally *making* people learn in school, work in a company, participate on a team, act as a family, and so on? Of course not.

Even when we do make people behave in specific ways, typically we do not unilaterally make them do what we want done. Instead, we depend greatly on their assistance. As parents, you may have or will experience how difficult it can be to change the diapers of an infant or to dress a toddler who does not cooperate with you. The same holds true for police who handcuff citizens and place them in police cars. Even when we (almost) make others do what we want them to do, we still depend on their help.

People almost always make themselves do what they do. People, not outside forces, move themselves about, come, leave, attend, work at, goof off, try again, give up, talk with, talk back, and do all the things that people do.

Even when people are threatened with death if they do not give up their money, when they give up themselves or submit in some other way they are not being "made" to do what they do. They can still behave otherwise. People do refuse; they do resist. At times, we even perversely realize this when we claim that women who were sexually assaulted did not resist "enough."

But don't misunderstand me. I am not suggesting that we should refuse or resist whenever we are threatened; nor am I implying that, if we obey the threat, then we are morally culpable. I do not mean that, because the threat does not make us submit, the person who threatened us is not legally or morally responsible for what happened. All I am saying is that, even when we are threatened, the threat does not make us do anything. We make ourselves do what we do.

Many social scientists and people believe that we are propelled by forces in the world. Recall from Chapter Two the principles of social life that objective social knowers are trying to discover. These principles demonstrate which forces are important. We have little or no control over the forces that make us do what we do. Stimuli produce responses; the environment causes behavior (Gottfredson and Hirschi, 1993: 48; Kohn, 1993).

For example, if it begins to rain, people outside scurry for cover or open an umbrella. The rain caused them to do so. If people are praised for some act, then they tend to act that way on similar future occasions. The stimuli, in this case praise, causes the future behavior. When people grow frustrated, they become aggressive. Frustration causes aggression. Like the marble knocked about by the flippers in a pinball machine, according to some social scientists, people are propelled by the forces in their world. What do you think?

Self-directing People

Others do not see people as pinballs. Instead, they believe that people direct themselves to act in order to meet their concerns. These concerns may be vital physiological states, such as the biochemical balance of their bodies or such "goals" as "doing well in school" (Powers, 1973; Ford, 1987; Kohn, 1993). People may or may not be consciously aware of their concerns; rarely are they aware of their vital physiological states. But they are all aware when they tell themselves that their cars need gas or that they will go grocery shopping later that day. When people notice a gap between their concerns and their present conditions, they may consciously direct themselves to act. They can often act in many ways to meet their concerns, even changing these concerns. But the concerns never dictate how people will act in order to achieve them (Powers, 1973; Robertson and Powers, 1990). People fundamentally direct themselves.

For example, if we feel hot at home, we may take off some clothing, change the thermostat, open a window, turn on a fan, get a drink, or do many other acts so that our perceptions fit our concern of "being comfortable." Or, if we cannot make ourselves comfortable, we may turn our attention to other concerns, such as finishing painting a room, and act to meet that concern. Later, we may get comfortable. Not wishing to be shot when an armed robber confronts us, we turn over our money or plead with him. Not willing to be robbed, we flee or strike back. While adults may take shelter when it rains, children may not mind getting wet or even delight in it. We act to meet our concerns. The world does not make us act.

Of course, people have many concerns, from physiological ones that they are sometimes not even aware of, to such mundane desires as buying the latest outfit, to grand goals and dreams. The worlds we inhabit provide us with all kinds of concerns that we may choose to take up but cannot be "made" to embrace. Once we embrace them, however, they become our concerns by which we direct ourselves to do what we do.

Some of you who have graciously put up with my discussion might protest that I have gone too far. Even if we do not "make" or "cause" people to act, surely we "influence" them. For example, teenage friends may urge, dare, kid, or ridicule someone to make that person take drugs. They may exert a lot of "peer pressure" on the person. They may not have caused the person to ultimately try drugs, but surely they have influenced that person.

But what is meant by "influence"? Isn't influence one of the many words that we use without thinking too much about what we mean? Isn't influence an indirect, "softer" way of saying that something or somebody caused a person to act? Influence implies that there is some kind of connection between prior conditions and what people do. But what is that connection? And does that connection lessen people's responsibility for what they do?

Shared Responsibility

People direct themselves, and only rarely can they literally be made to do what others want them to do. This view may be opposed by some and misused by others.

Many who are concerned about people who are least well off in society argue that it is not the fault of those who have not succeeded. Poor education, few job opportunities, and other unequal treatments have kept some people down. But the above view states that people are responsible for what they do. Nobody and nothing can make people not pay attention in school, not do their homework, cut classes, drop out, become pregnant, not look for work, show up late for work, and so on. Those who are sympathetic toward fellow citizens who lead difficult lives may denounce this view, because they believe it blames these people for their own troubles. Do you agree?

However, others will take comfort in this view by misusing it. Many believe that ample opportunities exist for all. Therefore, those who do not succeed have only themselves to blame. They may not be competent enough, work hard enough, or behave well enough in order to succeed. Critics of such people will embrace the view that people control their behavior. The critics understand this view to mean that each person alone is responsible for what he or she accomplishes. After all, people do not control others; they control themselves. Both those who denounce this view and those who misuse it misunderstand it.

Social life is shared responsibility. People cannot control others. But through their action, they help to create worlds that others encounter. The opportunities and obstacles that they create for others are their own responsibility. In turn, how others manage these opportunities and obstacles is the responsibility of those others. We do not live as isolated individuals in worlds that we have made by ourselves, a fundamental point that many of us overlook.

Therefore, we should not demean our fellow citizens who live troubled lives by assuming that they have no capacity to act on their own behalf. How condescending that would be. But we also should not play them for fools by claiming that what they accomplish is completely "up to them," and that others had no responsibility in creating the worlds in which they act.

People make and encounter very different "social landscapes" throughout their lives. The social landscapes that some people encounter are smooth and grassy with plenty of shade and beautiful scenery. Some landscapes even slope gently toward one's destination so that it is relatively easy to get there. But others encounter landscapes with all kinds of rocky terrain, gorges, and other obstacles to cross. Many people make these social landscapes; they have made them in the past and continue to maintain them in the present. Those who have helped to make and maintain these landscapes are responsible for their own handiwork. All those who move about in these landscapes are responsible for how they move. But getting from here to there is never merely a matter of each person's own effort. Yet, without one's own effort, a person will not get anywhere.

So, what might we mean by "cause," "make," "influence," and the like? Perhaps our language fails us; after all, language is a tool for marking and managing our experiences. And, as I have already explored, not every marking and managing serves us well (Humphrey, 1992: Chapter 2). Perhaps this time we have failed ourselves through our language of cause, make, and influence. Maybe living and interacting together is more subtle, more complex than the way in which these concepts enable us to think about social life.

What is the connection between prior conditions, including the actions of others, and what people do? Perhaps my metaphorical discussion of social landscapes will begin to help you make a useful connection. Through our words, deeds, and larger social actions, we help to create, continue, and change the social landscapes that we and others encounter. But these landscapes in no way make people successfully traverse them or force people to give up part of the way across.

Now, if we cannot make people do what we want them to do, how do we "get" people to do what we want them to do? The challenge may be greater than you think.

Three Control Approaches

If we cannot literally make others do what we want them to do, then what can we do? What would you do to get employees to work industriously and imaginatively, students to try their best, or children to behave well? People attempt many strategies. Force, payoffs, and commitment are three important ones (Collins, 1982: Chapter 3). Each strategy has its shortcomings. We often use a mix of the three, trying one, then another, or a combination.

Force

When we force others to do what we want them to do, we hurt or threaten to hurt them in some way. We "punish" them. We beat them, restrict their movement, or take away or harm someone or something that we believe is dear to them; or we threaten to do so. As I previously explained, we almost never literally make or force anyone to do anything. Instead, we assume that people do not like to be punished. Therefore, they will avoid our force by doing what we tell them to do.

We use force on a wide scale. Government officials incarcerate, fine, even execute, in order to get citizens to do what they expect them to do. In America, we have more than one million people incarcerated in jails and prisons. Adults beat children and one another; children do likewise. Millions of family members are assaulted by fellow family members each year, and almost all young children are hit by their parents (i.e., spanked or struck in other ways) (Straus and Gelles, 1988). Teachers paddle students, "write" them up, and send them to detention. Some bosses beat their workers, but usually they fine them, demote them, fire them or punish them in some other way. Nations withhold aid that they had promised to other countries, embargo them, and even bomb them.

When we are not harming others, we are threatening to do so. Teachers threaten their students with detention, demerits, a trip to the principal's office, a call to their parents, or bad grades. Parents threaten their children with all kinds of punishment. Management threatens to fire workers or dock their pay. Governments threaten to punish its citizens. Nations threaten to wreck havoc on their foes. Force is everywhere.

Ironically, when we use force we often claim that we "had" to do it. The others against whom we use force—misbehaving children, law-violating citizens, unruly students, or recalcitrant countries—made us do it. By now we should realize that others almost never make us do anything. Certainly they cannot force us to use force against them.

What might we accomplish when we claim that others made us use force against them? Is this claim an important way to construct our world? Does this claim attempt to absolve us of our responsibility for harming others? Is it an attempt to maintain the humane selves that we know ourselves to be? I will leave you to wonder about these issues.

Force may be a distasteful strategy for getting others to do what we want them to do, but it would seem to be effective. After all, who wishes to be harmed? But how useful is force?

Flawed Force

Imagine that force is the sole means for getting others to do what we want them to do. That can be difficult to imagine. Even in extremely coercive relations—master and slave, tyrant and subject, guard and prisoner, abusive mate and abused mate—force is only part of the relations. Much more may be going on in such coercive relations. Nevertheless, try to imagine that force is the sole means for getting others to act.

Most of us do not like to be punished. Wouldn't we rather do what we are commanded to do than be punished for failing to do it? Perhaps. Yet, who likes to be forced to do something? Force does not affirm ourselves; it negates ourselves. It attempts to take away our fundamental capacity to direct ourselves. This capacity is perhaps our most important feature. Force attempts to subjugate our will, demanding that we submit to another.

When you are forced to do something, do you become more willing or more resentful? Do you perform more imaginatively and industriously? Or do you work more reluctantly?

If possible, people may try to escape. The slave, the student, the child, or the spouse may flee after being beaten or when threatened. If escape is not possible, then people may become sullen and withdrawn. They may escape into themselves. The more people are forced, the less willing they are likely to become. They may also become aggressive and violent (Kohn, 1993: 165-169).

To avoid another's force, people may do what they are commanded to do. Yet, how well will they do it? Typically people will do whatever they are told to do with minimal effort and skill (Collins, 1982: Chapter 3). They may do just enough not to be punished, maybe not even that much. People may devise various ways of appearing to work without accomplishing much. Coerced children appear to clean their rooms as they rearrange their mess. A recalcitrant country appears to comply with an ultimatum as it stalls or provides reasons why it cannot proceed promptly. A slave chops and hoes but not very quickly or effectively. Threatened students stare into their books but do not read.

Consider the "practical" requirements of using force. Those who use force must be able to martial more force than the other against whom they use it. Many adults, both parents and teachers, are learning how difficult it is to use force to control their children and students. As people have grown larger in size and have become more physically mature at younger ages over the past century or so, force has become more difficult to use against youth (Stark, 1992: 127-129). Nations, too, must calculate how forcefully they can act. Those who use force may not know well enough the strength of the other's defense. Will the use of force result only in a Pyrrhic victory which has been won only at great cost to the victor? Weak people, groups, organizations, and governments may find it very difficult to use force against others.

When people threaten to use force, they must make their threats credible. Otherwise, those who are threatened may ignore the threats or even preempt them with an act of force of their own. Through a "show of force"—size, number, demeanor, display of arms, and other means—people try to make their threats credible.

Force requires monitoring. If force is the only way people can get others to act, then they will have to observe closely what the others do. Remember, they cannot count much on anyone's cooperation, so they will need to monitor others so that they do not rebel or escape. They will also have to monitor the others' efforts to comply with their commands (Collins, 1982: Chapter 3). Yet, how well can those using force tell that others are complying with their commands? As I noted above, coerced people can act in many clever ways as if they are complying without accomplishing much. The extensive monitoring that force involves takes time and resources that could be used elsewhere.

People who use force to get others to do what they want them to do often complain how incompetent those others are. The slave, the student, the child, the foreign leader are thought to be lazy, hard-headed, or simply incompetent. But who is the incompetent one when force is used—the enforcers or those being forced (Collins, 1982: Chapter 3)?

Force is not only ineffective for getting people to do what we want them to do, it is particularly ineffective for getting people to do their best. I have mentioned some of the reasons why that is so. We should not be surprised that employees do not work well when coerced, students do not learn well when threatened, children do not behave well when beaten, and people do not perform well when forced (Kohn, 1993).

Through force we can stop people from acting. If we are forceful enough, we can restrain people or even eliminate them (Collins, 1982: Chapter 3). Sometimes that may be all we wish to do or can do, as we try to live and interact with one another. If force does not work very well and if it is repugnant to you, then what can you do?

Payoffs

Why not pay people to do what we want them to do? As we all know, rewards are much more effective than punishment in getting people to perform well. Wouldn't you rather be paid than be forced to perform?

We pay people in many ways to do our bidding. We pay workers with money, medical, and other benefits, vacation time, stock options, choice parking places, chauffeured automobiles, and other things. We pay children with candy, toys, allowances, the use of the family car, later bedtimes and curfews, and so on. We pay students with extended recess, longer lunch periods, bonus points, good grades, and many other kinds of rewards. School officials, not just parents, even pay money for grades. A high school near my home has recently joined with thousands of other

schools in an "incentive" program. Based on their grades, students at
this school will become eligible for privileges and drawings that include
a variety of incentives, such as $50 cash, double lunch periods, free
gasoline, test exemptions, and haircut discounts (Farrington, 1993). We
pay countries with loans, most-favored trading status, the sales of arms
or other technology, and in many other ways. Surely pay works effectively enough. But does it (Collins, 1982: Chapter 3; Kohn, 1993)?

Possible Problems with Pay

Try to imagine that pay is the only basis for the relationship between
the payer and the payee. Again, this may be difficult to do because the
relationships with which we are familiar are much more complex than
those solely based on pay. What do you think may happen? Let's explore
some of the possible problems with pay.

Pay pits people against one another. It may create conflict between
the payer and the payee, between those performing for pay, and even
pit each person against herself or himself. Instead of working at what
is personally meaningful to them, people are manipulated to work on
what others want done. Like force, pay can be a coercive experience.

Consider the relationship between those paying for production and
those paid to produce. They payer and the payee are likely to disagree
about or haggle over the amount to be paid, what is to be paid, how
much will be (or was) produced and how well, when the pay is to be
provided, and the like. Participants may find it difficult to decide about
these and other matters.

For example, employers may aim to keep pay low; employees to raise
it. Parents and their children may disagree about how clean the children
have made their bedrooms or how well they have raked the yards. A
house painter may want to be paid at the beginning of the job; the home-
owner may wish to wait until the work is done. Neither party may trust
the other party to live up to its part of the agreement. Does this last
point raise the issue that relationships primarily based on pay must
also require some trust in order to work (Collins, 1982: Chapter 1)?

Such problems as the amount to be paid, what will be paid, and the
specific examples just illustrated may occur in any relationship based
on pay. Why don't you try to develop other examples? For instance, it
is not just employers and employees who may haggle over how much
will be paid. Teachers and students haggle over grades ("Why is this
essay worth only a B?"), as do parents and children over how much
children should be paid for washing the family car.

Those who pay and those who produce for pay may often participate
in production-for-payoff markets. Payers and producers often have possible alternatives, as they try to establish their payoff arrangements.
Employers are not necessarily limited to the first person who walks in
the door looking for work, and workers may have other employment

possibilities. Even students do "shop around" for teachers and courses. With such alternatives as grandparents, other relatives, and part-time jobs, children need not rely on their parents to get their spending money. And parents may have other neighborhood youth whom they could pay to do chores besides their own children.

When payers and payees have alternatives, the possible problems of payoffs may become more complex. Each party can try to play off the other party against the alternatives that each has. For example, employees may demand more money, less work, or other desirables by threatening to work elsewhere. Parents may offer their child no more than a certain sum of money to do a chore, because they know they can hire a neighborhood youth to do the task at the same price. What others are paying or producing may become a benchmark against which payers and producers calculate what they will offer or accept to make a deal. And still other complexities may appear in these payoff-for-performance markets.

Bosses, teachers, parents, and others who rely heavily on pay to get others to produce often complain that their employees, students, and children will only work if they are paid. "They won't do anything unless they get something in return!" they lament. Consider high-paid athletes who demand to be traded or have their contracts renegotiated. Who is responsible, however, for this crude calculation? If bosses, teachers, parents, and others have made payoffs the primary basis for their relationships with others, then they should not be surprised that others will play their game only when they are paid (Collins, 1982: Chapter 3).

But payoffs also pit payees against one another. When teachers grade on a curve, how well classmates do will affect each other's grade. The worse others do, the better one's chances of a good grade. When bosses provide merit raises, the less other employees have produced during the year, the more likely one's own performance will merit a raise. Even when people are paid based on what their groups produce, one group may benefit at the expense of another. And members of a group may resent having their pay adversely affected by the contributions of fellow members. Those who are paid may also be able to compare their pay to what their fellow payees or those elsewhere receive. They may not be pleased with the comparisons. Rather than being collaborators, those who are paid may become competitors and even saboteurs of their co-workers' efforts. Hence, payoffs may create a wide variety of conflict and resentment among those paid (Kohn, 1993).

Payoffs may create many other problems, too (Collins, 1982: Chapter 3; Kohn, 1993). But perhaps the primary shortcoming is that payoffs deflect people from what is personally meaningful to them. People perform better when they do what gives meaning to their lives. Of course, how meaningful a task is need not be the only basis for performing well. "Meaningful" is difficult to define. But when people do what interests them, what is important to them, what they love to do, what enlivens them, they are likely to do better (Kohn, 1993).

Even though payoffs are emphasized so much nowadays, surprisingly workers do not typically rate pay as their first priority. Instead, they rate first the type of work or "interesting work" they do. Pay may be ranked only fifth or sixth out of ten factors. And people who are unhappy with their jobs do not usually cite salary as the major issue. Instead, their jobs lack "challenge" or "variety," or conflicts exist with others at work. Perhaps only those who have difficulty earning a living are most concerned about money. Pay is not the motivator that many of us think it is (Kohn, 1993: 130-131).

When people perform primarily for pay, they may become at odds with themselves. They are doing what others want, not what is meaningful to them. They may come to experience payoffs to be as coercive as the use of force, by denying their capacity to direct themselves. To get what they wish, they must do what others tell them to do; they must submit. For example, as students, how often have you felt coerced when teachers paid you with grades to do what the teacher wanted done? You *had* to do what was assigned if you wanted to pass the course. But how well did you do your assignment (Kohn, 1993)?

Payoffs do not typically work well to get people to do their best. Instead, payoffs improve performance in limited situations. When we ask people to do tasks that are meaningless to them, our continuing payments or promises to pay may get them to do more of what we ask, but not necessarily to do it better (Kohn, 1993: 46). Even then, the problems that I explored earlier may still occur.

Payoffs, like force, are not as effective for getting people to perform as well as we might imagine. Certainly we often need to pay people to get them to do what we want them to do. For example, when people make their living through work, we need to pay them to do our work. Can you imagine many people working long hours at a demanding task each day without being paid for it? Would you do so? Furthermore, we may increase people's pay to get them to work for us rather than for others. However, paying them to work does not guarantee that they will do it very well. What else can we try?

To answer the question above, I can easily imagine people working long hours at a demanding task without being paid to do it. Doesn't that describe being a parent or family member, a member of a voluntary organization or club, or even a member of a religious group? How do you explain that?

Commitment

If force and payoffs are not the best means for getting others to do what we want, is another strategy available? Yes. But it too is difficult to use and has shortcomings. Done well, however, it may also be the most satisfying. It can affirm the dignity of each of us and create bonds among one another.

Imagine those occasions when you did your best, such as those times that you worked exhaustingly hard, you worked longer than anyone expected you to, or you were not satisfied with what you did and redid it. Imagine those moments when you were proud of what you accomplished. Perhaps you even surprised yourself with what you produced. You may be imagining some occasions at work, or perhaps in some voluntary organization or team, among friends, within your family, in school, or by yourself. Did someone force you to do it? No. Was pay the motivating factor? I doubt it, though you may have been paid for what you did.

Instead, I imagine that when you tried your very best, you were committed to what you did and very likely to a group of which you were a part and for which you acted. You affirmed yourself in the work and by working for the group. You gave yourself fully to that which gave meaning to yourself—the activity and the group. Who you were was powerfully bound with others. To do less would be to disappoint yourself and those comrades who depended on you. Collective commitment can wed our own concerns to other people who make us part of something grander than ourselves. Through this solidarity, we turn "doing my own thing" into "doing *our* thing."

Commitment is one of the most powerful means for getting people to do well what we want them to do. If we can enable people to become committed to the task and, much more importantly, to the group that depends on the task, then they may literally give up their lives for others.

For example, soldiers do not typically fight well because they are forced to with guns at their back. Instead, as many of Saddam Hussein's soldiers did during the war over Kuwait several years ago, they desert whenever possible. They do not fight well because they are paid, nor do they fight harder in order to earn more. They may not even fight for their country in some abstract way. Instead, "soldiers fight well when they are members of cohesive small groups and led by officers they trust. . . ." (Wilson, 1989: 46). They fight to uphold what supports them and makes them meaningful—their comrades.

Some of you may object that I am belaboring the obvious. Commitment to others is natural, you may contend, because humans are naturally social. Collective commitment—call it solidarity—springs out of who people are. Family members are naturally committed to one another; so too are friends, teammates, citizens of a nation, and so on.

Not necessarily so! The troubling amount of neglect, abuse, and violence within families indicates that families do not naturally experience solidarity. Close friends are committed to one another, but close friendships do not arise on their own. How many close friends (e.g., those with whom you share personal information about yourself and whom you would neglect your own interests to assist) do you have? Many people have few close friends. Teams often flounder due to dissension.

Neither can nations always count on their citizens' allegiance. Civil wars, intergroup strife, and profound skepticism about one's government and country indicate that national commitment does not happen on its own. While we take for granted that citizens hold allegiance to their country, such allegiance is only a recent accomplishment. Citizens and leaders did not widely create national allegiance in Europe until the nineteenth century and did not commonly produce allegiance to states outside of the West until the twentieth century (Chirot, 1986: 71-72). As the turmoil in Eastern Europe and elsewhere indicates, that allegiance may often be in jeopardy. We must *create* commitment to be enriched by it.

How can people produce commitment? How can they create solidarity, a sense of belongingness, or a shared identity that ties them together? How can they create what we call allegiance, loyalty, trust, duty, even love that express a profound merging and intertwining of people? Commitment may not always be so intense. But however strong it may be, how can people create it?

I will not take up all the possible ways in which people may create commitment, but will primarily explore two of them: *rituals* and *responsibility* (Collins, 1982). First, consider the following examples.

Commitment Scenes

I imagine that you have attended religious services. While services vary greatly, many are similar to the following. Members congregate at particular places and specific times, participating collectively in common, coordinated activities. They listen, clap, sing, pray, recite passages from their scriptures, even dance and chant together. They do this in what all know to be the proper way. They create shared emotions of reverence, awe, excitement, pride, contentment, hope, even jubilation. While their ministers, priests, or other religious officials may lead the services, the members have responsibility for many parts of it. They talk and learn about beliefs that bind them together and separate them from others. They make books, beads, crosses, words, and other objects sacred and conduct their services around these objects.

Consider the military. The process of becoming a soldier begins with basic training. What does that involve? The military separates young men and women from their homes, families, and friends and puts them together with others who are similarly disattached. The military shears them of their civilian identities and provides them with a common, military one, symbolized by their standard uniforms and treatment. The recruits eat, sleep, drill, train, march, go on maneuvers, and do almost everything together. They must depend on one another in order to get through the rigors of basic training; when they "screw up," they screw it up for their entire group. They compete against other platoons of recruits for honor. They learn about the history and tradition of their branch and are trained in esoteric skills unfamiliar to most civilians. Those who are successful graduate in ceremonies attended by families and friends that mark the solemnity of their passage into the military (Zurcher, 1983: Chapter 2).

Think about fraternities and sororities. Some of you may be members, others may become members, and many of you know people who are members. Pledges, who wish to become new members, go through a pledge period. What happens? They attend classes with other pledges where they learn about their fraternities and sororities—about the history, philosophy, ideals, and other features of their organizations. Much of this is secret, to be revealed to no one outside of the Greek organization. Students whom I teach will not tell me—and I am glad that they don't. To do so would dishonor their organization and themselves. Pledges participate in social, civic, and other activities of their organizations. They may be paired with other members; for example, their "big sisters" who provide companionship, advice, support, and more personal ties to their organizations. Some may be asked by their "brothers" or "sisters" to accomplish various tasks and even endure some hardships, though I believe that hazing is on the decline. After weeks or months of these activities, the successful pledges will be initiated in a secret ceremony that stresses the specialness of their new membership, even the sacredness of the organization that they are joining. The Greek letters that identify each organization, its motto, the pins and other emblems all become important objects to the new members.

Imagine being a parent. Some of you who read this are parents, and most of you will become parents. Personally, I find it a great challenge. Some parents meet that challenge in part by being "with" their children in important ways and by giving them the opportunity not only to decide for themselves but also to help make family decisions. Instead of watching television or doing housework as little ones swarm around them, some parents give their children special attention. They cuddle, rock, and talk to their babies. They read to, walk hand in hand with, "roughhouse" with, or share the thrill of a sports contest or the magic of an artistic performance with their older ones. They and their children re-count the day's activities at the dinner table, and they tell bedtime stories at night. Parents listen carefully to their children's concerns, and some even tell them their own hopes and fears. Together, they celebrate and they embrace.

Some parents also allow their children to make many decisions for themselves. Younger children are given guiding choices. Older children are encouraged to make such decisions with the advice of the parents if they want it. Together, parents and children decide where to go out to eat, what to do on the weekends, what vacation to take, even what automobile to buy, and more, just as husband and wife do with each other as they become a committed couple.

Consider the following business scene. A group of workers on the production line meet in a conference room early Monday morning. They exchange greetings and pleasantries with one another, ask about their families and weekends, then discuss the possibility of manufac-turing a new product to be sold by the company. That discussion, at times in meetings with executives, will go on for several months as they explore the feasibility of the new venture. The workers also discuss some recent difficulties on the production line and how they should handle them, deciding whether to suggest to managers that a new production process would work better than the present one. Later in the week, the chief executive meets with the workers in a weekly, informal session, during which the participants discuss whatever they wish. They may decide to establish a committee to explore some recent safety concerns, the availability of overtime pay, community volunteering on company time, or other matters. Later in the month, some of the workers in the group may agree to exchange jobs in order to become more versatile in their skills. Have you ever worked in a business where you had as much input as the above workers do?

What means for producing commitment can we extract from these scenes of religious worship, military recruits, Greek organizations, families, and businesses? There are at least two that I would consider important in these not-so-hypothetical scenes: rituals and responsibil-ity.

Rituals

Social rituals are the ways in which people obligate themselves to act when they are in the presence of what they regard as profoundly significant, even sacred, or when they are in the presence of a repre-sentative of what is sacred to them (Durkheim, 1965; Goffman, 1967, 1971: Chapter 3; Collins, 1982: Chapter 2). Rituals are means through which people show their great respect for that which they exalt. Rituals may vary in intensity, formality, and the degree of respect that they create. Done well, social rituals bind people to one another.

Through rituals, people assemble, separating themselves from their ordinary, everyday existence. They separate themselves from those not part of the group. They collectively participate in common, coordinated, even rhythmic activities. They pray, sing, chant, march, listen, and clap together. They create shared emotions. They may feel awe, excitement, reverence, pride, contentment together. They make sacred objects and emblems that embody their group and its ideals. Those banners, holy books, Greek letters, names, mottos, clothing, and other objects and emblems make concrete what otherwise is ethereal—the significance, even sacredness, of their group. To mishandle these sacred objects is to disrespect the group. Done well, rituals produce commitment (Collins, 1982: Chapter 2).

Rituals create moral and emotional energy. In acting with others, members experience being a part of something larger, more powerful, than themselves. Their actions and beliefs are not those of an isolated individual, but of a group of people bound together. Their shared experiences, training, and knowledge set them apart from others. The collective, even rhythmic chanting, drilling, dancing, singing, pledging, and other activities increase the emotional energy of the participants. From quiet contentment to increased esteem to spiritual glow to elation to even manic frenzy, rituals charge participants. They become emboldened to act when they would not do so alone. Consider the extra boost of athletes who seem to play beyond themselves at the deafening urging of the hometown crowd, the zeal of the political party after a rally, the renewed dedication of church members after a moving religious service, or the increased determination of family members to meet their family's challenges after an emotional reunion.

However, when members of the group disperse, the commitment and moral energy may dissipate. Separation from one's companions and immersion in everyday activities lessens one's solidarity. Gazing upon, manipulating, thinking about, or in other ways experiencing the sacred objects that embody the group can re-energize the dispersed members. They read from holy scriptures, put on uniforms and wear special colors, recite mottos, attach pins, look at pictures of family members, and the like. However, members may sometimes find it difficult to energize themselves only through manipulating these symbolic objects. So they maintain that solidarity by reassembling to ritually reproduce the sacredness of their group. Weekly worship services, regular meetings, reunions, celebrations, and the like enable committed members to renew themselves through ritually participating with one another (Collins, 1982: Chapter 2).

Rituals can be a powerful means for creating social commitment. In what rituals do you participate? I would imagine that you may be participating in anything from intimate, two-person rituals to large-scale, national rituals. How do you feel when you do so?

Responsibility

Rituals are not the only means for producing commitment. Responsibility can be effective, too. When people have responsibility for acting for or on behalf of their groups—for representing them to others and making decisions about the operation of their groups—they are likely to become much more committed to their groups. Through responsibility, members have the opportunity to extend themselves for others.

When you and I represent our groups to others, we become identified with our groups. Others identify us as members of those groups. They act toward us not as isolated individuals, not even merely as individuals, but as part of overall groups: our teams, organizations, sororities, schools, families, and so on. Thus, they make salient our membership in the groups that we represent. We also identify ourselves as part of the group, publicly proclaiming that we are its members. By speaking for them, we "stand for" our groups. We judge ourselves through the eyes of our teammates, classmates, and colleagues. Who we are becomes tied more forcefully to our groups. Representation creates identification, and identification encourages commitment (Collins, 1982: Chapter 3).

Responsibility for decisions in groups also increases people's commitment. In giving people responsibility for making decisions for the groups, their members entrust themselves to their fellow members. In making decisions for their groups, the members invest themselves in their groups. Their decisions become fateful for the groups and for themselves.

Furthermore, if the responsibility is collectively exercised, then commitment may become even stronger. Members deliberate with one another to decide for all, their participation with one another increases, and their collective decisions may become shared beliefs. Workers given responsibility for helping to make decisions about their work and about larger company policies, volunteers given responsibility in their civic groups, students given responsibility for helping to run their schools and classes, and children given responsibility in family matters all become more committed to their respective groups. Responsibility for others provides an opportunity to create commitment among one another (Ford, 1987: Epilogue; Wood, 1992; Kohn, 1993). Instead of being coerced to act, people with responsibility have the opportunity to direct themselves in the service of one another.

Other Means to Create Commitment

Beyond rituals and responsibility, people use other means for creating commitment. For example, in opposition to outsiders who threaten the group, its members may draw more tightly together. National leaders may rally citizens against the credible or the trumped-up threat from other countries, though opposition to outsiders can develop into scapegoating or demagoguery.

Some groups use a mix of strategies to create commitment among their members. Consider for a moment Utopian communities, which flourished in America during the 1800s, especially the 1840s, then again during the late 1960s and early 1970s.

Utopian Communities and Commitment

Utopian communities strove to develop physical, social, and spiritual harmony in which people lived and worked together "closely and co-operatively" (Kanter, 1972: 1). Utopian communities in America generally developed out of a

> desire to live according to religious and spiritual values, rejecting the sinfulness of the established order; a desire to reform society by curing its economic and political ills, rejecting the injustice and inhumanity of the establishment; or a desire to promote the psychosocial growth of the individual by putting him (or her) into closer touch with his (or her) fellows, rejecting the isolation and alienation of surrounding society. (Kanter, 1972: 8)

Some utopian communes developed out of a mix of these concerns.

Those utopian communities of the 1800s that were most successful, lasting for several decades or more, created and maintained collective commitment. This commitment enabled these communes to "survive crises, persecution, debt, and internal dissension" (Kanter, 1972: 75). The strategies involved *sacrifice, investment, renunciation, communion, mortification,* and *transcendence.*

Successful utopian communities required their members to sacrifice for the community, such as abstaining from sexual activities, alcohol, tobacco, meat, or other common objects and activities. Through austere sacrifices, members gave up things that had been desired in order to belong, thereby increasing the significance of each commune.

Members invested their time, energy, and resources in these successful communes. They were often required to donate financially and assign their property to the communes, as well as turn over what they received while members of the communes. These donations were often irreversible. Through investment, members tied their future to the success of the communes.

Through renunciation, members gave up outside ties that would weaken their attachment to the entire group. They were also discouraged or forbidden to develop smaller subgroup ties within the group. Geographical isolation from mainstream society; the provision of all that members needed within the communes; the labeling of all mainstream society as outside; distinctive language and dress to further separate the commune from the outside; restrictions on contact with outsiders; restrictions on the formation of couples; and the lessening of the importance of the family were all means that successful utopian communities used in creating and maintaining attachment to the entire group.

Successful communes created communion among their members in the form of collective unity. Religious, social, ethnic, or any other homogeneity of members promoted communion. Sharing property with the commune; collectively working for the commune rather than for individual pay; rotating work assignments and working together as a commune, such as during harvests; communal meals, meetings, and other regular group activities (which left little time to be alone); group rituals and celebrated special occasions; and facing together the persecution of the outside world, all promoted the communion of its members.

In successful communes, members mortified themselves. They lessened individualistic pride and tied their identities to their communes. They publicly confessed all wrongful ways from the past and mutually criticized one another for continuing any of these errors. Successful communes often distinguished members according to how well they lived up to the communes' ideals. Special privileges might be provided to those who more successfully embodied the ideals of the communes; otherwise, the communes did not typically differentiate the members. For example, members might wear similar clothing and be buried in similar coffins.

Finally, through transcendence, communes created the belief and faith that members were part of some higher, all-encompassing system that made their lives meaningful. Successful communes developed ideologies that explained humanity and directed its members in many areas of living, including their daily schedules. The ideologies justified the requirements of the communes by appealing to such higher, transcendent principles as God's will. Some communes claimed that, by being a member, one had special powers of revelation, wisdom, and the like.

Though members participated greatly in making daily decisions together, they were often separated from the spiritual leaders of their communes. These leaders were the charismatic founders who "served as the link between members and those higher sources of wisdom and meaning, who represented for their followers the greatest growth to which a person could aspire. . . " (Kanter, 1972: 116-117). By separating the leader from the followers, perhaps in a special residence and with a special title, and by making some decisions through revelation, the communes manufactured mystery and the "awe-inspiring magic of the community."

The mystery and awe of these charismatic leaders were protected by a system of leadership that handled everyday matters. The failure of everyday matters to go as planned could have discredited the leaders had they been handling these matters. This routine system of leadership also enabled successful communes to continue when founding fathers died (Kanter, 1972: Chapter 4).

Successful nineteenth-century utopian communities used many strategies to develop and maintain the commitment of its members. You might consider whether some of the groups in which you are a member use any of those strategies. I think you may be surprised.

We may not wish to participate in communes. I personally wouldn't, nor would I find all of their strategies agreeable. Some of them appear quite coercive, which could lead one to wonder if some of these successful communes created respectful collective commitment or oppressive dependence. But that is not my point. Rather, it is that people may use many strategies and go to great efforts in order to try to create commitment. Commitment does not appear naturally on its own. And not all of these strategies may be acceptable to you or me.

Shortcomings of Commitment

Commitment, like force and payoffs, has its drawbacks. Rituals take time. Organizing and participating in collective, coordinated activity take members away from working on behalf of the group. The more time and resources are spent on producing commitment through rituals, the less time and resources are left for tackling other tasks (Collins, 1982: Chapter 3).

Commitment may also create conflict. Rituals produce group loyalty, but group loyalty implies that those who are not members are outsiders. Outsiders do not hold dear what is sacred to the group; they are not bound to the group. Worse yet, the actions and beliefs of the outsiders, whether intentionally or not, may threaten one's own group. Outsiders may become enemies. Thus, school spirit may evolve into vandalism and fights between schools. Business loyalty may develop into sabotage of other businesses. Religious fervor could turn into persecution of other religions. Ethnic solidarity may be transformed into oppression of other ethnic groups. Patriotism may result in international belligerence, and so on. Commitment can produce serious conflicts.

Another possible drawback of commitment—at least from the stand-point of those who wish to get others to do what they want done—is that they may need to give up control in order for others to control themselves. But to myself and others, and hopefully to you, this "draw-back" can be a great strength of commitment.

When others are given responsibility to act on behalf of the group, those in charge have less control. Those used to being in charge place their future in others' hands.

Even more potentially threatening to those in charge is the fact that members with great commitment may care deeply about their group. Since the business, the church, the Greek organization, the military, the voluntary organization, or the country are deeply meaningful to those committed members, they may be concerned about what those in charge are doing. After all, it is *their* group, too. Are the leaders living up to the ideals of the group? Are the leaders successful in managing the group? Are their plans appropriate for the group's future? If not, then the members may eventually challenge the leaders whom they see as undermining the group.

Commitment can not only jeopardize those who wish to be in charge, it may also endanger the committed individuals. Others can take ad-vantage of those who trust them. Furthermore, members may become so immersed in the group, so bound up with each other, that they find it difficult to exercise any independent judgment. To do so would be to assert themselves against that which encompasses them. To do so may risk divorcing themselves from what gives them meaning. To those of us accustomed to the strong emphasis on individualism in America, "losing" one's individual self may appear frightening. The tragedy in Waco, Texas, in which members of a religious cult went up in flames with their leader, provides chilling testimony to the power and the dan-ger of commitment. But I don't think we have to look to the unusual to notice the corruption of commitment. From families and friendships to companies and nations, trust can be betrayed and commitment can overwhelm the individual.

Getting others to do what we want them to do is a neverending chal-lenge. It does not happen naturally on its own. Instead, we devote enor-mous effort to that challenge. Unfortunately, we often fail. Out of our attempts to control one another, we create conflict.

Control and Conflict

Control produces conflict. How people try to control one another, their failure to do so, and how others manage those people's attempts to control them is what produces conflict. Social inequality, intergroup conflict, and crime are three such areas of conflict. Much has been said about them, but I will briefly discuss them in relation to control and conflict.

Inequality

Consider your social worlds, both large and small. Do you find equality in them? Are people equally wealthy? Do they receive the same amount of respect from others? Do they have the same capacity to decide what will be done? Do you find that people enjoy the same amount of whatever is desired?

Consider your society. Mine is America. When I look at my society, I notice that some people live in mansions; others live in shacks. Some eat lavish meals; others literally eat garbage. Some attend schools and universities that provide everything imaginable to help students to learn; others go to schools where everything seems to be broken. Some citizens in my country are honored; others are despised. Some work at jobs that are challenging and personally meaningful; others repeat the same task thousands of times each day. And still others cannot find work no matter how long they look or how long a line they stand in. In still other ways, people in my society have more or less of what is desired; while many people are in the "middle." I am not criticizing my society. In other societies, members are more unequal than in mine. I am simply observing that people are not equal. Are they equal in your society?

How about in your smaller social worlds? Are people equal where you work? Do they receive similar pay? Do they have equal authority for managing the work? Do they perform equally interesting jobs? How about school? Do administrators, teachers, other staff, and students equally run the school? How about clubs or other voluntary organizations of which you are a member? Are some members officers of the club with more authority than others? Are all members given equal respect? Perhaps your family enjoys equality. But are children and adults equal in your family? Are the parents equal? Who in your family tells whom what to do? Who controls the resources of the family? Who makes the decisions? Consider other groups and organizations in which you participate. Are the participants equal? Inequality is everywhere.

Does that make you suspect that inequality is inevitable, or that social life cannot exist without inequality? Social scientists have argued this point. Some have argued that, whenever people live and interact together, they must coordinate their actions. To do so requires leadership. Leaders direct others; therefore, whoever the leaders are have more power than those who are not. Furthermore, if humans are naturally self-seeking, as many claim, then those who are the leaders will use their superior positions to increase their well-being (Mosca, 1939 cited in Stark, 1992: 241-242).

I'm not so sure. We do need to direct one another if we are to live together. But must we create fixed positions of leadership that only some people are permitted to occupy? Or should we create ways to increase the participation of people in governing themselves? Perhaps people could do so through collective decisionmaking, or they could rotate the positions of leadership. From small communities to organizations that are alternatives to bureaucracies (as I will explore in the next chapter), people have reduced the inequality of leadership. Fixed leader positions may work fairly well, perhaps more so in larger groups. But is it inevitable that we create such arrangements of unequal power?

I'm also not sure that humans are merely self-serving. I believe that we have a tremendous capacity to serve ourselves and others. But creating commitment to one another is a difficult challenge.

Even if inequality is inevitable, people are not similarly unequal everywhere. Societies vary dramatically in how much inequality their members have created. For example, in some societies a small elite is in control; in others, members widely participate in governing themselves. Companies, organizations, families, and other groups vary greatly too. Inequality is widespread, but it also varies in many ways. How can we begin to make any sense of inequality?

Controls Create Inequality

I think that our attempts to control one another go far towards creating our relationships with each other. Through how we try to control one another, we create more or less inequality. We also produce other qualities in our relationships, such as the warmth or lack of warmth we have for one another.

Through force, we put people down; through payoffs, we put people at varying distances; through commitment, we begin to put people together. Force creates the most inequality, while commitment has the potential for producing the least inequality.

Dominating Through Force

Through force, we dominate people. We place others beneath us and make them less worthy than us, even unlike us. We create relationships of master and slave, nobleman and serf, oppressor and oppressed. Wherever we use force, we create tremendous inequality. The "great" agrarian societies of the world, such as ancient Egypt, Rome, China, the Aztec empire, and the nations of medieval Europe, created the most inequality. By monopolizing military force, a small ruling class controlled much of society. Serfs, peasants, and slaves toiled for the ruling class, not for themselves. Perhaps one fourth of what they produced was taken by the ruler; as much as one half by the elite. The elite often came to think of themselves as a "superior human species" (Stark, 1992: 256-260). Nowadays, in the developing countries of South America and Africa, where leaders still rely greatly on force in order to rule, inequality is much higher than it is in the advanced industrialized societies (Braun, 1991:75-76).

People dominate others through force in all kinds of relations. Parents beat or threaten to beat their children. Educators spank, paddle, scream at, detain, and expel students, or threaten to do all that and more. Coaches intimidate their players. Bosses fire or threaten to fire workers. In past times they broke the attempts of common workers to organize and improve their laboring conditions with bloody force (Zinn, 1980). The state directs most of its sometimes deadly force toward the poor, especially impoverished minority groups (Black, 1976; Reiman, 1990). I will return to this point near the end of the chapter. Through force, people suppress others and create great inequality.

Ranking Through Pay

When we pay people, we create an impersonal, instrumental relationship. What can others do for us? Apparently they cannot do the same, because we do not equally pay people or the positions in which they produce, nor do we give equal prestige to what they do.

For example, the average pay of chief executive officers in America is almost three quarters of a million dollars, twenty-five times as much as the average wage of a manufacturing employee (Shapiro, 1992). Of course, some executives are paid millions of dollars each year, while some laborers do not make enough to keep them out of poverty. Skilled corporate lawyers in a large city might earn $75,000 or more the first year out of law school. Skilled teachers might earn $25,000 that first year.

We respect people and what they do differently, too. For example, we respect more the position of an engineer than the position of a clerk (Stark, 1992: 465-468). How would you explain this inequality?

I believe that a widespread response, though not by everyone, would be the following: those who earn more deserve it. They deserve more pay because they are smarter, have more talent, studied longer, work harder, do more important work, and so on than those who earn less. They have earned their just rewards (Kluefel and Smith, 1981; Shepelak, 1987; Kohn, 1993: Chapter 2).

Some social scientists have developed a similar argument (Davis and Moore, 1945; Horan, 1978). However, they focus on the necessity of unequal payoffs in order to ensure the success of the social group.

Imagine that your group accomplishes a variety of tasks as it sustains itself. These tasks vary in their importance for the success of the group. Some are crucial; others are less significant. Wouldn't you want the most skilled, hard-working group members to perform the most crucial tasks and to do their best? If so, then what could you do? If payoffs are the means for "motivating" people, then your group should provide the greatest pay to those who do the most important tasks. Otherwise, your group may not sustain itself.

The above illustrates the basic argument of some social scientists who believe that inequality is useful to social groups. Inequality in payoffs is the means by which social groups insure that the most important tasks are performed by the most competent members.

Some social scientists have clarified that basic argument with the idea of "replaceability": the degree to which positions or those who perform the tasks of the positions are hard to replace (Stark, 1992: 243-247). Some positions and the people who occupy them are more difficult to replace than others. For example, the position of mailroom clerk and the people who occupy that position in a large business are quite replaceable. Others could easily be hired to do that job; secretaries, accountants, executives, and others in the company could, if need be, perform the tasks of mailroom clerks. The position of accountant and those who perform those tasks would be more difficult to replace. Those positions and people who are difficult to replace are important to the group. The more difficult it is to replace the position or its occupant, the greater the pay. In other words, the greater the demand for people to perform particular tasks compared to the supply of competent people available, the higher the pay (Stark, 1992: 243). Does that make sense to you?

This explanation is not satisfactory to me, however, nor to many other social scientists for a variety of reasons (Collins, 1975; Horan, 1978; Baron and Bielby, 1980; Coverman, 1988; Strang and Baron, 1990). I will not take up all those reasons; nor could I, since I have not studied them all.

Restraints

Indeed, tasks are not equally important. Some positions require more training and talent than do others. Some people and positions are more or less replaceable than others. But I and others believe that *restraints* are also important in producing inequality in payoffs (Collins, 1975:

420-424). Restrictions that people apply to who can do what produce inequality.

If people created a social world in which all members could act freely, then inequality would lessen greatly. If payoffs were the "motivator" in this world, then tasks that paid well would attract many people and perhaps more than needed. Likewise, tasks that paid poorly would attract few people and perhaps not enough to perform them. Pay could be reduced for the well-paying tasks, but then it would need to be increased for the poorly paid work in order for it to get done. Eventually the pay for all tasks would become more similar (Collins, 1975: 420-424).

But restraints disrupt the free actions of people. They interfere with who can do what, and they produce inequality. Recall the great inequality that force creates. When people pay one another to perform, they may create more subtle restraints, which in turn produce less inequality than force. I think we can be pleased about that, but I do not believe that we should ignore the restraints.

Those who argue that inequality is a useful means by which social groups sustain themselves recognize what might be called "individual" restraints. People differ in their intelligence, conscientiousness, pleasantness, and other personal qualities. These differences may restrain some people, limiting what they can do. They presumably limit the supply of people who can perform the more demanding, important tasks. But those who argue that inequality is useful for society primarily focus only on individual restraints. They ignore or pay less attention to social restraints, those that people create.

Social scientists who disagree have emphasized the restraints that people create. I briefly mention just a few of those restraints. People limit others to develop themselves. For example, they do not provide equal educational opportunities to everyone. Public schools may now be available to all, but they are not equally educational for all students. And few have access to exclusive private schools. Educators and others in charge limit who can take what classes, who can go to college, who can major in what disciplines, who can attend graduate and professional schools, and so on. Many people who could benefit from increased educational opportunities are turned down or turned away.

People are also limited in their opportunities to work. Most obviously, not enough jobs exist for everyone who wishes to work. Millions of Americans are unemployed, and other countries suffer even greater unemployment. When pay is used to get people to perform, those who have few alternatives are more likely to accept jobs that they otherwise would not, particularly low-paying positions. Educational and licensing requirements also limit who can do what. Even worse, people are discriminated against by not being hired or promoted into positions they may deserve. Women, black Americans, those with disabilities, and others have historically experienced such discrimination in America.

More subtly, but perhaps more significantly, the way social groups organize their tasks also limits what people can do. Often the structure of work causes restraints. Social groups must structure work in some way in order for it to be done. They must arrange for who to do what through which social arrangements.

For example, by organizing work into fixed jobs that only the occupant of each position is allowed to do, groups limit people's opportunities to learn to perform a wide variety of tasks. Work could be organized more flexibly and fluidly, so that more diverse tasks could be available to more people within the group. Classifying jobs into many separate categories, with distinct titles, descriptions, and requirements, can become a means for some workers to protect their privileged positions by keeping their distance from other workers (Strang and Baron, 1990). Creating "job ladders" within an organization, such that those on one ladder (e.g., a series of production positions) cannot easily move to another ladder (e.g., a managerial "track"), also restricts who can do what. Assigning categories of people, such as men and women, to different job tracks further restricts workers.

A country's entire economy can become structured. Organizations create relations among themselves. Social scientists have argued that some organizations are part of the core or advantaged sector of the economy. They are large, have relatively few competitors, depend on sophisticated technology, and yield high productivity and profits. For example, major "high-tech" computer companies would be part of the core economy, while other organizations are not part of the mainstream and remain peripheral. The latter tend to be small, depend more on the labor of their workers, compete with many other organizations, and yield low productivity and profits. Small retail stores are one example. Those who work within core organizations are likely to be better paid, given more opportunities for advancement, and have greater job security than those similarly qualified workers in peripheral organizations (Coverman, 1988).

These and many other arrangements restrict who does what. Some of these restraints may be useful for accomplishing tasks, while others may not. Some people may support certain restraints; others may disagree with them, though they may not be able to do much about them. While payoffs may produce rankings of people and positions, they do so through the many restraints that social groups create.

Are you satisfied with what is implied by those who argue that unequal pay is a means to insure that positions difficult to replace will be competently filled? Doesn't it imply that pay is what primarily matters to people, perhaps mostly to those who take up the more challenging positions? Or does it?

Creating Equality Through Commitment

Through commitment, we begin to join ourselves with others and produce solidarity among one another. Through rituals that bind and shared responsibility that unites, we can move toward equality with one another. In which of your relationships are you and the other parties most equal? I would imagine that these are relationships in which much commitment has been created. Perhaps in your families, among friends, in some of your voluntary organizations, or elsewhere, you and the other members have begun to produce more equal relations through commitment. Are these also your most satisfying relations?

Social groups of all kinds, even whole societies, vary by their commitment. For most of human history people have lived as hunters and gatherers. While they produced little surplus to divide unequally, they also relied greatly on commitment to function. Small bands of kin folk, daily interacting with one another, ritually sharing what they had, worshipping the supernatural together, taking collective responsibility for their survival, created a great deal of commitment to and equality with each other. These bands did create inequality based on the sex and age of their members. But if some member tried to become a leader and control others, the others would probably regard this would-be leader as mad and either ignore him or her, or move away and set up another band (Harris, 1989: 344- 351).

Nowadays, while America and other technologically advanced societies rely greatly on payoffs, they produce considerable commitment, too. From public schools that aim to educate all children equally, to national celebrations and rituals of patriotism, to democratic government in which citizens collectively exercise responsibility for their governance, to greater responsibility in the workplace, technologically advanced societies depend greatly on widespread commitment to survive. Today's despots, on the other hand, do not depend as much on this commitment. Strong commitment from their relatively few supporters and from the military is enough for them to wield their power. Through the way we try to control one another, we create inequality.

Intergroup Conflict

People also create intergroup conflict through how they attempt to control one another. They produce interethnic tensions, interracial antagonism, religious hostilities, international conflict, and conflict between other groups. While specific conflicts between groups vary in important details, I think they all develop out of people's attempts to control one another.

Consider a group of boys at summer camp. The boys are separated into two groups. They live in two different cabins; eat their meals separately from one another; swim, hike, and do other camp activities apart from each other. Several days later, counselors bring the two groups together to compete in athletic contests. What do you think might happen?

When Muzafer and Carolyn Sherif did what I just described, the boys created solidarity within their groups and bitter rivalries between them. When first separated, they developed nicknames for their groups, created flags and insignias, and deeply identified with their respective groups. They also viewed the boys of the other group as outsiders. When they all began to compete athletically, the boys created hostilities between their two groups. They fought, called each other names, and damaged the cabins and possessions of the opposing group. They created intergroup conflict (Sherif and Sherif, 1956: Chapter 9; 1966: Chapters 9 and 10). If 12-year-old boys can so quickly create intergroup conflict over what may seem to be minor matters, we should not be surprised that adults do even worse over seemingly more important issues (Stark, 1992: 290).

When people create solidarity among themselves and compete with others for payoffs, for what they find desirable, the participants will create intergroup conflict (Banton, 1983). When people create in-group solidarity, they necessarily create outsiders. Those who are not part of the in-group are outsiders. These outsiders have not participated in the rituals of the in-group, they do not share their common experiences, nor are their beliefs the same. They are strangers. Who are they? Can the in-group trust them? And, of course, the insiders are strangers to the outsiders.

When the insiders and the outsiders compete for what is desired—jobs, land, educational opportunities, control of the government, worldwide economic opportunities, and other desirables—the outsiders become threatening. They threaten the insiders' security and future, even their existence.

If the in-group uses force to counter that threat, even force in the subtle guise of such restricted opportunities as barriers to hiring "them" or quotas on "their" imports, then the insiders heighten the antagonism between the groups. Remember, force denies a fundamental feature of people—to direct themselves. If force succeeds, then the insiders have made the outsiders less worthy than themselves, perhaps even fundamentally alien to themselves.

The oppressors may then justify their force by arguing that the outsiders deserve to be oppressed. The insiders may stereotype the outsiders as brutish, foul-smelling, uncivilized, or in some other way less human than are the insiders. The outsiders' sexuality is not normal. They corrupt, seduce, or act in treasonous ways. They are loud, flashy, or in some other way overly visible. They are fundamentally different from the insiders (Adam, 1978). Therefore, the insiders must keep them in their subservient place.

If the outsiders have not yet created solidarity among themselves, then many are likely to strive to do so. Their common oppression becomes fertile soil in which to produce solidarity. But the solidarity will not blossom on its own. It must be nourished, as the outsiders come together to share their common plight, plan what to do, and collectively attempt to counter their oppressors. Oppression may be met with collective resistance.

Recall your high-school days. I would imagine that many of you went to a high school that had a strong rivalry with one or more other high schools. During the week of the "big game" with your rival, what did you and your fellow students do? Did you participate in pep rallies and other rituals and activities that increased your school spirit? By doing so, you increased the solidarity among your fellow students. But did you also increase the separation from, even antagonism toward, your rival? No doubt your rival did likewise. Did students from your school pull pranks on the other school? Did some of them paint your school colors on the rival's property? Did your rival pull pranks on your school? Did the pranks sometimes escalate into fights? How did you stereotype your rivals? Did you think they were less worthy than you? And all of this may have happened even though you knew students from the other school. Wherever people create in-group solidarity and compete with other groups for what is desired, they may produce intergroup conflict.

Until people create a larger solidarity that includes the antagonistic groups, intergroup conflict will continue. Through inclusive rituals, sharing of responsibility, and developing common goals toward which members of differing groups can contribute, people may create that larger solidarity. For example, when the Sherifs arranged for the feuding campers to tackle problems that required all of them to work together, such as fixing a water-supply system or getting a truck to start, the boys began to reduce the conflict between their two groups (Sherif and Sherif, 1956: 316-328).

Even conflict with a third group that threatens both the insiders and outsiders can momentarily enable the two antagonistic groups to join together (Sherif and Sherif, 1966: 285-286). However, that expedient alliance may collapse when the outside threat vanishes. Consider, for example, the uneasy cooperation among Israel and its Middle Eastern neighbors against Saddam Hussein. After Hussein was driven out of Kuwait, Israel and its neighbors resumed their antagonisms. Even allies, much less hostile groups, may have difficulty working together after a common threat is vanished. Witness the increased difficulty between America and its European allies to work together now that the Soviet Union has collapsed.

Reducing intergroup conflict is difficult. Often the dominant group has handled the conflict through force, having eliminated, removed, segregated, confined, or in other ways kept the less powerful group down. Antagonistic relations have been perpetuated for decades, even centuries. For example, consider what the European colonizers and then Americans did to Native Americans and to Africans. America is still grappling with those conflicts.

Ironically, out of producing what is useful for social life—solidarity—we may create what is harmful—intergroup conflict. We create intergroup conflict as we develop solidarity among some of us and compete with others for what we desire. Solidarity is inclusive, but it also creates conflicts of exclusion.

Crime

Crime is a third form of conflict that we produce when we try to control one another. I will briefly mention three ideas concerning crime that may be very different from what many of us "know" about crime: crime as social control, a justice system that is itself criminal, and seductions of crime. Each of these ideas concerns different connections between crime and control.

Crime as Control

What is crime? I think most of us take for granted that crime is illegal behavior. It violates our standards. We may even see it as immoral behavior. It is a failure of control, of both social and self-control (Hirschi, 1969; Gottfredson and Hirschi, 1990). Social groups have failed to restrain its members who commit crimes, and those who commit crimes have not developed proper self-control. Therefore, we must control crime. How to do so is continually debated. But perhaps we can also look at crime in another way.

Have you ever experienced the following? Some children are playing with one another until one of the children keeps the ball, repeatedly pushes another, calls the other names, or acts offensively in some other way. Assuming that no adult is present to handle the matter, the child who is offended retaliates against the offender, perhaps by assaulting him or her. What do you make of the child's retaliation? Is it a violation of morality? Or is it an attempt to uphold morality?

Some crime may be viewed as moralistic, perhaps an attempt to punish or control those who have wronged the "criminal." Maybe the criminal is the victim. Perhaps a great deal of crime, including even serious crime, can be understood as the "criminals'" attempts to pursue justice. When legal means are seen as not readily available to handle the alleged wrong, people may act "criminally" to uphold justice. And when people use crime to control others, the American legal system often treats offenders more leniently than we imagine. By doing so, it makes less unacceptable what we would otherwise take to be criminal (Black, 1983).

Consider vandalism or malicious destruction of property. Much of it seems to be wanton, without purpose. Cars are spray- painted, school property is defaced, store windows are broken, and so on. But at times, those vandals have a grievance with the property owners. They have been wronged in some way. Perhaps school officials have "put them down" or thrown them out; perhaps someone continues to park in their spot. Maybe the store refuses to hire any local teenagers. The vandals see themselves as victims who pursue justice.

What about assaults and even homicides? Most assaults involve people who know one another and have grievances against each other. Many homicides fit this pattern, too. Family, friends, and acquaintances are offended by the behavior of those they know and violently attempt to seek justice (Luckenbill, 1977). Spouses act unfaithfully; "friends" act disrespectfully. Even quarrels about mundane matters such as paying bills or fixing dinner may become deadly contests over respect and honor.

Please don't misunderstand me. I am not excusing such crime. I am not advocating that people "take the law into their own hands." But when the law or other means of social control are not easily accessible to some people, we should not be surprised when they sometimes act outside the law. When youth are wronged and authorities will not listen to them, when women are abused but our justice system does little to the abuser, when the concerns of impoverished people go unheeded, we should not be surprised if some help themselves. Crime may be partly an attempt to uphold morality rather than violate it (Black, 1983).

A Criminal Justice System?

The criminal justice system is the state-approved use of force against those who harm others. Through it, people attempt to reduce crime and control those who commit crimes. When you think about crime and criminals, what comes to mind? Do you ponder such crimes as murder, rape, assault, burglary, drug dealing, and other street offenses? Do you imagine a scruffy, tough-looking male, perhaps a young, minority youth? Would you be surprised to learn that most of the harm to people and their property comes not from young, minority males, but from managers, professionals, executives, and other successful people who are typically white? Most harm is committed by those in the "suites," not on the streets (Reiman, 1990).

Each year, more people die or are physically harmed through the hazards of their work than are murdered or assaulted. More money is stolen through white-collar crime—consumer fraud, embezzlement, insurance fraud, tax evasion, price fixing, and other crimes of those far from poverty—than is stolen by street criminals. But when people express concern about crime and politicians talk tough about crime, they are not typically thinking about business executives, bankers, lawyers, managers, white-collar workers, and other "respectable" people. Maybe the criminal justice system works in ways that we have not thought much about.

Perhaps the criminal justice system works in such ways that it produces a "visible class of criminals." This visible class is young, impoverished, often minority males who commit street offenses. When people worry about crime, they primarily look "below" them in order to protect themselves from harm. But they rarely consider the harm that comes from "above." This one-sided image of crime and criminals deflects people's attention from some of the greatest dangers to them.

How does a criminal justice system produce an image of crime that emphasizes the street offenses of the impoverished but neglects the white-collar offenses of more successful citizens? First, by not seriously addressing what is known about some of the social landscapes within which street crimes flourish—the widespread availability of guns, the impoverishment of hope and opportunity that many poor people experience, and a perhaps misguided war against drugs—society gives a helping hand to many impoverished people to commit crimes. Second, by focusing primarily on one-on-one harm such as murder, robbery, assault, and other street offenses rather than on occupational hazards, chemical assaults on citizens (through food additives, smoking, and pollution), and unnecessary and dangerous medical practices, society narrowly defines what is crime or at least what is serious crime. Third, by more likely arresting, prosecuting, and imprisoning poor minority offenders than well-off professional and corporate offenders, society fills up its prisons with only some of the people who harm its citizens. If you have never visited a prison, you should. But don't be misled. Prisons do not hold all of those who harm others, but primarily only the least powerful (Reiman, 1990).

The criminal justice system also produces an image of crime that deflects people's attention from unequal educational, occupational, and other opportunities that citizens experience. This distorted image of crime helps to protect the advantaged position enjoyed by those who are relatively well off in society, who have the greatest capacity to change the criminal justice system. Yet, they see little reason to do so. They, too, believe that the greatest harm to society comes from "below."

Most of those who are well off do not harm their fellow citizens, but neither do most of those who are impoverished. Many in the criminal justice system work with dedication and compassion to assist those who have committed crimes to become more responsible citizens. At the same time, people can act with good intentions, yet still create harmful arrangements. In that sense, social life can be very complex.

Nevertheless, I encourage you to wonder about what is accomplished through the criminal justice system. Are we controlling harm, or are we also protecting successful people's advantages, some of which does great harm (Reiman, 1990)?

You may believe that it is an exaggeration for Jeffrey Reiman, whose work I have drawn from, to charge that the criminal justice system is a system that is criminal. Yet, do you consider every legal system a system of justice? Do you consider the legal systems of Hitler's Germany, the former Soviet Union, South Africa when it embraced apartheid, China, and many other countries just? What about when America first embraced slavery then later segregation? Legal systems may be grossly unjust to us all (Reiman, 1990: Conclusion).

Criminals often use force, but so does the criminal justice system. If this system is to be superior to crime, then shouldn't it use its force to protect equally everyone and punish equally those who harm others? To the extent that the criminal justice system perhaps does not protect nor promote justice, then perhaps it is a *criminal* justice system (Reiman, 1990). What do you think?

Seducing Ourselves into Crime

How would you explain people committing crimes? Social scientists have developed many possible explanations, some of which argue that an internal or external cause makes people commit crimes. Some people are defective—they are wicked, biologically predisposed, have pathological personalities, and the like. Law-abiding citizens must restrain these people if they cannot reform them. Other explanations emphasize that social conditions are defective. People who experience broken homes, disorganized neighborhoods, inadequate schooling, few job opportunities, and other adverse social conditions become criminals. Conventional citizens must help these people. Though these explanations may be somewhat useful, each suffers a similar shortcoming (Collins, 1982: Chapter 4; Katz, 1988).

These common approaches assume that some condition causes people to commit crimes. As I have explored earlier in the chapter, almost never does anyone or anything make us do what we do. But as you might recall, we do encounter very different social landscapes within which we direct ourselves. Responsibility for social life is shared.

Nevertheless, many people who experience these internal or external "causes" do not commit crimes, while many people who do not experience these causal conditions do commit crimes. And even those who experience the causal conditions and commit crimes sometimes commit crimes and sometimes do not. If these conditions make people commit crimes, they work in very mysterious ways (Katz, 1988: Introduction).

I ask you to consider another view, that perhaps we seduce ourselves into crime (Katz, 1988). Perhaps we produce powerful feelings and understandings that seem to compel us to commit crimes. It is almost as if we "had" to do it, even though we are the ones who initially produced that sense of compulsion.

Have you ever stolen anything? Many ordinary people have. Try to remember what that experience was like. Consider the following scenario involving a young woman. It could just as easily be a young man, but the work I draw upon here primarily concerned women on this point (Katz, 1988: Chapter 2).

While a teenage girl is shopping, an item "catches" her attention. She cannot take her eyes off the perfume, the bracelet, or the lingerie. It seems to beckon to her. She knows she has to have it. It is there for the taking. It would be so easy. But are others watching? Surely they must sense her deviant desire. But how could they? What if she is caught? What would her parents say? She'd "just die." But nobody would have to find out. She could get away with it.

The teenager moves back and forth between the desire to do it and the horrifying thought of being caught. Her oscillation increases the attraction of the object. The excitement, the thrill, and the tension increase. The girl begins to act out the larceny in her heart while concentrating on maintaining a normal appearance. But how should she act like a shopper when she is no longer one? What she previously did without having to think about it now becomes a challenge when her desire has become deviant.

The teenager may produce one or several of a multitude of emotions. She experiences the thrill of courting danger but also the control to overcome it; the excitement of exploring the unthinkable without others sensing her desires; the satisfaction with winning the contest; the rush, almost a sexual rush, as the tension builds then releases when the getaway is made. All of these and more make her sneaky thrill profoundly compelling. The teenager may throw away what she stole or never use it. She may vow never to do such a "crazy" thing again. She may feel ashamed for having done it. But during the shoplifting, she made it an emotionally compelling experience. She created a challenge to herself.

Could she do it? Could she do what until then was unthinkable? Finally she did it—and succeeded.

She has seduced herself into crime, creating a powerful experience that compelled her to do it. The forbidden item, the emotionally charged scene, and the experience of it made her do it. Yet, of course, nothing made her do it. She made herself do it. Doesn't this seem odd? It almost seems magical. But it is not a magic trick performed only by those committing crimes. You and I conjure it up everyday.

Don't we experience much of our everyday behavior as compelled by outside (or inside) "forces"? Something "catches" our attention. A colleague made us mad. That movie made us laugh so hard that our stomachs started to hurt. We couldn't keep from staring at whomever or whatever. That book was so boring that it put us to sleep. The cookies or chips were so tasty that we couldn't stop from eating all of them. In these and many other moments we experience ourselves as compelled to act by something over which we have no control (Katz, 1988: Introduction). Yet, we create those compelling experiences.

Seducing ourselves into crime *and* into conventional behavior seems strange, doesn't it? Of course, that is not how we produce and experience all of social life. But perhaps our capacity to act, to create satisfying and horrific social life as I mentioned in Chapter One, is greater than we realize. After all, as I explored in the previous chapter, we create our worlds. Seducing ourselves is one way we do so. Now that is something to wonder about.

Conclusion

How we get people to do what we want them to do is a fundamental challenge in creating social life. It is difficult because nothing typically makes people act. Instead, people direct themselves. They direct themselves to meet all kinds of concerns. Some people's concerns at times may not be especially compatible with others' concerns. This basic self-directing feature of humans makes getting people to do what we want them to do a tremendous challenge.

We may use a mix of strategies for getting people to do what we want done. Force, payoffs, and commitment are three important ways that I have explored. We often use force or threaten to use force to get people to act. However, force denies the integrity of people. It produces resentment and creates great social conflict.

We also pay people to do what we want them to do. I think pay is a tremendous improvement over the use of force. However, it is not without its difficulties, as explored earlier.

Moreover, if you buy into the "pay-for-performance" scheme, have you sold yourself out? Certainly, given our economic arrangements, al-

most all of us must take up paid work in order to live. For most of
human history that was not so. There was no "paid" work. But the more
we do what we do because others pay us to do it, the less we save of us
for ourselves.

Perhaps the most satisfying way to get people to do what we want
them to do, and the most difficult of the three, is to create commitment.
By creating collective commitment, we can begin to give up the illusion
of control over others in order to create communion with them. We do
not impose our will on others but instead try to create a collective will
to which we can all commit. But with greatly different visions of the
world that we wish to create, we may find it very difficult to give up the
attempt to control others. And commitment can be corrupted, as I noted
earlier.

You must decide how you will try to get others to do what you want.
This is a challenge we face every day.

There is at least one other way that we use to get people to do what
we want them to do. We may not realize that we use this approach, as
it is so pervasive and difficult to detect. We mutually use it on one another. I did not cover it here because I already explored the basis for it
in the previous chapter.

When we create the world such that we make it an objective, taken-
for-granted, that-is-just-how-it-is-and-must-be world, then we greatly
control one another. We do not question how the world is. Instead, we
act within it as we "know" one must, as our entire being "compels" us
to act. Even fleeting thoughts of alternatives can repulse us. It can turn
our stomachs, as it does to the students in my class when they view a
film of college students at a fraternity ritual eating salamanders.

But consider eating people. How horrifying! Yet, a man in Milwaukee
did so a few years ago. Throughout history, different groups of people
have practiced cannibalism (Harris, 1989). Eating human parts was
part of their taken-for-granted world. I am thankful it is not part of
ours.

But to the extent that people create a taken-for-granted world, they
control themselves to a great degree. They do not recognize that they
could act differently. How do people create worlds that seem so powerfully objective that they are "obviously" as they must be? As you recall,
I took up that puzzle briefly in the previous chapter. I urge you to explore
it further.

In the process of trying to control one another, we create conflict.
We create inequality, intergroup conflict, and crime. Conflict and other
troubles seem to be everywhere nowadays. What has the world come
to? But has the world become worse? Let us now turn to the profound
changes in social life that people have created.

Chapter Five

Where Are We and How Did We Get Here?

I magine a world where people have improved their lives tremen-dously in a short period of time but now believe that their world is falling apart. For most of their existence, these people struggled to survive in small bands, often no larger in number than a kindergarten class. Moving every few weeks, they lived precariously on what they could catch or collect. Most of their children died during childhood (Stark, 1992: 529), and the average adult lived only thirty years. Gen-eration after generation, the lives of these people remained much the same. After thousands of generations, fewer of these people existed than now live in any of the great cities of our world. For most of their history these people were an "endangered species" (Stark, 1992: 529).

However, in the past ten generations or so, these people have revo-lutionized their lives and their world. Billions of them now inhabit their world, living in enormous groups of tens and hundreds of millions of people. One group is more than a billion. Living over twice as long as did their not-so-distant ancestors, many of these people are vastly healthier, eat dramatically better, learn much more, live more comfort-ably, and experience more widely the wonders of their world. They can peer inside their bodies, travel into the heavens, and instantaneously view the activity of others all around their world. They enjoy great free-doms in making their lives. Their ancestors could never have dreamed of the world in which their descendants presently live.

Yet, these people, particularly those who enjoy most the benefits of their revolutionary progress, are deeply troubled about their world and their future. Though they live like no one has ever lived before, they are disheartened and even frightened. Everywhere they look, they see trouble. Their families are breaking apart, their educational system is failing, their economy is floundering, their racial and ethnic groups are feuding, their countries are warring, crime is flourishing, and values are flaunted (Kennedy, 1993: 310). Some believe that their world is surely about to end.

What do you make of these people, who have made such unimaginable progress, yet are so deeply dissatisfied with their lives? What do you make of *us*? We Americans and others throughout the "developed" world and, to a smaller but just as important extent, throughout the entire world live beyond our ancestors' imaginations. In many ways, we are making social life far more satisfactorily based on our present values than we have in the past. Yet, we are deeply troubled. How do you make sense of this? I wonder if our genuine concern fundamentally misunderstands social life and overlooks our own accomplishments. I wonder if we nostalgically look to the past which, if we were to live it now, we would not find as satisfying as we have made it out to be. And I wonder if we reminisce too much, instead of grappling with the uncertainty of social life today and tomorrow.

Many of us believe that social life is natural. After all, we are social creatures. We become who we are through living with others. Without that sustenance from others over the years, we would not survive. Our human nature virtually guarantees that we live and interact well together, doesn't it? If social life is natural, then any problems that we encounter must be unnatural. And they may become almost unbearable. We lament that life is not supposed to be this way.

Yet, nothing inside or outside of us assures us that we will succeed at social life. Often we don't, as I have shown throughout this book. Instead, we have the capacity either to produce wonderful social life or to fail miserably. If we realize that successful social life is not guaranteed, then perhaps we can better cherish our successes and strive to improve our shortcomings.

Many of us do not have a keen sense of where we have come from. I myself don't. We are historically myopic. We live in the present, anticipate the immediate future, and forget what little we knew or experienced of the past. Because we view life so shortsightedly and take social life for granted, we often lose sight of our amazing progress in creating social life. In just a few hundred years (though building on achievements from before), people have revolutionized their lives and their worlds. I will later explore some of these changes more fully.

In the process, however, we have created new challenges for ourselves. The challenge of living and interacting together never ends. We continue to create new social means for meeting our concerns but also new, unanticipated obstacles. We also create new standards by which to judge ourselves. The troubles that concern us today would not even exist had we not made so much progress in the past few centuries.

For example, our ancestors would not have been troubled by segregated education when they had no schools. The conflict between different races and ethnicities would not have caused them much heartache, since they lived in small, isolated bands of kinfolk. The poverty, inequality, and economic hardships that dismay us today would not have worried them in their hard struggles to survive. The challenges experienced by working mothers in managing the two careers of work and family would not have concerned our ancestors when all people worked at home or when women were expected to be housewives while men went to work. Through change, we have created a far different world of challenges.

Ironically, by advancing so far in such a short time, we have made for ourselves a fundamentally new challenge: the pursuit of progress. Because we have been so successful so quickly, we have come to believe that progress is natural. We tell one another so in many ways, not the least of which are the promises of our politicians and the blandishments of our businesspeople: if you elect me, I will make your life better; you deserve the best, so buy my improved product. Progress, doing better than the previous generation or even better than yesterday, becomes the standard by which we measure ourselves. The pursuit of progress is a fundamental feature of our world. But we do not always and everywhere make progress. Social life is not so simple. Maintaining present successes can be seen as failure when we expect progress.

If we assume that social life and progress are natural, then any setbacks, shortcomings, or so-called "stagnation" will create uncertainty and even despair. We handle such difficulties and feelings in many ways. One way, noted above, is to look back to what we believe were more satisfying times before we somehow went astray.

I will first explore four *social shortcomings* about which we often complain. However, I would argue that we should regard these shortcomings more usefully as our *social successes*. How have we revolutionized our world in such a short time? Many of us would answer that technological inventions have been crucial. From the steam engine to the computer and beyond, we have dramatically changed our world through scientific progress and its technological application. I would certainly agree. But *social inventions* have been important, too. Without them, sustained technological development would not likely have been possible. I will explore two such social inventions: capitalism and bureaucracy. Through these and more, we have revolutionized our world. But like all inventions, our social inventions have shortcomings.

Social Shortcomings or Social Successes?

Many Americans are troubled over their country. Wherever they look, this country seems beset with problems. But I wonder if any of those shortcomings might better be understood as successes.

If we look more closely at how we lived in the past, we may be surprised at how much we have presently achieved. Nostalgia for a golden past that in reality never existed needlessly troubles us today. Many of us would not want to return to the "good old days," even if we could.

Consider four important arenas of social life: *families*, *education*, *material comfort*, and *social relations*. We are more successful in these four arenas than we realize. Yet, we continue to face significant challenges.

Families

Many believe that American families are in danger. About half of all marriages end in divorce. A million children are born out of wedlock each year, about 25 percent of all those born. Around one fourth of all children under the age of 18 live with a single parent, primarily their mothers (Saluter, 1989). By the time they become adults, most youth have been sexually active: almost 80 percent of males and more than 70 percent of females have had sexual intercourse (Hofferth, Kahn and Baldwin, 1987; Sonenstein, Pleck and Ku, 1991). Domestic violence is rampant. Millions of children, women, and men experience physical abuse each year at the hands of their families (Straus and Gelles, 1988). And on and on it goes (U.S. Bureau of the Census, 1991: 67). Families, the bedrock of society, seem to be crumbling.

Americans gaze wistfully upon traditional families from the past. They look nostalgically at the situation comedies of the 1950s, such as *Father Knows Best* and *Leave it to Beaver*. These programs show what many Americans long for in a family: stability and security, with the mother at home, the father at work, and a couple of children in school. Our yearning for bygone days has distorted our image of so-called traditional families and has misunderstood our changing creation of families (Coontz, 1992).

Traditional families, particularly from the 1500s to the 1700s in Europe, did not fit our nostalgic image at all. They were often cold, impersonal groups of people typically crowded into one or two filthy rooms, perhaps with lodgers and hired hands. Spouses were emotionally distant, as their marriages had often been arranged by their parents in order to create or strengthen ties among families and for economic purposes. Because death came early, few spouses lived long together. Families with one parent or with a step-parent were common. Sex was often strictly functional, without emotion or joy, designed to produce children, maintain family lines, or appease an employer.

Many parents were indifferent and inattentive to their children. Children were not the "apple of their eyes." Many died in infancy or childhood. Many parents boarded out their infants to wet nurses who suckled them, though the parents knew that they would not be able to nourish all the children under their care. Those that did not die early typically left their families in early childhood, as young as 7 or 8, to work elsewhere as servants, apprentices, or shepherds. Parents neglected their young children as they worked from sunup to sundown, sometimes even later for the mothers. Infants suffered skin diseases and sores from being left in dirty swaddling. Harvest time was especially dangerous for young children; many perished when they strayed too close to the hearth fire or were eaten by barnyard hogs. Others were simply abandoned outside churches or foundling homes or, if they were dying, were discarded like trash. Some parents did not know how old their children were, others reused the same name when a child died, and many showed little regret over their children's deaths. These parents were not monsters. It was simply out of their struggles and their conceptions of children as creatures "barely possessing a soul" that traditional parents were so indifferent to their children (Shorter, 1975: 169).

Domestic privacy did not exist, nor was it sought. Family members did not turn to one another for companionship. Instead, they sought companionship among their peers, perhaps at a tavern or an evening's sewing bee. Privacy further decreased as lodgers and hired hands crowded with the family into one or two rooms. The citizens of small villages knew one another's affairs, often disciplining those who were errant and supervising the courtship of the young.

What many of us take for granted or long for today in our families did not typically exist in traditional families of old. Western society began to develop a concern for romantic love, the welfare of children, and family privacy in the late 1700s and early 1800s, which eventually led to the creation of what some call the modern family (Shorter, 1975). Near the end of this chapter, I will briefly explore our development of the modern family. At this point, do you still yearn for traditional families?

What about the tight-knit "nuclear" families portrayed by the sitcoms of the 1950s? Real families of the 1950s were more complex and not as successful as their television counterparts. They did not solve all their problems in 30 minutes. The 1950s were "an era of suppressed individuality, of national paranoia, and of largely unrecognized discrimination against minorities, women, the poor, foreigners, homosexuals, and indeed most of those who dared to be different—the era that came to an end with the onset of the '60s was a time bomb waiting to explode" (Conger, 1981: 1477-78 cited in Skolnick, 1991: 50). Many women were bored by their housework and found it difficult to care for several young children. Wives who worked were regarded as abnormal. Observers were concerned about the delinquency, drinking, gang fighting, and educational shortcomings of youth in the 1950s (Skolnick, 1991: Chapter 2, 207). Clearly, the 1950s was not by any means the golden era for which many of us now nostalgically yearn (Coontz, 1992: Chapter 2).

Perhaps more importantly, the nuclear families of the 1950s were not typical of our continuing development of families. A family with the mother as housewife and the father as breadwinner was an uncommon arrangement, which peaked around 1890. Before the 1800s, all family members in a household contributed by working. With the rapid development of factories in the 1700s and more greatly during the 1800s, husbands went off to work while women remained at home—in part because men forced them to do so.

Since World War II, however, women and in particular wives and mothers have left home for work as well, primarily out of necessity. (Statistically, black women have worked for pay or looked for paid work more frequently than white women.) With the proliferation of relatively low-paying, white- and pink-collar jobs, such as for clerks, fast-food workers, secretaries, receptionists, and teachers (especially after World War II), and with the cost of living since the mid-1960s rising more quickly than the income of the average working male, married women have increasingly become paid workers (U.S. Bureau of the Census, 1975: 134, 1992: 387; Harris, 1981: Chapter 5; Skolnick, 1991).

Mr. and Mrs. Cleaver, who represented those adults who formed families in the late 1940s and especially during the 1950s, were an anomaly. Since at least the early 1800s, families have been having fewer children. Women in the early 1800s gave birth to an average of 7 or 8 children. One hundred years later, they had about 3 children. Today, women average about 2 children. Since the mid-1800s, marriages have increasingly ended in divorce, though the divorce rate has recently leveled off and declined slightly. Most young men and women at the turn of the century did not marry in their early twenties, nor will they likely do so at the end of this century (Cherlin, 1981; Saluter, 1989).

But the "Cleavers" and many others who became adults in the late 1940s and the 1950s married somewhat earlier, had larger families, and were more likely to remain together than the trends Americans have been creating for the past hundred years or more (Cherlin, 1981). Why? How is it that these young adults momentarily reversed the American trend of the past century? Several possibilities have been suggested (Cherlin, 1981; Easterlin, 1987), but I will mention just two of them.

First, many of the young adults from this era grew up during the Depression. In order to help their families survive, they often took on adult responsibilities as children, working and helping extensively at home, even leaving home to work. They were ready to begin a family by their late teens and early twenties. They also realized how important children were for families, having themselves played important roles in their own families' survival. Finally, many experienced disharmony in their childhood families due to the economic difficulties of the times. Therefore, they cherished family security and stability. Out of these family experiences from the Depression, many young adults in the late 1940s created their own families. If this explanation seems useful, should we follow its implication? I don't think so.

A second possibility is based on World War II and its aftermath. America had mobilized for war, diverting its industrial capacity from producing consumer goods to military weapons and materials. The pent-up demand for consumer goods and the might of America's corporations throughout the post-war world helped to fuel a strong economy that enabled people to marry sooner, support several children, and experience fewer of the strains that often undermined marriages. Furthermore, our government's gratitude toward the veterans who served their country was in effect a pro-family policy. We made available to fourteen million veterans, most of them young, single men, "substantial severance bonuses, cheap life insurance, guaranteed low-cost mortgages, and tuition and monthly stipends for education with dependency allotment" (Harris, 1981: 83). Whether we intended to do so or not, we provided a massive subsidy for young people to form families. While I realize that the implications to be drawn from this possible explanation are more complicated, would we want another earth-shattering war in order to proliferate the mythical families of the 1950s sitcoms?

The housewife/breadwinner family is only one kind of family that we have created. Because many American adults today were either parents or children during a brief resurgence of that family form, many yearn for it and mistakenly assume that it has been the dominant form throughout history. But that hasn't been the case at all.

Instead, with the continuing development of our modern society, we have created new family arrangements in response to the changing challenges we experience: economic struggles, new job opportunities for women, declining job opportunities for those poorly educated, greater equality between women and men, lengthier dependency of youth as we keep them longer in school and out of work, extended life span, greater emphasis on emotional satisfaction, and more. We are struggling to create loving, emotionally satisfying, more egalitarian families, something that we have never done so prolifically before. We should not be surprised if, as a result, we experience many setbacks (Skolnick, 1991).

We even mislead ourselves with our statistics about family failure. For example, while about half of all marriages now end in divorce, that does not mean that half of all married people divorce. Most married people do not divorce, but some of those who do divorce do so several times. Their repeated divorces and continuing search for fulfillment mislead us about the stability of marriages. Twenty years ago, approximately 21 percent of those over fifty who had ever married had divorced; today, the figure has risen to about 27 percent (Stark, 1992: 389-390).

About 70 percent of married Americans claim to have very happy marriages; only a small percentage say that they are unhappily married. Americans are more content with their families than with their work, friends, or hobbies; and they are happier with their families today than during the 1950s (Caplow, 1991: 62; Coontz, 1992: 35-37).

Consider family violence. Some statistics show a dramatic increase in domestic violence. Typically, these are official statistics reported to social service agencies. But much of that increase is due to our heightened awareness of such violence and our increased efforts to record and reduce it (Straus and Gelles, 1986; Skolnick, 1991: 172). What we tolerated in the past or even considered natural, we abhor today. Family violence rightly troubles us because we are trying to make more emotionally satisfying, respectful relations among family members. Moreover, other studies that do not rely on reports to official agencies show a decrease in child abuse by parents and no increase at all in abuse among spouses (Straus and Gelles, 1986). What appears to be a problem has perhaps become a stunning achievement!

Minority citizens, particularly black Americans, are experiencing great challenges in creating stable, emotionally satisfying families. Black Americans are less likely to be married, more likely to have children without being married, and more likely to head single-parent households than white Americans. For example, slightly less than half of all black Americans 18 years and older are married; almost two thirds of white Americans are married (U.S. Bureau of the Census, 1991: 43). More than half of all black households are headed by women, as opposed to less than 20 percent of white households. Approximately 60 percent of all black infants are born to unmarried mothers, while less than 20 percent of white infants are born out of wedlock. More than half of all black children live with a single parent, while approximately 20 percent of all white children do (Saluter, 1989).

Primarily since World War II, black Americans have diverged from white Americans in their patterns of forming families. Why? No one is certain (Cherlin, 1981). Some social scientists believe that an important reason, but certainly not the only one, is the imbalance between the number of young black women and black men. For every 100 unmarried black women ages 20 to 24 there are only 72 unmarried black men ages 23 to 27 (men being typically a few years older than the women they marry) (Stark, 1992: 350). This imbalance is worsened by many black men's (and black women's) lack of training and economic opportunity to make and sustain families (Wilson, 1987; Lichter et al., 1992).

Why is there such an imbalance? Poor nutrition and health care affect male fetuses and infants more than female fetuses and infants. By their first birthday, black females outnumber black males. This is not so for white infants. As the children grow older, black males are more likely than black females to die through accidents, drug use, or violence (Stark, 1992: 363-5).

Unfortunately, many of the surviving black men have great difficulty in making a living that could sustain a family. For example, only about one unmarried black man with an income above the poverty level is available for every 3 unmarried black women in their 20s (Lichter et al., 1992). Many young black men have been caught up in the criminal justice system (as many as one fourth, according to some studies) and/or are unemployed or have poorly paying jobs. As I will note shortly, we are educating our black citizens more successfully today than in the past. Yet, we fail to educate all of our black citizens. Moreover, as we have decreased the availability of unskilled jobs, particularly those that pay a "livable" wage, inadequately educated citizens, whether black or not, have great difficulty making a living. Furthermore, with high school- and college-educated women increasingly working since World War II, black men who are often not as well educated have experienced even more difficulty in becoming employed. For these and other reasons, many black men face enormous obstacles in making a living and supporting a family (Harris, 1981: Chapter 7).

Should we be surprised that black women and men find it difficult to marry or to remain married? Yet, they live in a world where we heavily emphasize sexuality. Incidentally, when "suitable" white men are less available, white women also find it more difficult to marry (Lichter et al., 1992). Americans face great challenges in their attempts to form families. However, compared to past eras, families are in much better shape than many of us imagine.

Education

Many people give schools a failing grade. They believe that too many students learn too little. Respect appears to be down, violence is up, and teachers seem poorly prepared. Inner city schools are crumbling, and most of their students are dropping out (Kozol, 1991). American youth are falling behind those of other nations. Some do not even know where America is on a map, let alone other countries. We are producing a nation of incompetent youth, or so it seems to many. But are we really? Or have we once again overlooked our successes and misunderstood our shortcomings?

In many ways, we are educating our youth better than ever. However, we are not teaching them as well as many of us would like. We have made tremendous progress in the education of our minority youth, though that progress often goes unnoticed. Nevertheless, we continue to struggle in that endeavor, especially for those who live in inner cities and rural areas.

For most of human history, people have educated their youth within the family and the small groups within which they lived—hunting and gathering bands, clans, and small villages. Young children learned as they watched and helped older children and adults with chores and the other activities of life. With the development of an industrialized society, people began to more formally educate their youth. They did so primarily in order to provide them with the basic skills necessary to be productive workers in the newly built factories, to enable them to be responsible and aware citizens, and to bring together within a common culture the diverse people that populated the country.[1]

At that time, a grade-school education was deemed enough, often more than enough, for the vast majority of American youth. At the turn of the century, only an elite few finished high school or went to college; less than 10 percent of Americans graduated from high school in 1910 and only 3 percent of those between 18 and 24 were enrolled in college. Today, over 70 percent of Americans graduate from high school. The majority of Americans now start college and almost one third earn some kind of degree (Caplow, 1991: Chapter 8; Stark, 1992: 477). Until recently, Americans expected youth to leave school before they graduated; thus, the term "dropout" did not exist in 1950 (Meier, 1992: 271). Throughout this century, Americans have opened the schoolhouse doors more widely than ever before. Consequently, Americans are much better educated than they ever have been.

Some argue that in the past when Americans educated a smaller percentage of their children, especially in high school, they did so more successfully. The elite who graduated from high school a century ago were better educated than those who graduate today, because high schools imposed high standards on the few who attended. Those who could not keep up or measure up were not allowed to stay in school (Stark, 1992: 478-479). Perhaps this is so.

Or perhaps it is not. Seventeen-year-olds, from the 1930s to today, have not changed much in how competently they have answered questions concerning the laws of science, dates of wars, names of Presidents, and other basic scholastic information (Meier, 1992: 271). Fifty years ago, "talented" students "rarely took more than two years of high-school math, science or history, and virtually none took calculus—a college course in those days" (Meier, 1992: 271). Today, educators offer to and require from many students much more than they ever did before.

America now more broadly educates its citizens. While some lament the nation's grand obsession with television—American households watch an average of 7 hours each day (Caplow, 1991: 103)—we are also reading much more now than we did before industrialization. We have the time, the money, and the ability to do so.

American students may not do as well in math, reading, science, and other academic areas as do students of other advanced industrialized countries (Stevenson and Stigler, 1992). When Americans finish high school, however, most of them start college. Far fewer do so in other countries. And many foreign students come to America to study at its colleges and universities (Stedman and Smith, 1985; Caplow, 1991: Chapter 8).

Much has been written recently about what is wrong with America's schools. Certainly we can and should improve them. But perhaps the broader lesson to be learned is that we and other industrialized countries are educating our citizens far better than in the past, while developing countries are striving to do likewise.

Many citizens remain appropriately concerned about the failures in educating less advantaged youth, particularly black Americans and other minority youth (including those with disabilities). However, black youth have made great advances in the past several decades. Before then, black youth were much less likely to finish high school than white youth. In 1950 less than one fourth of black Americans (and other "non-white" citizens) between ages 25 and 29 had finished high school, while more than half of white Americans in their late twenties had done so. Today, 86 percent of white Americans aged 25 to 29 have attended 4 or more years of high school, while 83 percent of black Americans (and others who are "non-white") have done so. The median years of school completed for white and black Americans aged 25 to 29 is now 12.9 and 12.8 (U.S. Department of Education, 1991: 17). Are many people overlooking the great improvements that America has made?

Challenges continue, however, in the education of America's black youth. They and the youth of other minority groups are less likely to go to or graduate from college. Many who live in the inner cities do not finish high school. Dropout rates exceed 50 percent in some areas (Kozol, 1991). As a group, black and other minority youth do not perform as well on proficiency tests as do white students, but they have made some impressive gains, especially in reading (U.S. Department of Education, 1991: 112-121, 1993: 115-124).

Americans have asked their schools to do more and more—to educate all of their increasingly diverse youth, to prepare them for a more complex society in which fewer and fewer unskilled jobs exist, to counsel and guide them, to feed them, to encourage their personal and social growth, and still more. Certainly, improvements can be made. But the shortcomings can better be understood as partly the result of the greater educational demands that Americans have placed upon themselves. While important challenges exist, Americans (and citizens of many other countries) can take credit for their successes. If people cling to the myth that schools were more successful in the past, then they may not very well meet the challenges that they now face and will face in the future (Meier, 1992).

Material Comfort

Rising prices, mass unemployment, poverty, homelessness, the increased layoffs of white-collar and professional workers, stagnant wages, savings and loan scandals, the increasing cost of medical care, the bankruptcy of large companies, the soaring cost of a college education, and more trouble us all. So they should. The "American Dream" seems to have become an economic nightmare for many. But again, I wonder if it would be more useful to view our economic concerns within a larger context. I do not wish to overlook suffering, but we should not ignore our successes. As we achieve more, we expect more. What appropriately troubles us today, we took for granted in the past.

Let's go back only several hundred years ago, for example, to the era of the European exploration of the New World. Peasants, between 90 and 95 percent of people in preindustrial European societies, lived wretchedly (Stark, 1992: 256 quoting Sjorberg on percentages). Many survived worse than the members of our ancestors' hunting and gathering societies thousands of years before. For example, the typical medieval English peasant had

> little more than a hunk of bread and a mug of ale in the morning; a lump of cheese and bread with perhaps an onion or two to flavor it and more ale at noon; and a thick soup or pottage with bread and cheese in the evening. . . . Beds were uncommon; most peasants simply slept on earthen floors covered with straw. (Lenski, Lenski, and Nolan, 1991: 179)

Life was a grim struggle for peasants surviving on their farms. Many did not. Crops failed and livestock died. Taxes, tithes, fines, "gifts" to the lord, and loan interest of more than 100 percent drove many peasants off the land. By the late 1700s in France, millions of dispossessed peasants drifted throughout the country. With survival so precarious, many families directly or indirectly killed their infants, especially girls. Death rates were high and life was short. Peasants could expect to live only 25 years (Lenski, Lenski, and Nolan, 1991: 173).

Life was not only a struggle for peasants, but often their lives were not even their own. The governing elite was only a few percent of the agrarian population, and yet they owned much if not most of the land; perhaps as much as two thirds of all arable land. They also often owned the peasants, who with their primitive technology could support themselves and provide a surplus for their masters. One Russian nobleman of the nineteenth century owned 2 million acres of land, more than twice the size of Rhode Island, and almost 300,000 serfs. The czar of

Russia owned more than 27 million serfs (Lenski, Lenski, and Nolan, 1991: 178).

For almost everyone then, life was short, harsh, and grossly unequal compared to today. Even the elite, with all their possessions, lived short, difficult lives compared to most of us in contemporary Western society, even those classified as poor.

Most citizens in America and other technologically advanced countries enjoy the health, comfort, and material well-being that the kings and queens of past ages could not even dream of: sanitary living conditions, effective health care, a sufficient supply of nutritious and diverse foods, adequate housing, rapid communication and transportation, and so on.

For the past several hundred years and especially in this century, Westerners in particular have prospered. The income per person in Western Europe has increased more than ten times since the mid-1700s, with the United States in the lead (Fukuyama, 1992: 76; Chirot, 1986).

> The great majority of people throughout the world today are healthier, better fed, longer-lived . . . better protected against pain and suffering . . . better educated, better housed, and more frequently entertained than any preceding generation. (Caplow, 1991: 25)

Others appropriately point out the continuing challenges to Americans' material well-being: the increase in the poverty of children in the past twenty years, the continuing extensive poverty of some of America's minority populations, a decline in weekly incomes in the past twenty years (Kennedy, 1993: 294), the relatively unchanged income inequality since World War II, the difficulty for less well-educated citizens to make a living, the increase in the average unemployment rate for each decade since World War II (Cloward and Pivens, 1993), the recent increase in the unequal distribution of wealth (e.g., such assets as stocks, bonds, real estate, and other forms of accumulated resources) (Nasar, 1992), the higher cost of housing relative to people's income (Braun, 1991: 6), the millions of citizens without adequate health care coverage, the competition from abroad and our relative decline compared to other industrialized countries, and so on (Caplow, 1991: 40; U.S. Bureau of the Census 1991: 462). These are important concerns. However, I do not believe that we should overlook the great strides that people have made in America and in other technologically sophisticated or industrializing countries.[2]

Perhaps the greatest challenge is to enable the least technologically developed countries to grow more fully in order for its citizens to enjoy the health, education, nutrition, and other comforts taken for granted by many of us (Kennedy, 1993). Approximately one third of the world's countries produce less per citizen than the United States or England produced almost 200 years ago (Chirot, 1986: 59). The gross domestic production (i.e., the value of all goods and services produced within a country) per person in the United States, West Germany, and Japan (excluding farming and such extractive industries as mining) is between $16,000 and $17,000 per year. The GDP for Bangladesh, Ethiopia, Uganda, and other economically troubled countries is less than $100 (Lenski, Lenski and Nolan, 1991: 241-242). The heartrending impoverishment of more than one billion people, primarily in parts of Asia, Africa, and elsewhere, and the increasing gap in the material well-being of citizens in technologically advanced societies, compared to those in some of the less developed societies, trouble many (Chirot, 1986: 207, 233; Kennedy, 1993: 49). For example, more than 100 infants die out of every 1,000 born in some countries. In America less than 10 do, even fewer in some other countries (Population Reference Bureau, 1992). Many people throughout the world are more materially comfortable than they ever have been. But others still live under harsh conditions.

Social Relations

Americans are divided, not united. Relations among citizens are strained. Members of ethnic and racial groups are wary of one another, if not hostile toward each other. Intergroup strife in our cities, including riots and "hate crimes," alarm and sadden us. Many white Americans believe that black Americans have as equal an opportunity to advance themselves as do whites; whereas, most black Americans do not believe that they are getting a fair chance (Gallup, 1992: 165-170). The recent immigration of people from Central America, Asia, and other non-European countries seems to be changing the face of America in ways that many white Americans find uncomfortable. "Does anyone speak English any more?" complain some of them. And others demand that Americans in government agencies and elsewhere do something about it.

Americans are "culturally warring" with one another (Hunter, 1991). Those who believe that absolute truth is divinely revealed and those who hold that truth and values are evolving and relative each compete with the other for America's "soul." The conflict over abortion, school prayer, the Supreme Court, homosexuality, family, and other issues deeply divide the country.

Everywhere you look, Americans appear to be at odds with one another. Many women are challenging men for equal opportunities in education, business, politics, the professions, at home, and in public; yet, they fear a backlash. Men are having difficulty managing these changing attitudes. Citizens with disabilities demonstrate for equal rights, but critics argue at what cost. People who are homosexual refuse to stay or be shut in the closet, even and especially with the widespread prevalence of AIDS. Generations clash. Adults complain about the violence and loud, obscene music of youth, while the youth complain that they get no respect. Adults have forgotten their responsibilities to their elderly parents. On the other hand, senior citizens seem to have more political power, maintaining such entitlements as Social Security and Medicare, than non-voting children (Caplow, 1991: 140). And the clashes among citizens throughout Europe, Africa, the Middle East, and elsewhere, many of which are similar to ours, show that conflict among people is worldwide.

But are we once again forgetting the improvements that Americans and others have made in living together while we appropriately attend to the conflicts that we continue to create? And are we assuming that people naturally get along? If we do, then any failure to do so would indeed be deeply troubling.

As I have explored earlier, I do not believe that anything inside or outside of us guarantees that we will live together successfully. The fact is, we do *not* naturally get along with others. Until we make ourselves known to each other and develop solidarity among ourselves, we will continue to be wary of one another. As long as people are strangers to us, then we will remain suspicious. If others are not "one of us," if we have not made them part of our kind, family, clan, group, community, country, religious body, or common humanity and joined them to us in some other way, then we are watchful. We do not know who they are, what they will do, or whether we can trust them (Stark, 1992: 283; Collins, 1982: Chapter 1).

Therefore, when we do live and interact together successfully, we should take credit for our success. While we continue to experience great difficulty and suffering in trying to live together, we have also made tremendous progress within our country and throughout the world.

Compare America today with its past. Americans enslaved black people, raped black women, lynched black people (more than 4,000 have been documented), and legally segregated them until just a few decades ago. Americans killed Native Americans by the thousands, then marched their survivors off to reservations. Americans restricted the "dangerous, turbulent flood of immigrants" with harsh immigration laws in the 1920s that favored Anglo-Saxons at the expense of those not "white" (Zinn, 1980: 373). The American government rounded up approximately 100,000 Japanese-Americans and detained them in relocation camps for three years during World War II (Zinn, 1980: 407-408). Businessmen and politicians pitted ethnic or racial groups against one another in order to better control them, as strikebreakers, in preferential hiring, as recipients of patronage, and the like. America did not enfranchise women until the passage of the Nineteenth Amendment to the Constitution in 1920. Until recently, women and men had typically only men to vote for. And it was not until 1960 that Americans elected a president who was not Protestant. America forced people who were gay into the closet and kept those with disabilities at home or warehoused them in large institutions.

America has always been a nation of diverse people struggling to live together. By the next century, it will be even more diverse. Sometime during the twenty-first century, most Americans will not trace their ancestors to "white" Europe (Takaki, 1993). Yet overall, Americans succeed more in many ways today than they ever have.

Civil rights laws and other government regulations and programs promote fair treatment for people regardless of their age, ethnicity, race, religion, sex, or disability. Citizens may not always abide by these laws or vigorously enforce them as some would like, but this legislation makes it officially clear that America will not tolerate the kind of discrimination that was once taken for granted. The outrage that many of us feel now when we hear of the beating of minority citizens by majority officials, the sexual harassment of women, the desecration of places of worship, and other acts of violence and intimidation is testimony itself to our heightened expectations. The increased interaction of diverse people on the job, in politics and social organizations, and in non-coercive intimate relations (during slavery, coercive intimate relations occurred often between white masters and black slaves) speak to the improved social relations that we have created. (However, in the last several decades schools, especially big-city schools, are becoming more racially segregated (*Newsweek*, 1993, December 27).)

Much of the social conflict that concerns Americans today is due to their improved relations and increased expectations. What troubles Americans today about relations among one another was often of little concern or notice to them in the past. The oppressive behavior toward black Americans, women, those with disabilities, and others that now offends many of us was often the typical, accepted behavior of the past.

With a broadened, worldwide view, people have made great strides in living together. But they continue to experience great difficulty in doing so. Many of us take for granted our industrialized societies. However, for the past 2,000 years most people have lived in agrarian societies. For several thousand years before then, humans lived primarily as horticulturalists, herding animals and cultivating crops (Lenski, Lenski and Nolan, 1991: Chapter 4).

Our agrarian ancestors would make us look pacific, were it not for our advanced warfare technology. Their societies were constantly at war. Their crops, their surplus, their land, and even their people were always worth raiding. Two thirds of a sample of premodern agrarian societies warred every year. Perhaps as much as fifty percent of the time, European agrarian societies were at war (Stark, 1992: 257).

While warfare has become dramatically more destructive than ever before, some societies are warring less. During the 1700s approximately four and one half million people died in wars. In this century alone, on the other hand, wars have killed more than 100 million people (Caplow, 1991: 26). Yet, liberal democracies have either never warred with one another or have not done so since the early 1800s. The United States, Canada, England, Australia, France, and now Germany, Japan, Italy, and other countries whose governments recognize human and political rights have not warred with one another. Liberal democracies still war with other countries, but some societies have created peaceful international relations (Fukuyama, 1992: 42-45, 262-265).

As meager as international assistance may sometimes be and as often ineffective as such international organizations as the United Nations may seem, both speak to the growing solidarity that we diverse people have created among ourselves. Even the Olympics and other international athletic events address the worldwide solidarity that people are creating. We have always struggled to live together, but I believe that in many ways we are more successful than we have ever been.

But how have we done so? How have we revolutionized our world even as we continue to create and confront the challenges of social life?

Social Inventions

People have dramatically remade their world in just a few ticks of the earth's clock. Consider that life began on earth more than 3 billion years ago, and that our distant ancestors appeared perhaps 5 million years ago. Only about 100,000 years ago did homo sapiens appear. Just 10,000 years ago, humans lived primarily in nomadic bands that moved every few weeks or months in order to forage for food and other necessities. Fewer than 10 million of us existed throughout the world in 100,000 to 300,000 of these tiny bands with their endangered lifespans of about 30 years (Harris, 1989: 14-19; Lenski, Lenski, and Nolan, 1991: 45, 97; Stark, 1992: 530).

Five hundred years ago, populations had increased considerably, but they were still small compared to today. Europe had about 80 million people; the world about 425 million. Just a century and a half earlier, the bubonic plague killed between one quarter and one third of the population of Europe (McEvedy, Jones, 1978, 1979: 18, 342; Lenski, Lenski and Nolan, 1991: 178).

Today our world is dramatically different. More than 5 billion of us inhabit it. We live in fewer than 200 societies, each averaging between 25 and 30 million citizens. China has more than 1 billion people, and India is approaching that number. We have created huge metropolises of millions of residents. The life expectancy of people in technologically developed countries is now 70 years and more. The sorcerers, shamans, and "men of science" of centuries ago would marvel at what many take for granted today: computers, air travel, space exploration, vaccines, antibiotics, CAT scans, organ transplants, dialysis, cellular phones, microwave ovens, silicon chips, and genetic engineering (Harris, 1989: 501; Lenski, Lenski, and Nolan, 1991: 45, Chapter 9).

How did we accomplish all this so quickly? How did we remake our world in such a short time?

The conventional answer is science and technology. Through increasing scientific understanding and technological applications, people have revolutionized the world. Science and technology have been and continue to be important. From the small band of hunters and gatherers who stalked their prey with sticks and spears, to the medieval farmers with plows, to the large-scale managers of agribusinesses; from the sorcerers who tried to appease the spirits, to the medical men who let blood and drilled holes in people's skulls, to high-tech doctors with their CAT scans and laser tools; from the belief in supernatural powers to the knowledge of nuclear power; from the use of fire to the use of solar energy and the silicon chip. Our astonishing technological developments have enabled us to transform our world.

But science and technology are not enough. They provide us with possibilities, but we may not necessarily use and benefit from them. Without supportive social arrangements, science and technology will not flourish. Instead, they will wither away.

Consider China. It was more technologically advanced than Europe hundreds, even thousands, of years ago. Yet, it did not modernize as Europe did after the 1600s (Caplow, 1991: 20). Actually China did begin to industrialize long before Europe. By the eleventh century, northern Chinese industrialists had begun manufacturing iron on a large scale. They produced almost twice as much iron as England and Wales did 700 years later. These industrialists recognized the demand for iron and realized that they could send their iron to distant areas by river and canal. They quickly made large profits which they reinvested in their iron foundries, reaping even greater profits. With the increasing availability of iron, farmers began using iron tools that dramatically improved their production of food. By the thirteenth century, however, these Chinese industrialists were marketing very little iron, and eventually they abandoned their foundries. What happened? How did China's iron production collapse?

Most likely, the imperial court, having noticed that commoners were getting rich, began to closely supervise the manufacture of iron weapons, monopolized the sale of agricultural tools made of iron, then taxed the production of iron and set prices so high that industrialists could not continue their high levels of production. Invasions by nomads and the flooding of the Yellow River, which destroyed the system of canals, added to the difficulties of sustaining the production of iron (McNeill, 1982: Chapter 2; Stark, 1992: 506). Without supportive social arrangements, China's iron industrialization floundered.

If science and technology are not enough to revolutionize our world, what else is crucial? Without social inventions that encourage and enable people to work industriously, to produce more effectively, to strive to improve their performance, our modern world would not exist.[3]

Almost all of you have been employed at one time or another, and many of you are employed now. How hard did you or do you work while on your job? Do you extend yourself, even developing new ways to do your job more efficiently and effectively? Or do you "goof off" while pretending to work diligently?

People have the capacity to either work hard or be slothful. They have the capacity to either strive to increase and improve what they do or be satisfied with what they presently accomplish. Throughout history, people have worked casually compared to today's practices. They have often avoided work, performed little when they did work, and did not continually try to develop ways to be more productive. Hunters and gatherers of the past worked daily for about 3 to 5 hours, just as they do today (Csikszentmihalyi, 1990: 143); medieval peasants farmed carelessly (Stark, 1992: 504). Some of us may claim that this description of our ancestors' casual stance toward work applies to us today. No doubt it does to some of us. (And it does partly due to a shortcoming of our new social arrangements, which I will discuss later.) But people today typically work harder, striving more industriously to improve their productivity than their ancestors ever did.

An important exception to this is the labor of our predecessors during the early industrialization of Europe, America, and elsewhere. The industrial workers of the 1800s often worked twelve hours each day, six days a week, in unhealthy, dangerous conditions (Csikszentmihalyi, 1990: 143). Today, many recent immigrants may work long hours in unhealthy conditions. That most of us who live in technologically advanced countries work shorter hours (often less than forty hours each week) in much improved conditions is not any testimony to our laziness, but to our smarter productiveness. It is also testimony to our increased equality among citizens and our enhanced emphasis on individual gratification.

What then enabled England and other European countries to modernize so quickly around the 1600s? While the steam engine and other inventions powered the West into the modern age, science and technology were not enough. A variety of conditions and practices may be considered important here, but I will focus only on two (Chirot, 1985; Caplow, 1991: 20). England and other countries of the West that modernized at that time developed and implemented a new way of living and interacting together, a new social invention—*capitalism*. In turn, large-scale capitalism created and operated through *bureaucracies*.

Capitalism

Capitalism is the provision of human needs through private business seeking profits. A revolutionary social invention, it is the rational, calculable, methodical, predictable, and routine pursuit of profits. Through a free market, the foundation of capitalism, individuals freely choose how they seek to maximize their gain. They calculate and choose for whom to work, whom to employ and how, in what to invest their resources, what to make and how much to sell it for. People conduct business, knowing that their products and profits are secure from arbitrary seizure by the government. Through capitalism, they direct and organize themselves to pursue profits in a rational way.

Capitalism encourages and even requires people to work harder and smarter, rewarding their industriousness and inventiveness. Those who work harder and more effectively will prosper, as opposed to those who do not. Capitalism spurs technological development, necessitating that entrepreneurs develop ever more productive operations and new technologies. If they do not, then their competitors who have improved their own operations may drive them out of business. It "compels" people to work hard or be replaced by others who will (Collins, 1980; Stark, 1992: 505). Through the competitive pursuit of individual gain, capitalism increases the welfare of the society.[4]

I have presented a very brief, basic description of capitalism and the logic of how it operates. However, no people has ever created capitalism as neatly as described here. Perhaps they could not and should not. Perhaps they did not as some tried to protect their own advantages. When western societies began to develop capitalism, they did not have a blueprint to follow. Societies have since modified their capitalistic arrangements. Today capitalistic societies differ in their arrangements.

In and out of capitalist societies, people have debated whether and how capitalism should be implemented. Because the term "capitalism" has become pejorative to some, others have begun to use the term "free market" instead (Fukuyama, 1992: 44). As I will explore later, like all social arrangements that people make for living together, capitalism creates new challenges for social life and may not be satisfactory to everyone.

Nevertheless, capitalism is radically different from other means for living together. As a recent social invention, it is not the natural way that people must organize themselves. Many of us may not realize this, because we take capitalism for granted.

Precapitalism Exchange

While elements of capitalism existed thousands of years ago, it did not become the "indispensable" means for providing for human needs until the middle of the 1800s in Western Europe. Before the creation of capitalism, people exchanged goods and services primarily in three ways: ritual exchange, commanded exchange, and exploitative exchange. We continue to exchange in these three ways in capitalist societies, though not as the major means for producing and exchanging goods and services.

People have traditionally exchanged goods and services as part of a set of ritual practices that tied group members together and maintained the status of their relations. For example, a married couple in a clan gave their in-laws some item, and, either then or later, the in-laws presented the married couple with a gift. Or the lords of their manors gave to their church and remained in good standing with their fellow church members. There was no encouragement to produce more efficiently or to develop new products. People exchanged simply in order to maintain solidarity and stability, both important means for living together.

In another way, people exchanged with one another when others forced them to do so, the master forcing the slave, the ruler forcing the ruled, and so forth. Through taxes, tithes, rents, compulsory labor, "gifts," and other means, rulers took much of what peasants produced (Lenski, Lenski, and Nolan, 1991: 176-178). When elites commanded others to work or forced them to give up what they had produced or acquired, people usually had little reason to work hard or smart. If elites took the surplus produced by people, then those people were more likely to consume all that they produced than save some of it to invest in future production. They were also more likely to revolt, as peasants often did. For example, from 1801 to 1861 Russian peasants rebelled more than 1,400 times (Lenski, Lenski, and Nolan, 1991: 187). As I explained in the previous chapter, force is obviously not a very effective means for getting people to work effectively.

Furthermore, as the centralized economies of Communist countries and their recent dissolutions indicate, centrally commanded societies have great difficulty in effectively managing all the decisions and production processes necessary in a national or even international economy (Fukuyama, 1992: 93). Can you imagine having a central bureau of officials reviewing and setting hundreds of thousands, if not millions, of prices and making countless decisions about what will be produced by whom and with what resources? The Soviet Union and other Communist countries tried to do that but failed disastrously. Command societies that force exchanges simply do not work very well.

Merchants and traders also developed exploitative exchanges with those outside their solidarity group. Dealing suspiciously with those whom they did not know, they tried to cheat and price-gouge others before the others took advantage of them. Such exploitative exchanges did not promote the kind of stable, mutually beneficial relations that supported a free market economy (Collins, 1980, 1981: Chapter 1; Fukuyama, 1992: Parts I and II; Stark, 1992: Chapter 17).

Most of us participate in ritual, commanded, and exploitative exchanges in one way or another. Gifts and assistance of all kinds are often ritual exchanges. When parents, teachers, and spouses order their children, students, and spouses to work or perform, they are creating commanded exchanges. The "get-something-for-nothing" schemes that some of us fall for over the phone, through the mail, or on the streets, as well as the shady bargaining of our childhood and youth, are also exploitative exchanges. Now, back to capitalism.

The Rise of Capitalism

Imagine that you are an entrepreneur. You consider raising and spending large sums of money to develop and produce a new product, a "whatizit," or to build a large plant to produce products already on the market. Would you do so if you could not calculate and predict with some certainty what your costs and profits would be? If you could not be somewhat sure of obtaining the large amounts of raw supplies, labor, and continuing investment that you would need, would you try to start at all? If regulations that governed your business changed whimsically or the value of money fluctuated widely, would you undertake this venture? If you were not certain about the availability of safe and effective means for transporting raw materials to your plant and shipping your finished products to customers, would you take the risk? If the government might capriciously seize your profits, would you "take the plunge"? If you could not trust other businesspeople to honor agreements, would you want to go ahead? Probably not. Before the widespread development of capitalism, people had not created the social arrangements conducive to rationally, methodically, and calculably producing goods and services for a profit.

Capitalism depends upon other social and technological practices. Without them, a thoroughly calculable capitalism would not be possible. Management must be able to acquire the means of production in order to calculate how to use them. Land, buildings, materials, machinery, and other resources needed for production must be sold as private goods on an open market. Mechanized technology that enables the businessperson to carefully calculate costs improves the process of planning. People must be free to choose any work opportunity and experience the necessity to do so, because they have no other means for sustaining themselves. (Are shortcomings now beginning to become apparent to you?) Capitalists can calculate how much labor will cost, so they can set wages as needed to acquire workers. Any irrational restrictions on trading must be reduced. Restrictions on who can do what kind of work, who can buy what products, who can trade, and other movements of goods and the means of production must be minimized for capitalism to flourish. Finally, rational law that applies to all and enables all participants to systematically enforce their contracts and rights is needed in order to sustain capitalism. Such law must provide for private property rights over the various means of production, legal freedom for laborers, transferability of rights through stocks and other financial instruments, and all the other ingredients of capitalism (Collins, 1980).

These essential components of capitalism enable the investor, the executive, the worker, the customer, and all other participants to calculate and predict reasonably, if not perfectly, what course of action is most profitable for them. Without that economic rationality, without that predictability, large-scale capitalism will not flourish.

Before large-scale capitalism developed in the west in the mid-nineteenth century, previous societies lacked these essential ingredients. All kinds of irrational restrictions existed on the "free movement or economic transfer of labor, land, and goods" (Collins, 1980: 930). Often only aristocrats could own land; townspeople could not. Certain groups monopolized occupations or were prohibited from occupations, such as the prohibition of knights and peasants from trading. Slavery, serfdom, and other restrictive arrangements limited or prohibited citizens from moving wherever they could find work. Technologies of mass production were not widely available. The law was magical, personal, and/or corrupt. Warfare, robbery, poor transportation, an unreliable supply of money, and other barriers existed to hinder the rational, methodical pursuit of profit.

Through the ultimate development of a "liberal, bureaucratic" state, people created the ingredients for capitalism to flourish. The west developed the "highly bureaucratic state, based on specialized professional administrators and on a law made and applied by full-time professional jurists for a populace characterized by rights of citizenship" (Collins, 1980: 932). This liberal, bureaucratic state finally broke down the barriers to capitalism. It

> broke down feudalism . . . freeing land and labor for the capitalist market . . . pacified large territories, eliminated internal market barriers, standardized taxation and currencies . . . provided the basis for a reliable system of banking, investment, property, and contracts, through a ra-

tionally calculable and universally applied system of law courts. (Collins, 1980: 932)

In a liberal, bureaucratic state, individuals are citizens with political rights. We take the possession of citizenship rights for granted, but for most of history people did not have such rights. Instead, they had obligations to the ruler.

The development of military-fraternal cities acting to oppose the tyranny of a central ruler led to the development of these rights. By banding together, warriors created brotherhoods and city guilds fielded disciplined infantries to protect themselves and their interests against kings and lords. The rights of these urban elites later became enjoyed by others, even as the cities finally allied themselves with the central rulers.

Religion, which many of us see as incompatible with capitalism—one sacred, the other crassly secular—was important in the development of capitalism. The Church provided literate administrators, an education system, and its own bureaucratic structure as a basis for rational organization. The development of universal religions that worshipped one God for all people (though never completely so) broke down barriers between clans and tribes. Universal religions enabled strangers to form military alliances that opposed a central ruler and provided the trust necessary for methodical, large-scale economic practices.

Furthermore, the Protestant Reformation of the 1500s abolished monasteries and emphasized individuals' responsibility for their salvation. This shifted the ethical, methodical, and disciplined organization of life from the religious world to the secular world. Through disciplined, ascetic efforts, people could achieve salvation. In the process, capitalism flourished (Collins, 1980).

Technology certainly fueled the rise of the west, but it was not the only reason for modernization. The industrial revolution would not have been feasible without the social arrangements that constituted capitalism.

Large-scale mechanization depends on mass production. Even relatively simple machines, such as steam-powered looms, would be too costly without mass production. But mass production is feasible only when businesspeople can predict (though not always accurately) that large-scale consumer markets will be available and that the factors needed for mass production will be available at a reasonable cost. Otherwise, mechanization is worth little. Recall what happened in China almost a thousand years ago without social arrangements that supported the rational pursuit of private gain. Capitalism incorporates these necessary ingredients. The industrial-technological revolution occurred as capitalists sought ways to lower their costs and improve their profits. Through capitalism, which developed out of the liberal, bureaucratic state, people modernized the west (Collins, 1980: 929).[5]

Bureaucracy

Bureaucracies? Yuck! Have you ever waited in long lines only to learn that you were in the wrong line? Have you ever been passed from one staff to another when you asked for assistance? Have you ever received a bill that was in error but that multiplied itself month after month? Have you ever filled out a form in triplicate only to learn that you were handed the wrong form? As an employee, have the rules, procedures, and paperwork of your bureaucracy ever made your head ache? Many irritating experiences like these underlie our frustrations with bureaucracies.

But where would we be without bureaucracies? They are not perfect. No invention is. But bureaucracies enable people to create the modern, technologically sophisticated, free societies that many people enjoy and take for granted.

Bureaucracies have been indispensable to capitalism. Recall what I mentioned earlier about the importance of a liberal, bureaucratic state for the development of capitalism. Bureaucracy is a means for rationally and deliberately organizing people and their activities, particularly in large organizations. It is a way to control and coordinate what people do in order to calculatingly achieve the stated goals of the organization (Blau and Meyer, 1987: Chapter 1).

Imagine that you plan to produce and market television sets, selling them by the thousands, hundreds of thousands, even millions. How might you organize your company?

You might arrange for your employees to specialize. Each employee does one task or a small number of tasks to produce and market your product. Specific employees would design the sets, manufacture the parts, assemble the parts, create a marketing strategy, develop relations with wholesalers, and so on. No one employee would be responsible for doing everything. Through specialization, employees can become experienced and skilled at what they are doing. By dividing the production and marketing of the television sets into many small, less complex tasks, you are more likely to obtain people who can do the job effectively. (Of course, you may also be able to hire people with fewer skills at lower wages to perform the less demanding tasks. Could this be another source of concern to some critics of capitalism?)

If you divide the complex task of mass-producing and marketing television sets into many smaller tasks, then you will need to supervise many employees. As head of the company, you cannot possibly directly oversee all your hundreds or thousands of employees. You cannot make sure that they are performing as you have asked them to, that difficulties are handled satisfactorily, that the results are achieved as you had intended, and the like. Instead, you may employ some people as supervisors. High-level administrators may supervise various branches or departments of your company. Beneath each administrator may be other supervisors who manage the employees within the different units of each branch. Still other, lower-level supervisors may be used to manage the employees. Through this hierarchy of authority you are better able to manage your company, directing what others do and learning about the results of their actions.

While supervision will help you get your employees to do what you wish them to do, that by itself may not be enough. Supervisors cannot watch all workers do everything. So rules will be made to provide additional supervision. These rules may specify what size to make a particular component, how to obtain needed parts from another company, when employees should have breaks. Without directions to tell the employees what to do and how to do it, their actions may not be coordinated well enough with the actions of the many other employees in the company.

In order to be more certain that your employees are doing what you have asked them to do and in order to be aware of how your company is doing, you may use written records. People document what they are doing and the consequences of their actions. These records provide you and your administrators additional information about who is doing what in your company. The reports are another means for supervising your operations.

In order for your company to succeed, you will want qualified people who can do their work efficiently. You will hire people based on their skills, training, and experience. You will require them to attend to their work. Personal matters, family concerns, likes and dislikes, emotions, and other personal concerns are to be kept out of the company, as they could cause disruptions. You will stress impersonal, professional relations focused on "getting the job done."

The above are basic features of bureaucracy: specialization, a hierarchy of authority, rules, written records, and professional impersonality. All of these features enable those who run large organizations to more calculatingly and rationally manage their operations (Weber, 1968: 956-1005; Blau and Meyer, 1987).

Through bureaucracy, people have also produced better government. Many of us are disappointed by government inefficiency, corruption and "good-old-boy" politics. Several years ago, my own state experienced a scandal in its state government. But through bureaucratic procedures and principles, we have created more effective, responsible, and honest government.

Through a bureaucratic state in which professional officials implement rational laws that are applied to its citizens, leaders and citizens can enable their government to make a diverse people a nation of citizens. A bureaucratic government enables officials to reach throughout the country to routinely "touch" its citizens in so many ways that we take for granted or do not realize: the schools you attend; the roads on which you drive; the money that you earn and spend; the regulations that provide you with health and safety; the laws that structure business, finance, insurance, health, and all arenas of social life; and countless other arrangements. A bureaucratic state more effectively and stably governs a large territory of people. Repressive, non-bureaucratic governments may terrorize their people, but on a daily basis they do not touch their lives. And some people in countries where the government is not part of their everyday lives may not even think of themselves as members of a nation (Collins, 1980: 932).

Through bureaucracy, citizens encourage officials to carry out the obligations of their offices and not plunder the government for their personal gain. In past eras, rulers and officials understood the country, the government, and their offices to be their property and to be used to their own advantage. Favoritism, payoffs, and plunder were common. Many of us who are concerned about government corruption may not fully realize what vast improvements people have made (Lenski, Lenski and Nolan, 1991: 187-189; Blau and Meyer, 1987: 3).

Recently, even smaller and non-profit organizations have become bureaucratic. Apparently, they have adopted bureaucratic procedures in order to comply with government regulations. More than 90 percent of American employees work in bureaucratic organizations (Caplow, 1991: 92).

No organization of people operates solely according to bureaucratic principles. Perhaps they should not, as I will explain later, or perhaps cannot. Nevertheless, bureaucracy is a crucial social invention that has enabled people to revolutionize their world.

Revolutionizing the World

Through capitalism (and certainly much more), people have created enormous social changes that many of us now take for granted. Not realizing how revolutionary these changes are, we often assume that our present arrangements are how people naturally live. But we would be wrong.

Using the past 200 years as a rough benchmark, with the time varying somewhat by country and previous developments, Americans and others in technologically sophisticated societies have dramatically changed their worlds. To a lesser extent, so have the people of developing societies. Advanced and developing nations have changed in many different ways, but I will not explore the differences here. I will mention briefly a few of the more commonly known changes, besides those already explored earlier in this chapter. Then I will discuss a few of the less commonly known changes that may speak to the fabric of social life.

The people of technologically sophisticated societies have industrialized, bureaucratized, urbanized, and suburbanized; dramatically increased their economic wealth while emphasizing more the merits of one's efforts and less the station of one's birth; reduced the number of their children but greatly increased their population, as well as their divorce rates; created organizations of all kinds and sizes, often massive ones; increased their health and life expectancy; increased the size and scope of government, while reducing the importance of hereditary monarchs to symbolic and ceremonial roles; established free public education; improved the opportunities for women and others who have been oppressed; created and disseminated more widely new ideas, in particular the idea of progress; and developed tremendous weapons of mass destruction and used them, thereby questioning the idea of progress (Lenski, Lenski and Nolan, 1991: Chapter 9).

Many of us are aware of the changes noted above, even if we do not know much about them. I hope to learn more myself. I will briefly mention some changes that you may be less aware of.

1. We have separated work from the rhythms of natural life. The provision of food, clothing, and shelter used to be integrated with all other aspects of life. Throughout human history, people worked on tasks necessary to sustain themselves. They hunted, gathered, planted and harvested crops, raised and tended animals, made clothing and shelter, and attended to other tasks as part of the "natural" rhythm of life (Thompson, 1991: Chapter 6). When cows gave birth to calves, the peasant or farmer had to attend to them. Those who fished attended to the tides. Crops were planted in the spring, and grains were harvested before the arrival of thunderstorms in the summer. Cows were milked as their necessity demanded, and so on (Thompson, 1991: 357-58).

Today, we work in rationally organized businesses that follow the logic of profit, divorcing ourselves from the rhythms of the natural environment. Here is a minor example to illustrate part of the major point here: can you imagine your boss taking for granted that you will not come to work on the first glorious day of spring?

2. We have developed new stages in the lives of people: adolescence, empty nest, retirement, even middle age. We have come to view teenagers as both vulnerable to exploitation (as in factories) and as possessing tremendous potential. We now require youth to remain in school and thereby lessen their opportunities to work, both for their own sake and to protect adult's opportunities. We have segregated young people from the adult world and kept them from meaningful adult responsibility, a marked contrast to the past. (For example, in 1910 half of all

15-year-old boys and one fourth of all 15-year-old girls were working or looking for work (Skolnick, 1991: 167).) We have increasingly pitched our products to youth, from music to movies to fashion and beyond. We tell them that they are an important, distinct segment of our population. With the development of the modern family and more intense emotions among its members, adolescence has become an awkward, turbulent period in the development of young people (Skolnick, 1991: 156-161).

With fewer children and longer lives, women (and their spouses) experience what we now call the empty nest—a home without children. Today, women can expect to live more than 30 years without children at home (Skolnick, 1991: 14).

With our increasing health, we have created for most of us a new concept of old age—an age when we are retired, yet still healthy, but often without meaningful responsibilities.

More recently, we have created a period of middle age when adults are caught between the needs of their children and their parents and often wonder what they will do with the rest of their lives. We have created longer, more complicated lives for ourselves (Skolnick, 1991).

3. We have created the modern family from which developed a sense of emotional attachment among its members and privacy from the outside world. With the economic independence that jobs have provided for young people, with increasing economic prosperity, with the growth of large cities and the demise of small villages, and with the emphasis on the capitalistic pursuit of individual gain, we have created social conditions that have enabled and encouraged people to emphasize romantic love among spouses, emotional attachment to children, and a desire for family privacy from the watchful gaze of neighbors and from the demands of the working world. We have come to expect the enjoyment and fulfillment we experience with our families. Our higher expectations may also mean that we often fall short of them. Hence, divorce has become a major result of our unfulfilled expectations for personal satisfaction (Shorter, 1975).

4. Ironically, as we created the modern family, we also diminished its place in social life. The family was always the fundamental organization of society (Black, 1993: 59; Coleman, 1993). For a large part of human history, our small societies of perhaps several dozen people were families and related kin. Even as societies became more complex, people to a great extent lived their lives in their families and among their kin. The family organized people's lives. Child rearing, work, play, worship, and all aspects of social life took place within the family. Families were legally liable for the misdeeds of their members. One's identity was bound up with that of one's family and kin. People's lives were enmeshed within a web of family relations and responsibilities.

Capitalism did not start the phenomenon of the diminishing family, but it certainly has continued it and perhaps even increased it. We learn and earn outside of the family. Who we become is now less dependent on who our family is. We have supplanted the family in social life with a variety of "narrow-purpose" organizations—educational, economic, social service, financial, legal, civic, and others (Coleman, 1993). We look to public and private organizations for sustenance in time of need, for assistance with our troubles, for a means to pursue our grievances, for a way to mobilize our concerns. Consider that many households are completely empty during the day. In the past that would have been unheard of. We should not be surprised when we encounter great challenges to find new means for providing the support and control that previously came from the all-encompassing family.

5. As technologically sophisticated countries have become competitors in the world economy and the world of politics, we have both homogenized our societies and increasingly interconnected them.

We have dramatically reduced the number of independent states, a trend that has been developing for about 3,000 years. At one time, perhaps as many as 500,000 separate societies existed. Today, only about 200 do. For example, over three centuries ago Germany existed as 900 separate states. In contrast, some claim that today we are beginning to create a global society; one person has even forecasted that in 300 years the world will be one global country (Harris, 1989: 501).[6]

In our competitive world, businesses often develop and adopt similar, sophisticated technologies and processes or go bankrupt. So do governments through political competition with one another. Countries develop or purchase comparable military technology and organization in order to protect their sovereignty (Fukuyama, 1992: Chapter 6).

Governments have often extended their reach into their undeveloped territories, unfortunately sometimes destroying the native people's way of life or transforming them into "modern" men and women. Businesses have sold their products worldwide, lessening the vitality of distinctive, locally produced goods and services. Our mass media and compulsory educational system have reduced cultural differences in speech, style, understanding, and so on.

Yet, through the increasing interconnection of our world, we can taste much more of the variety of life that various people have produced, even if we have made that variety somewhat less distinctive. We can dine at ethnic restaurants and go to ethnic community celebrations, see foreign films, wear clothing from other countries, communicate with people from other places in our neighborhoods and in our schools, watch television programs that are beamed in by satellite from around the world, visit and vacation in other lands, and so on. We have also created more opportunities, desires, and the time and money to experience what remains of our world (Caplow, 1991: Chapter 3).

6. Perhaps most fundamentally, we have created a social life of *personal choice* and *uncertainty*. Until capitalism was widely developed, most people lived *circumscribed lives of chance* (Skolnick, 1991: Chapter 6).

In past eras, who you were and what you did was greatly circumscribed at birth. You lived as your predecessors had done for generations before you. You did what your fellow hunters and gatherers, peasants, or elite did. You often did not grow up to become something other than what you were born to be. The chance of birth presented a specific life for you to adopt. You knew who you were—a member of your tribe, clan, village, noble lineage, and so on. But chance of another kind played havoc with the life laid out before you. Death came frequently and uncertainly to all. You would make your life within narrow avenues, but at any moment that life might end.

"Only in the twentieth century could a majority of people expect to live out (what we now take to be) the normal life course of growing up, marrying, having children, and surviving with one's spouse until the age of fifty" (Skolnick, 1991: 14). Today, three fourths of all people live beyond the age of 65; in 1850, only 2 percent did (Skolnick, 1991:153). Today, a white baby girl has a "greater chance of living to be 60 than her counterpart born in 1870 would have had of reaching her first birthday" (Skolnick, 1991: 153).

> Contrary to the myth of a stable past, our ancestors did not progress through life in an orderly way. For example, before 1900 only about 40 percent of the female population of the United States followed the "normal" family cycle of leaving home, marrying, raising children, surviving to age fifty with one's spouse. The rest never lived to marriageable age, never married, died before having children or before their children were grown, or were widowed before age fifty. (Skolnick, 1991: 166)

With the development of our modern world, we have created a life of personal choice and uncertainty. More so than in previous eras, we have presented ourselves the opportunity to choose in making our lives. We even require it. A liberal, free-market society provides opportunity for people to move far from their place at birth—geographically and socially, up or down. As I noted earlier, families are no longer so all-encompassing. They continue to provide opportunities and at times obstacles for making our lives, but they do not dictate what lives we make. Choices and the uncertainty that come with them abound: marrying, having children, friendships, schooling, work, leisure, retirement, participation in politics, religious affiliation, and more. Individuals, rather than family and kin as in past eras, make these choices. What are we

doing? What can we do? What should we do? With the future less similar
to the present in our modern era, as compared to past eras, uncertainty
increases.

Furthermore, we celebrate more the individual, often crudely so
through our emphasis on self-gratification. The tremendous variety of
businesses that cater to people's personal desires and interests embody
this emphasis. More importantly, we emphasize the personal rights of
the individual to worship, participate politically, speak, and live in many
ways as one chooses (within certain bounds) (Fukuyama, 1992: Chapter
4). We also emphasize more the legal obligations of the individual and
less the liability of people as part of a family or clan (Black, 1993: 58-59).
We have also become "more introspective, more attentive to inner experiences" (Skolnick, 1991: 17). We have become concerned about our
feelings. What are our feelings? Are we in touch with our feelings? How
should we feel? What are you feeling? Our concern with emotions can
produce immensely satisfying experiences and disappointment. It can
produce great uncertainty.

Who we are, who we will become, and what we will do has become
much more the product of our efforts and less the chance of our birth.
This has grown increasingly so, as we diminish the role of the family
in social life and emphasize the rights and responsibilities of the individual. We provide new opportunities for developing ourselves (through
education and leisure), but experience much greater uncertainty as we
make who we become.

Much of what we take for granted about our lives and our worlds
today we and our ancestors have created over the past several hundred
years, at times even more recently. Within a very short span of time,
people have revolutionized social life. They have done so by building
upon previous changes and developing new social inventions for managing the challenges of social life. As useful as the two powerful social
inventions of capitalism and bureaucracy have been, many people today
have become increasingly concerned about them. Like all inventions,
social inventions often come to be regarded as falling short of expectations.

Shortcomings of Our Social Inventions

Through capitalism and bureaucracy people have profoundly
changed and continue to change their world. Of course, the development of science and technology and other arrangements have been important, too. But as with all inventions, people may become dissatisfied
with social inventions. So it is with capitalism and bureaucracy.[7]

I believe that we can usefully understand these shortcomings within
the scope of our increased accomplishments and greater expectations.

We have produced a world that is far more satisfying in many respects than ever before (at least as seen through our present values). In doing so, we have taken for granted our vast accomplishments and have increased our sights as to what is an acceptable way of life. For example, through much of human history, people had no individual rights, only obligations to those who ruled. Today, we protect our rights and claim ever new rights. Throughout the past, people lived physically burdensome lives. Today, we expect much more comfort in our lives—in our work, at home, and elsewhere.

Through our increased expectations and new concerns, we often make shortcomings out of our past accomplishments and present practices. We find fault in the progress that we have made. But that can be very useful. By doing so, we challenge ourselves onward to create new worlds rather than merely maintain our present ones.

Criticisms of Capitalism

Capitalism is the rational, methodical pursuit of profit within a free market. The essence of capitalism is both its strength and its fundamental flaw, according to some people. I have explored its revolutionizing strength. Now let's discuss its flaw.

Have you ever asked what was "in it" for you before agreeing to do something for another? Have you ever looked down upon others who have not had much material success? Have you ever decided to get to know someone because you believed that person could help you "get ahead"? Or decided not to get to know someone because that person could not? Have you ever approached learning primarily as a means for "making a buck"—taking courses only because you had to in order to get your degree and not working very hard at courses that didn't matter? Have you ever "sold yourself out" in order to get what you wanted? Even to the detriment of others? Have you ever you considered a job that you thought you might enjoy but then decided that the pay was not good enough, so you took another job that you hated?

Through capitalism, we persuade ourselves to narrow the diversity of life and the complexity of people to what is profitable (Stewart, forthcoming). Wealth is the measure of worth in capitalist societies. Costs and benefits become the calculus for our lives. How much will it cost? What will the return be? In all realms of social life—from family to education to religion to work to politics and beyond—"what's the payoff?" becomes the common concern.

Companies calculate the cost of improving the safety of the products they make versus the cost of lawsuits due to the wrongful harm or death of customers as a result of unsafe products (Ermann and Lundman, 1987: 247-48). Governments usually calculate the cost of regulations

on businesses versus the lives that will be saved through those regulations. Depending on how the "numbers add up," safety improvements
may not be made or the regulations may not be enacted. Governments
also calculate the costs and benefits in deciding whether to help other
countries. "If it's not in our national interests, then we shouldn't intervene," goes the reasoning. Juries and judges calculate the cost of a person's life in wrongful death suits or in injury claims. Potential earnings,
loss of companionship, and other concerns are figured into the award
(Black, 1993: 49). Non-capitalist societies also put a price on the harm
done to people, but they do not do so as thoroughly and as carefully as
in capitalistic societies. Health professionals and others also calculate
the cost of keeping people alive.

We turn each other into *human capital*. We become synonymous to
money, land, factories, and other resources that are capital for the entrepreneur to assemble and manage in the pursuit of profit. We exploit
ourselves in order to increase the net worth of the company or the country. Of how much worth are those who are of little economic value (Higgins, 1992: Chapter 7)?

One well-known social scientist has argued, without intending to be
tongue in cheek, that we should pay parents (and other adults) a
"bounty" for increasing the value of children to the state beyond what
otherwise would have been expected without the efforts of those parents
or adults. For example, foster parents would be paid more for doing a
"good job" with difficult children than with easy children. They would
be paid more because they had increased the value of the difficult children to the state more so than the foster parents who satisfactorily
raised easier children. Social science would be used to predict the "expected costs and benefits to the government of a given child." The difference between the prediction and any improvement would be
considered the amount of the bounty (Coleman, 1993: 13).

Or, education becomes an *investment* in order to improve children's
productivity, rather than a means to encourage them to wonder and to
discover. If children cannot be profitable, then people may resist in-
vesting in them. Many people oppose the equal distribution of educational resources because they want their children to have an
advantage—and they do not believe that "those" people's children could
benefit very much anyway from more resources (Kozol, 1991). That
would not be a rational use of resources. Thus, parents move to the
suburbs to distance themselves from those who are not as well off, so
that their children can hopefully go to better schools. Or they pay for
better schools by sending their children to private ones, at the same
time often complaining that their children are receiving no benefit from
their property taxes that support public education.

The rational pursuit of profits, the free market, becomes the means by which people increasingly organize social life. We privatize what we took for generations to be public responsibility and what throughout history was the collective responsibility of the clan or village. We turn over to entrepreneurs, who claim that they can make money and that the community can be better and less costly served, our schools, prisons, day care, garbage collection, hospitals, bus systems, fire protection, police, and other services that we used to provide through the collective efforts of government (Wolfe, 1989: 74). Some have even argued that we should turn over our national defense to private enterprise (Wolfe, 1989: 75).

Young people have always worked. Now even *students* have increasingly joined the work force. Perhaps as many as 75 percent of young people between ages 16 and 18 have jobs. Most high-school students work while attending school. They often do so not to help their families make ends meet, but to buy the latest in fashions, music, and automobiles. They have become the consumers that a capitalist society wishes all of us to be (Wolfe, 1989: 72-73). They may have little time for learning, since they tend to sacrifice so much of it to earning money.

We turn time into a commodity that we often feel we have short supply of. "Time is money." We charge people for our time (e.g., lawyers bill by the hour, as do many people who service and repair our products). We limit how much time we will give to others (e.g., fifteen minutes to see a patient.) We manage our time with great concern. We require people to use it wisely and productively and punish them when they do not (e.g., fining workers or disciplining students who arrive late). We try to get as much out of it, "squeezing" it as much as we can. We save it up in order to take off work early. We trade it with others by switching schedules with our co-workers. We punch in and out and work on and off the clock. We complain when we lose some of it. "Passing time" is regarded as wasteful and irrational (Thompson, 1991: Chapter 6).

In the rational pursuit of profits we harm, even degrade, ourselves. We endanger our health through unsafe working conditions and our environment through polluting production. We relocate our businesses, even to other countries, if by doing so we can boost earnings, no matter how much we damage the communities from which the businesses moved (Kennedy, 1992: Chapter 3). When our government bans the sale of hazardous products, we ship them abroad to be sold in other countries. We mislead one another to purchase our products. We imprison the petty criminal, but merely fine the corporate officers who massively defraud the public. After all, we may rationalize, they were just engaging in sharp business practices (Reiman, 1990).

We minimally assist those in need, so that we do not undermine our free-market society. If people can receive a "generous" handout (i.e., one through which they can live in dignity until able to work), the argument goes, then why should they work for a living (Stone, 1984)? We use sex to sell goods to one another and, by doing so, cheapen our sense of intimacy. We manage broken families by wrangling over how to divide the money in the marriage. "Wise" newlyweds sign premarital contracts to protect what they have accumulated should the marriage fail. We, including our school districts, pay youth to learn in school, with A's valued as "top dollar." Universities are touted as worth the tuition because of the increased earnings of college graduates. Never mind that college students may expand their minds or become more complex people.

Money becomes the measure of all that matters, or it sometimes seems to. What is something worth? Let the market decide. It is worth whatever people will pay for it. Should we act in this way or that, provide this program or establish that one, let us decide through a cost/benefit analysis. While I do not believe that any object we create has inherent value separate from what we give it, isn't how much people will pay for that object (which may be something as complex as justice, learning, or people) a narrow-minded way of deciding worth? While I do not believe that we can do all that we wish to do, therefore we must make choices, doesn't a cost/benefit analysis that turns the complexity of our lives into dollars and cents cheapen us all? We mask the terrifying enormity of what we do—"making" one another and sometimes causing anguish to ourselves or others—behind our coolly impersonal calculations.

Ironically, through capitalism we have expanded our world and ourselves; yet, in doing so, many of us have come to believe that we are also degrading ourselves. With our increased accomplishments and expectations, we find that through this social invention we have diminished ourselves by valuing people for their payoffs.

How might people respond to this possible crisis of capitalism? Some argue that we need more forceful rulers who can direct the development of the society. Too much freedom is dangerous. Some Southeast Asian countries have presently taken this approach, by which economic rights and growth are emphasized more than political and civil rights (Fukuyama, 1992: 44-45; 100-103; 122-125). Others claim that we need a more supportive, collectively oriented society. Government should provide more fully for the welfare of all of its citizens and foster their responsibility for one another, rather than allow individuals to pursue only their personal interests. Social welfare states in Scandinavia have been pointed out as such alternatives to capitalism (Wolfe, 1989: Chapters 5 and 6). Still others argue for closer ties between government and business, so that government can work to enable big business to prosper and thereby increase the economic might of the country. Japan has taken this corporatist approach. As you can see, capitalism is not the only alternative to command societies.

The Burden of Bureaucracy

Through bureaucracy, people systematically organize themselves to rationally and calculatingly pursue the goals of their organizations. Bureaucracy enables people to coordinate the complex activities of many persons, even over great distances and time. Bureaucracy enables people to modernize the world, to effectively mass-produce goods for millions of people, and to govern their complex societies more effectively and fairly. However, bureaucracy may also be burdensome. Let me explore some of the shortcomings in terms of work, which can also be applied to bureaucracies in other areas of social life.

Throughout the course of history, people integrated work—the provision for the basic necessities of life—into their lives and the lives of their families and communities, as well as into the natural environment in which they lived. Hunters and gatherers, alongside family and clan, worked three to five hours each day to provide themselves food, shelter, clothing, and tools. The remainder of the day they rested, conversed, or danced. They mastered a wide variety of skills in order to sustain themselves: hunting, tool making, house building, food preparation, making animal skins into clothes.

> Pre-industrial craftsmen also integrated their work and their lives. For example, English weavers had their looms at home and worked with their entire family, according to self-imposed schedules. They set their own goals for production and modified them, according to what they thought they could accomplish. If the weather was good, they quit so they could work in the orchard or the vegetable garden. When they felt like it they would sing a few ballads, and when a piece of cloth was finished they all celebrated with a . . . drink. (Csikszentmihalyi, 1990: 153)

Certainly the work of people in pre-modern eras must have been difficult and dangerous. It provided few material comforts. But many of them controlled their work, worked for themselves and their kin together, and sustained themselves through their work. To accomplish this, they did a wide variety of tasks that challenged them. Certainly not all of them enjoyed such work—slaves, serfs, and others controlled by masters or by harsh environments were burdened by work. But many gave their work great meaning.

Bureaucratic work may not be as meaningful to many of us today. We often work with people we do not know very well, for owners and managers we seldom see, producing products and services for customers we never meet, through tiny, specialized tasks that we endlessly repeat. The intimate relations, the commitment among workers and between workers and consumers of past eras, often does not exist to any great degree today (Harris, 1981: Chapter 2). As you might recall from the previous chapter, the strength of collective commitment enables people to work efficiently. But many of us today work in situations where our organizational arrangements and our work control us.

Of course, not all of us work in this way. But many of us do. The food preparer at a fast-food restaurant who can be trained in twenty minutes and reach top speed in about half an hour, or the assembly-line worker who repeats the same task every 30 seconds, may not be able to make their work very meaningful (Whyte, 1991: 110; Garson, 1992). Even surgeons who specialize in taking out appendices may not be greatly challenged by the work they do (Csikszentmihalyi, 1990: 155).

When we cannot make work meaningful, it may become difficult for us to work well (Berg, 1970; Rothschild and Russell, 1986; Csikszentmihalyi, 1990: Chapter 7; Kohn, 1993). Many of us are concerned about the shoddy goods and services that we purchase. Recently, one of my family's vehicles languished for four weeks in the service department of an automobile dealership. Have we squandered our great technological advancements through organizational arrangements that now discourage careful, meaningful work (Harris, 1981)?

If people repeat small, specialized tasks that bore or even debilitate them, methodically producing products for total strangers alongside other strangers, controlled by the commands of others or the pace of the assembly line, then should we be surprised if they make shoddy goods? If an arrow, a canoe, a basket, or a garment failed for pre-modern workers, it failed directly and sometimes fatally for the workers and their family or clan. Today, our failures beset unknown people. Can any of us imagine producing something today that would last several millennia—except perhaps toxic waste? Can we imagine weaving a basket so well that it holds boiling water without leaking (Harris, 1981: 22)?

Bureaucracy was a response to the challenge of coordinating and controlling many people and their activities, especially in large organizations. It met a challenge that businesspeople experienced a century or two ago. But it may not effectively meet some of our challenges today.

A century or more ago, many potential workers in America were immigrants who were poorly educated, did not speak very good English, came from rural areas with little industrial experience, and had little attachment to the local community or the company. (This also more or less describes the industrial workers in Europe when it began to industrialize before that time.) Through specialization and hierarchical control—two basic features of bureaucracy—managers (particularly in the 1800s and early 1900s) turned these poorly educated workers into useful workers for the company. In a fixed fashion they trained them to do specialized tasks that required little skill or thought. The factory machinery and the production process embodied the skill of the scientists, inventors, and managers. Managers controlled workers through specialization which reduced whatever skills the workers might themselves contribute. By being required to do less and less, these workers became more expendable. If they left, then managers could easily replace them (Kanter and Stein, 1980). Recall my discussion in the previous chapter about replaceability.

The view that owners and managers held of workers greatly diminished those who labored in their factories. Such a view attempted to turn people into machines. Other approaches that liberated rather than limited these poorly educated, unskilled immigrant workers may have worked satisfactorily (Zwerdling, 1980: 105-116). Today, however, such controlling procedures simply do not work at all.

With the creation of modern society, we have emphasized far more the inner life of ourselves and our personal, emotional satisfaction. We have educated one another more than we ever have before. We have provided ourselves with the opportunity to sample the diversity of our world. We have emphasized the rights of individuals. We claim that we provide ourselves the opportunity to meaningfully make our lives and not merely lead those lives already laid out for us. We have become an imaginative people.

Bureaucracies, however, often do not adequately fit who we have made ourselves to be; nor do they fit very well the sometimes complicated work that we ask ourselves to do. To a great extent we require many people to do tiny, specialized tasks in repetitive fashion with little control over what they do; or we may ask them to do complicated tasks without any meaningful control over how they do these tasks. What we require of many people in work conflicts mightily with the complex, highly capable, self-directing, fulfillment-seeking individuals that we have made ourselves to be.

Whenever we try to get people to do what we want them to do, we always depend on their imagination. It is not possible to provide directions so complete and precise that people merely "go through the prescribed motions." They must always make some decisions of their own about what to do next. We cannot, not even through a bureaucracy, direct people so automatically that they work in "robot-like" fashion. (Incidentally, the robots that some firms, many of them Japanese, are now using do not work in robot-like fashion either. However they are programmed, many of them must make complicated decisions as they perform tasks.) Even if we could direct people to work in this way, I do not believe that we should. Do we then suppress people's imagination, or do we encourage it? Bureaucracies have too often done the former.

Note the irony here. Through bureaucracies (and other means), we have produced a society in which we emphasize more now than in past eras the importance of the individual. In turn, as we savor our importance, we too often find bureaucracies constraining and confining our individuality. Yet, we experience little of the gross coercion inflicted upon slaves, serfs, and indentured servants of past eras and in other places today. Nevertheless, with this new understanding of who we are and what we can become, bureaucracies no longer suit us. Instead, they burden us.

In response to this dissatisfaction with bureaucracies, people have created alternatives. In various ways, to different degrees, and with more or less genuine commitment, people have created organizations that are more participatory. Some organizations are collectively owned by the workers. Others may be democratically managed by the members who vote for representatives who, in turn, decide the policy. In many organizations members of work groups may decide how they will do their tasks and provide suggestions to management. Some create more flexible arrangements in such a way that members rotate among jobs, share tasks, and organize and reorganize themselves into shifting teams on each work project.

People have created these and other alternatives to bureaucracy in order to increase the collective participation of members in their organizations. Instead of bureaucracies running the workers, the workers manage themselves. In doing so, participants reduce restraints on who can do what and thereby reduce inequality among themselves. In some worker-owned firms or worker collectives, the ratio of the highest to lowest pay may be only 3 to 1 or 2 to 1, instead of 100 to 1 as it is in other businesses (Rothschild-Whitt, 1979; Rothschild and Russell, 1986; Caplow, 1991:94-96; Whyte, 1991).

Like all social inventions, these bureaucratic alternatives are not without their own shortcomings. Can you imagine what some of the difficulties might be? To mention one, the process of governing democratically can be "messy." In bureaucratic organizations, decisions are handed down. In participatory alternatives, members discuss, debate, then decide, perhaps even trying to create a consensus and not merely a majority decision. This takes time. The emotional intensity of the decision-making process can be great. Participants may put a lot of themselves into the debate. Disagreements can be interpreted as personal rejections. Participatory management can be exhausting (Rothschild-Whitt, 1979). To say the least, no social invention can solve all of the challenges of living and interacting together.

Conclusion

Where are we and how did we get here? Where we are troubles many people. We are alarmed by our schools, families, economy, social relations, and much more. I do not think that we should be satisfied, but we might also recognize our successes. If we believe that nothing guarantees successful social life, then we may be pleased by the great improvements that we have created.

Furthermore, we might better understand what troubles us as due in part to the increased expectations that we have created for ourselves as we revolutionize how we live. Matters that throughout time people have seen as "natural" or taken no notice of, such as poverty or intergroup conflict, now trouble many of us. Indeed, present shortcomings are often great improvements over past conditions. Yet, with our increased expectations, we are properly dissatisfied with what we have achieved. For example, we educate our citizens better today than we have in past eras, but we do not satisfactorily teach everyone and we demand more from ourselves.

Through science, technological inventions, and, just as importantly, social inventions, we have revolutionized our world. Through capitalism and bureaucracy, the two social inventions that I have explored, and through others that I did not, people have changed social life and their individual lives immensely. Yet, most of us take for granted how we presently live.

Such rapid, profound changes create challenges and concerns. We become uncertain about how to create our social world, how to handle the dissatisfactions that we produce for ourselves. Some are concerned about both capitalism and bureaucracy and have tried or urged people to develop alternatives to them. Others are grappling with the enormous changes in the family, economy, social relations, education, and other arenas of social life.

We have now made many of these challenges global ones. People throughout the world are increasingly interconnecting their lives and their social worlds (Kennedy, 1993). For example, through global economic competition, workers in a factory in the Midwest may lose their jobs as executives relocate the work that was done in that factory to one in another country. Or, because of wars and other armed conflicts, poverty, anticipated opportunities abroad, and still other reasons, millions of people are migrating throughout the world (Meisler, 1993). The challenges of creating social life interconnect us all.

We do face many challenges in making our lives, in making our worlds. I have briefly explored some of them earlier in this chapter. I urge you to learn for yourself what challenges others believe we experience, identify what challenges you believe we should address, and participate with others to meet them (Kennedy, 1993).

I do not know what social life we will create for ourselves in the future. I hope that it will be one in which all of us, here and throughout the world, enhance one another and do not diminish ourselves. But I do know that nothing will guarantee our success. Social life can crumble, as many horrific conflicts throughout the world have demonstrated. While nothing guarantees that we will produce satisfying social life tomorrow, we have a tremendous capacity to do so. That capacity, our previous and present achievements in creating social life, and many people's concern about creating social life more humanely in the future, give me hope. Perhaps they give you hope, too.

Endnotes

1. Critics argue that the widespread, compulsory education that America instituted in the 1800s and intensified in this century was primarily designed to control youth; to make them compliant workers; to "civilize" children of lower class, immigrant families; and to maintain separation among the different segments of society (Sarason and Doris, 1979).

2. Those who are not finishing high school, even those who do but do not go to college and graduate, are finding it increasingly difficult to find adequately paying jobs, if any at all. Low-paying, low-skilled jobs are being increasingly shifted to other countries. Americans with only a high-school diploma and especially those who do not graduate at all experience great difficulty in earning a satisfactory living. The gap in earnings between the college graduate and the high-school graduate has increased in the past 15 years. For example, a 30-year-old man with a college degree in 1979 earned 29 percent more than a 30-year-old man with a high-school degree. Today, that same man with a college degree earns 65 percent more, while the one with a high-school degree is earning less today than his equal did in 1979, taking into account inflation (approximately $23,000 compared to $27,000) (Levinson, 1992). Even many college-educated people are experiencing difficulty making a satisfactory living. About one fifth of recent graduates work at jobs that do not typically require a college degree (Samuelson, 1992).

3. Without social practices that also enable large numbers of people to live and interact together, the world we take for granted would not be possible. Remember that, for almost all of human history, people were only able to produce tiny bands of a few dozen members. Part of this stemmed from their inability to produce enough food to sustain larger groups and their difficulty in creating social arrangements that enabled larger numbers of people to live together. I cannot explore here the range of social practices that people have created throughout history, but these practices typically separate people into categories and arrange who can do what where, so that people do not interfere too much in one another's affairs. This separation and distribution of people and their activities typically favors some at the expense of others (Cohen, 1985; Harris, 1989: 344-347).

4. Capitalism and the industrialization it spawned profoundly disturbed the prevailing social life. These changes wrenched people from village life, from their friends, neighbors, customs, and habits. Peasants were displaced from the land and craftspeople were displaced from small shops, as agriculture and manufacturing became increasingly mechanized. Industrialization took from workers their control over their work and compelled them to labor for others. Instead of coming and going and taking holidays as they pleased when they worked at their own trades, laborers were now required to submit to the discipline—the regulations, routine, and time requirements—of those who ran the factories. These factories were often associated with prisons, workhouses, and orphanages from which the new industrialists acquired involuntary labor. The working class did resist such changes through protest, violence, destruction of the agricultural and industrial machines that were threatening their way of life, political organizing, and what nowadays would be called "job action," such as staying away from work or abandoning

the job (Thompson, 1963, 1991: especially Chapter 6; Pollard, 1965: Chapter 5; Kennedy, 1992: 6-8).

5. But modernization can be pursued through other means. Once scientific and technological developments occurred, as they did based on capitalism, other countries could adopt these developments and further them without developing as the original capitalist countries did. Southeast Asian countries such as South Korea, Singapore, and Thailand have modernized remarkably in the past two decades without transforming into the liberal democracies that western capitalist countries have become (Chirot, 1985: 193; Fukuyama, 1992: 44-45; 100-103; 122-125). Those countries have emphasized economic rights and growth much more so than political and civil rights.

6. The number of independent states did increase in the past several decades. The "collapse of Western colonial empires" and the "disintegration of the USSR" have almost tripled the number of states that existed 60 years ago (Kennedy, 1993: 330). Nevertheless, only about 200 exist today.

7. Early observers, such as Karl Marx and Max Weber, recognized the power of capitalism and bureaucracy, but they were also concerned about their potential dangers. Marx worried about the alienation of people: people being controlled by what they have created which they no longer control. Marx was concerned that people did not realize or fulfill themselves in their work and with others. Instead, through capitalism, people became estranged from their work, from themselves, and from their fellow humans. He was also concerned about the great misery of working people that he noticed occurring in the early industrialization of Europe.

Weber was troubled by the rationalization of life that he saw occurring everywhere. The mystery, awe, and profound ties of people to one another that characterized earlier eras seemed to be diminishing by the onslaught of the rational, predictable, and calculable ways that people organized themselves in capitalist societies and bureaucratic organizations. Everyone and everything was "measured" and had to "measure up." See Coser (1971) for a useful introduction to exploring the concerns of Marx and Weber.

Epilogue

Well, you made it to the end of this short journey. How did it go? Are you puzzled, even bewildered? Are you now wondering more about social life? Does what seemed obvious to you before now no longer appear so certain anymore? I hope so. Or have you developed such new certainty that the puzzles explored here now seem even more obvious to you? Do you now take for granted ideas in this book that may have troubled you on first encounter? I hope not.

You and I have the capacity to create exhilarating social life. But we also have the capacity to create horrific social life. Nothing guarantees our success, nor dooms us to fail. Our nature, wants, and personalities are certainly important, but they do not dictate the social life we make. Instead, through what we *do*, we make social life.

We also *construct* what we know of our world. We may submit to the supernatural, or we may search for how the world "really," objectively is. Yet, I wonder if either of these two approaches are satisfactory for knowing. You will have to decide for yourself. I believe that, as we manage our concerns, we attempt to create new understanding. Whatever we produce that enables us to meet our concerns a little more satisfactorily than before is new knowledge. Knowing is doing. *Our* doing. Therefore, you must decide yourself if this book presents new knowledge or if it is nonsense. Does it enable you to meet your concerns any better?

The world is our doing, too. Through marking and managing our experiences, we make our world. We even make our selves. Although we cannot satisfactorily mark and manage our experiences in every possible way we choose, we can do so in ways that we have yet to try or even imagine. Can we mark and manage our experiences in ways that enhance all of us and do not oppress some of us?

In the process, how can we get others to do what we want? Perhaps the question itself creates the problem for us. We can try to force people to act as we want and we can pay them, but we can almost never make people do anything. Instead, people direct themselves. How can we direct ourselves in compatible ways? Perhaps by creating commitment among each other and to our activities, we can do together what we all "want" to do. Perhaps we succeed best when we give up control over others in order to create communion amongst ourselves. But social life is challenging. In our attempts to control one another, even through commitment, we produce conflict. Can we resolve the conflicts of inequality, intergroup conflict, and crime?

Many of us believe that our world is deeply troubled. But haven't we produced a far more satisfying social life today than ever before? Through science and technology, through such social inventions as capitalism and bureaucracy, we have revolutionized our world. Yet, we are not satisfied. I don't think we should be. We constantly change our world; but, as we do so, we change what we expect in that world and create new challenges to meet. The challenges of social life never end. Neither does our collective journey.

In this book I have only begun to explore the puzzles of social life, but a lifetime's journey still remains for you! Think of all the realms of social life in which you participate. I would imagine that you participate in a family, friendship groups, intimate relationships, school, work, perhaps religion, voluntary organizations, and perhaps in other ways: as a customer in retail stores, a driver on the road, a patron at the movies, a citizen in your country. What do you and others do to produce these realms? What are you producing? What are the consequences of your actions with one another? Can you produce social life more successfully?

Let me briefly mention one example that concerns me, a small but important part of the mosaic of social life. What puzzles me about it seems to apply to much of social life as well. Many students and professors are dissatisfied in one way or another with academic life in college. The men and women that I teach sometimes tell me that they feel burdened by being required to take courses of little interest to them. They are disappointed when they have to listen to professors who repeat what is already in their textbook. They feel alone in classes of several hundred students. They experience immense pressure to get good grades. And so on. But at times they are also intellectually stimulated by some of their courses (cf. Moffatt, 1989: Chapter 7).

Professors at my university are often dissatisfied with the large classes that they teach, by students who talk in class or act disrespectfully in other ways, by their lack of academic skills and intellectual enthusiasm, and so on. But they are also excited by those who seriously try to explore difficult ideas.

Observers frequently criticize professors, students, and others for the disappointing state of higher education in America (Moffatt, 1989: 271-272). On the other hand, men and women from foreign countries around the world flock to America to attend its colleges and universities.

For the sake of this discussion, let's put aside the larger institutional arrangements in college. What really goes on inside college classrooms? What are the men and women who produce these classes doing? What are the consequences of their actions? What could they do differently?

How do students and professors sometimes produce learning that soars, during which participants cannot wait for the next class to explore, debate, and question issues that they have made meaningful to themselves? Have you ever experienced such classes? I hope so. But what did you and the other participants do to produce such a high-flying state of learning? And how is it that you do not do so routinely in all your classes?

Beyond the classroom walls, how can people create any social world which they experience as profoundly meaningful? I think control is a crucial issue. Though you might return to Chapter Four to review that issue, I will not pursue it any further here.

When you wonder about social life, I urge you to look beyond your immediate world to the worlds of others. For example, how do people throughout the world create their families? They may do so very differently from what you are familiar with, but you can learn from "there" to help yourself "here." The same holds true for all of social life. All around the globe, people create diverse social life. Can you learn anything from others that you might use to create your own social life?

Wonder too about the seemingly distant actions of others that set the scene within which you live. For example, how do politicians and government officials govern? How do citizens organize themselves in order to be heard by their governments or to challenge present policy? How do executives and others arrive at their decisions to move their companies to other states or countries? How do the workers left behind handle these new challenges? How do nations develop cooperative, tolerable, or belligerent relations? These and many other large dramas set the scene within which you and I typically create our smaller social worlds.

Some of the larger world is so much a part of the fabric of social life that it may be hard to notice, much as we take for granted the air we breathe. Consider how we make fundamental characteristics of people: their gender, their age, and more. How do we make what we know to be males and females? For example, do we make females more nurturing than males? How do we make what we know to be people of different ages? For example, does America make both the young and the elderly persons without much responsibility? If so, then how is it done? And does that make sense? For whom? In what way? Social life is everywhere. There is so much to wonder about.

As you wonder about social life, have you developed any central idea that may have helped you to connect together my exploration of some of the puzzles of social life? To me, there is at least one key theme: responsibility.

We produce social life. Nothing inside nor outside of us forces us to act with one another as we do. We create knowledge, as we try to meet our concerns more successfully; we do not uncover our world. Through marking and managing our experience, we produce our worlds. The world does not come prepackaged. Though at times we claim that someone or something else "made" us do something, that is almost never so. Instead, we direct ourselves to act. Yet, we often direct ourselves in very different social landscapes, for which others are responsible. And through social inventions, such as capitalism and bureaucracy, and other means, we have changed our worlds. Social life is our collective responsibility.

I urge you to try to take this idea as seriously as you can, however overwhelming it may seem. Who are those people with whom you interact, and who are you? Does life have meaning to you? What is that meaning? What is honorable and horrific? How do we live our lives? How should we live our lives? Why do we use this or that social practice? Couldn't we do it differently? What should we do? These and all of the other troubling, exciting challenges of making social life are our responsibility.

We might wish to flee from that responsibility. We might yearn to escape to the certainty that social life must naturally be this way or that. "It must be so, because the divine or nature has made it so." "It must be so, because that is just how it is." While we might want to find refuge in this, I don't think we can. But we try to flee anyway, in so many ways. For example, how often have you replied that you didn't have time to do something that someone asked you to? Did you not *have* the time, or did you not *make* the time? Have you ever argued, when you or your colleagues harmed other people, that they "had it coming"? But did they have it coming, or did you *give* it to them? Have you ever hidden behind the rules of an organization when someone asked you to do something out of the ordinary? Did you claim that you couldn't do it? Or was it that you *wouldn't* do it? Perhaps, in part, you would not do it because you understood the extra effort you would need to do what was typically not done. From interpersonal action to international relations, people flee from responsibility.

But our responsibility for social life continually confronts us. We have the capacity to produce horrific social life—and to produce glorious social life. Ultimately, that is up to you and me. Our responsibility is awesome! Good luck to you, as you continue your journey and confront your responsibility.

References

Adam, Barry D. 1978. *The Survival of Domination: Inferiorization and Everyday Life*. New York: Elsevier.

Anderson, Margo J. 1988. *The American Census: A Social History*. New Haven, CT: Yale University Press.

Apple, Michael W. 1993. *Official Knowledge: Democratic Education in a Conservative Age*. New York: Routledge.

Baldwin, Frances E. 1926. *Sumptuary Legislation and Personal Regulation in England*. Baltimore: Johns Hopkins University Press.

Banton, Michael. 1983. *Racial and Ethnic Competition*. Cambridge: Cambridge University Press.

Baron, James N. and William T. Bielby. 1980. "Bringing the Firms Back in: Stratification, Segmentation, and the Organization of Work." *American Sociological Review* 45 (October): 737-765.

Berg, Ivar. 1970. *Education And Jobs: The Great Training Robbery*. New York: Praeger.

Berger, Joseph, Robert Z. Norman, James W. Balkwell, and Roy F. Smith. 1992. "Status Inconsistency in Task Situations: A Test of Four Status Processing Principles." *American Sociological Review* 57 (December): 843-855.

Berger, Peter L. and Thomas Luckmann. 1966. *The Social Construction of Reality: A Treatise in the Sociology of Knowledge*. Garden City, NY: Doubleday.

Best, Joel (editor). 1989. *Images of Issues: Typifying Contemporary Social Problems*. New York: Aldine De Gruyter.

Biklen, Douglas with Robert Bogdan, Dianne L. Ferguson, Stanford J. Searl, Jr., and Steven J. Taylor. 1985. *Achieving the Complete School: Strategies for Effective Mainstreaming*. New York: Teachers College Press.

Black, Donald. 1976. *The Behavior of Law*. New York: Academic Press.

Black, Donald. 1983. "Crime as Social Control." *American Sociological Review* 48 (February): 34-45.

Black, Donald. 1993. *The Social Structure of Right and Wrong*. San Diego: Academic Press.

Blau, Peter M. and Marshall W. Meyer. 1987. *Bureaucracy in Modern Society*. 3rd edition. New York: Random House.

Boswell, John. 1980. *Christianity, Social Tolerance, and Homosexuality*. Chicago: The University of Chicago Press.

Braun, Denny. 1991. *The Rich Get Richer: The Rise of Income Inequality in the United States and the World*. Chicago: Nelson-Hall.

Brinkerhoff, David B. and Lynn K. White. 1988. *Sociology*. 2nd edition. St. Paul, MN: West.

Brown, Donald E. 1991. *Human Universals*. Philadelphia: Temple University Press.

Brown, Roger. 1965. *Social Psychology*. New York: The Free Press.

Caplow, Theodore. 1991. *American Social Trends*. San Diego: Harcourt Brace Jovanovich.

Charon, Joel M. 1992. *Ten Questions: A Sociological Perspective*. Belmont, CA: Wadsworth.

Cherlin, Andrew J. 1981. *Marriage Divorce Remarriage*. Cambridge, MA: Harvard University Press.

Chirot, Daniel. 1985. "The Rise of the West." *American Sociological Review* 50 (April): 181-195.

Chirot, Daniel. 1986. *Social Change in the Modern Era*. San Diego: Harcourt Brace Jovanovich.

Cloward, Richard A. and Frances Fox Piven. 1993. "Punishing The Poor, Again: The Fraud of Workfare." *The Nation* 256 (May 24): 693-696.

Cohen, Mark Nathan. 1985. "Prehistoric Hunter-Gatherers: The Meaning of Social Complexity." Pp. 99-119 in *Prehistoric Hunter-Gatherers: The Emergence of Cultural Complexity*, edited by T. D. Price and J. A. Brown. Orlando, FL: Academic Press.

Coleman, James S. 1993. "The Rational Reconstruction of Society." *American Sociological Review* 58 (February): 1-15.

Collins, Randall. 1975. *Conflict Sociology: Toward an Explanatory Science*. New York: Academic Press.

Collins, Randall. 1980. "Weber's Last Theory of Capitalism: A Systematization." *American Sociological Review* 45 (December): 925-942.

Collins, Randall. 1982. *Sociological Insight: An Introduction to Non-obvious Sociology*. New York: Oxford University Press.

The Columbia Record. 1982. "Slave descendants challenge black classification." September 13: 3-A.

The Columbia Record. 1983. "Both sides await appeal of 'black-blood' ruling." May 19: 8-A.

Conger, John Janeway. 1981. "Freedom and Commitment: Families, Youth, and Social Change." *American Psychologist* 36 (December): 1475-1484.

Connell, R. W. 1987. *Gender and Power*. Stanford, CA: Stanford University Press.

Conrad, Peter and Joseph W. Schneider. 1980. *Deviance and Medicalization: From Badness to Sickness*. St Louis: C.V. Mosby.

Coontz, Stephanie. 1992. *The Way We Never Were: American Families and the Nostalgia Trap*. New York: Basic Books.

Coser, Lewis A. 1971. *Masters of Sociological Thought: Ideas in Historical And Social Context*. New York: Harcourt Brace Jovanovich.

Coverman, Shelley. 1988. "Sociological Explanations of the Male-Female Wage Gap: Individualist and Structuralist Theories." Pp. 101-115 in *Women Working: Theories and Facts in Perspective*, 2nd edition, edited by A. H. Stromberg and S. Harkess. Mountain View, CA: Mayfield.

Csikszenthmihalyi, Mihaly. 1990. *Flow: The Psychology of Optimal Experience*. New York: HarperCollins.

Davis, Kingsley and Wilbert E. Moore. 1945. "Some Principles of Stratification." *American Sociological Review* 10 (April): 242-249.

Davis, Phillip W. 1991. "Stranger Intervention into Child Punishment in Public Places." *Social Problems* 38 (May): 227-246.

Douglas, Jack D. 1976. *Investigative Social Research*. Beverly Hills, CA: Sage.

Durkheim, Emile. 1915 (1965). *The Elementary Forms of the Religious Life*. Translated by J. W. Swain. New York: The Free Press.

Easterlin, Richard A. 1987. *Birth and Fortune: The Impact of Numbers on Personal Welfare*. 2nd edition. Chicago: The University of Chicago Press.

Farrington, Carol. 1993. "Gilbert High to give incentives for grades." *The State*, October 10: 1A, 12A.

Feeney, Patrick G. 1992. "The 1990 Census and the Politics of Apportionment." *Footnotes* 20 (March): 5-6.

Ferraro, Kathleen J. 1989. "Policing Woman Battering." *Social Problems* 36 (February): 61-74.

Ferraro, Kathleen J. and John M. Johnson. 1983. "How Women Experience Battering: The Process of Victimization." *Social Problems* 30 (February): 325-339.

Ford, Donald H. 1987. *Humans as Self-Constructing Living Systems: A Developmental Perspective on Behavior and Personality*. Hillsdale, NJ: Lawrence Erlbaum Associates.

Fukuyama, Francis. 1992. *The End of History and the Last Man*. New York: Free Press.

Gallup, George H. 1979. *The Gallup Poll: Public Opinion 1978*. Wilmington, DE: Scholarly Resources, Inc.

Gallup, George H. 1983. *The Gallup Poll: Public Opinion 1982*. Wilmington, DE: Scholarly Resources, Inc.

Gallup, George, Jr. 1991. *The Gallup Poll: Public Opinion 1990*. Wilmington, DE: Scholarly Resources, Inc.

Gallup, George, Jr. 1992. *The Gallup Poll: Public Opinion 1991*. Wilmington, DE: Scholarly Resources, Inc.

Gallup, George, Jr. 1993. *The Gallup Poll: Public Opinion 1992*. Wilmington, DE: Scholarly Resources, Inc.

Garfinkel, Harold. 1967. *Studies in Ethnomethodology*. Englewood Cliffs, NJ: Prentice-Hall.

Garson, Barbara. 1992. "Permanent Temps." *The Nation* 254 (June 1): 736-737.

Geertz, Clifford. 1983. *Local Knowledge: Further Essays in Interpretive Anthropology*. New York: Basic Books.

Goffman, Erving. 1959. *The Presentation of Self in Everyday Life*. Garden City, NY: Doubleday.

Goffman, Erving. 1967. *Interaction Ritual: Essays in Face-to-Face Behavior*. Chicago: Aldine.

Goffman, Erving. 1971. *Relations in Public: Microstudies of the Public Order*. New York: Harper and Row.

Goode, David A. 1984. "Socially Produced Identities, Intimacy and the Problem of Competence Among the Retarded." Pp. 228-248 in *Special Education and Social Interests*, edited by L. Barton and S. Tomlinson. London: Croom Helm.

Goode, David A. 1986. "Kids, Culture, and Innocents." *Human Studies* 9 (1): 83-106.

Goode, Erich. 1994. *Deviant Behavior*. 4th edition. Englewood Cliffs, NJ: Prentice Hall.

Gottfredson, Michael R. and Travis Hirschi. 1990. *A General Theory of Crime*. Stanford, CA: Stanford University Press.

Gottfredson, Michael R. and Travis Hirschi. 1993. "A Control Theory Interpretation of Psychological Research on Aggression." Pp. 47-68 in *Aggression and Violence: Social Interactionist Perspectives*, edited by R. B. Felson and J. T. Tedeschi. Washington, DC: American Psychological Association.

Gould, Stephen Jay. 1978. "Biological Potential vs. Biological Determinism." Pp. 343-351 in *The Sociobiology Debate*, edited by A. L. Caplan. New York: Harper and Row.

Gross, Edward and Gregory P. Stone. 1964. "Embarrassment and the Analysis of Role Requirements." *American Journal of Sociology*. 70 (July): 1-15.

Hall, Edward T. 1959. *The Silent Language*. Garden City, NY: Doubleday.

Hardaway, C. Kirk, Penny Long Marler, and Mark Chaves. 1993. "What the Polls Don't Show: A Closer Look at U.S. Church Attendance." *American Sociological Review* 58 (December): 741-752.

Harris, Marvin. 1974. *Cows, Pigs, Wars, and Witches: The Riddles of Culture*. New York: Random House.

Harris, Marvin. 1981. *America Now: The Anthropology of a Changing Culture*. New York: Simon and Schuster.

Harris, Marvin. 1985. *Good To Eat: Riddles of Food and Culture*. New York: Simon and Schuster.

Harris, Marvin. 1988. *Culture, People, Nature: An Introduction to General Anthropology*. 5th edition. New York: Harper and Row.

Harris, Marvin. 1989. *Our Kind: Who We Are, Where We Came From, Where We Are Going*. New York: HarperCollins.

Henslin, James M. and Mae A. Briggs. 1988. "The Sociology of the Vaginal Examination." Pp. 140-152 in *Down to Earth Sociology*, 5th edition, edited by J. M. Henslin. New York: Free Press.

Heritage, John. 1984. *Garfinkel and Ethnomethodology*. Cambridge: Polity Press.

Hewitt, Paul G. 1985. *Conceptual Physics*. 5th edition. Boston: Little, Brown.

Higgins, Paul C. 1990. *The Challenge of Educating Together Deaf and Hearing Youth: Making Mainstreaming Work*. Springfield, IL: Charles C. Thomas.

Higgins, Paul C. 1992. *Making Disability: Exploring the Social Transformation of Human Variation*. Springfield, IL: Charles C. Thomas.

Hirschi, Travis. 1969. *Causes of Delinquency*. Berkeley: University of California Press.

Hofferth, Sandra L., Joan R. Kahn, and Wendy Baldwin. 1987. "Premarital Sexual Activity Among U.S. Teenage Women Over the Past Three Decades." *Family Planning Perspectives* 19 (March/April): 46-53.

Honigmann, John J. 1959. *The World of Man*. New York: Harper and Brothers.

Horan, Patrick M. 1978. "Is Status Attainment Research Atheoretical?" *American Sociological Review* 43 (August): 534-541.

Humphrey, Nicholas. 1992. *A History of the Mind*. New York: Simon and Schuster.

Hunter, James Davison. 1991. *Culture Wars: The Struggle To Define America*. New York: Basic Books.

Inciardi, James A. 1992. *The War on Drugs II: The Continuing Epic of Heroin, Cocaine, Crack, Crime, AIDS, and Public Policy*. Mountain View, CA: Mayfield.

Kanter, Rosabeth Moss. 1972. *Commitment and Community: Communes and Utopias in Sociological Perspective*. Cambridge, MA: Harvard University Press.

Kanter, Rosabeth Moss and Barry A. Stein. 1980. "Foreword." Pp. vii-x in *Workplace Democracy*, written by D. Zwerdling: New York: Harper and Row.

Karp, David A. and William C. Yoels. 1976. "The College Classroom: Some Observations on the Meanings of Student Participation." *Sociology and Social Research* 60 (July): 421-439.

Katz, Jack. 1988. *Seductions of Crime: Moral and Sensual Attractions in Doing Evil*. New York: Basic Books.

Kennedy, Paul. 1993. *Preparing for the Twenty-First Century*. New York: Random House.

Kephart, William M. and William W. Zellner. 1994. *Extraordinary Groups*. 5th edition. New York: St. Martin's Press.

Kluegel, James R. and Eliot R. Smith. 1981. "Beliefs About Stratification." Pp. 29-56 in *Annual Review of Sociology*, volume 7, edited by R. H. Turner and J. F. Short, Jr. Palo Alto, CA: Annual Reviews, Inc.

Kohn, Alfie. 1993. *Punished by Rewards: The Trouble with Gold Stars, Incentive Plans, A's, Praise, and Other Bribes*. Boston: Houghton Mifflin.

Kozol, Johnathan. 1991. *Savage Inequalities: Children in America's Schools*. New York: Crown.

Kuhn, Thomas S. 1970. *The Structure of Scientific Revolutions*. 2nd edition, enlarged. Chicago: The University of Chicago Press.

Lenski, Gerhard, Jean Lenski, and Patrick Nolan. 1991. *Human Societies: An Introduction to Macrosociology*. 6th edition. New York: McGraw-Hill.

Levinson, Marc. 1992. "Uphill Battle." *Newsweek*. (December 7): 38-40.

Lichter, Daniel T., Diane K. McLaughlin, George Kephart, and David J. Landry. 1992. "Race and the Retreat From Marriage: A Shortage of Marriageable Men?" *American Sociological Review* 57 (December): 781-799.

Lincoln, Yvonna S. and Egon G. Guba. 1985. *Naturalistic Inquiry*. Beverly Hills, CA: Sage.

Ljungqvist, Arne and Joe Leigh Simpson. 1992. "Medical Examination for Health of All Athletes Replacing the Need for Gender Verification in International Sports." *The Journal of the American Medical Association*. 267 (February 12): 850-852.

Luckenbill, David F. 1977. "Criminal Homicide as a Situated Transaction." *Social Problems*. 25 (December): 176-186.

Matalene, H. W. 1984. "Material Incompetence and the Rhetorical Ethos of the Ancien Regime." Pp.33-70 in *Romanticism and Culture: A Tribute to Morse Peckham and a Bibliography of His Works*, edited by H. W. Matalene. Columbia, SC: Camden House.

McEvedy, Colin and Richard Jones. 1978, 1979. *Atlas of World Population History*. New York: Facts on File.

McNeill, William H. 1982. *The Pursuit of Power: Technology, Armed Force, and Society Since A.D. 1000*. Chicago: The University of Chicago Press.

McPherson, J. Miller, Pamela A. Popielarz, and Sonja Drobnic. 1992. "Social Networks and Organizational Dynamics." *American Sociological Review* 57 (April): 153-170.

Meier, Deborah W. 1992. "Get the Story Straight: Myths, Lies and Public Schools." *The Nation* 255 (September 21): 271-272.

Meisler, Stanley. 1993. "U.N. foresees 'crisis' in forced migrations." *The State* (July 7): 1A, 12A.

Milgram, Stanley. 1974. *Obedience to Authority: An Experimental View*. New York: Harper and Row.

Miller, Dan. 1986. "Milgram Redux: Obedience and Disobedience in Authority Relations." Pp. 77-105 in *Studies in Symbolic Interaction*, volume 7, edited by N. K. Denzin. Greenwich, CT: JAI Press.

Miner, Horace. 1956. "Body Ritual Among the Nacirema." *American Anthropologist* 58 (June): 503-507.

Minow, Martha. 1990. *Making All the Difference: Inclusion, Exclusion, and American Law*. Ithaca, NY: Cornell University Press.

Moffatt, Michael. 1989. *Coming of Age in New Jersey: College and American Culture*. New Brunswick, NJ: Rutgers University Press.

Mosca, Gaetano. 1939. *The Ruling Class*. Edited and revised by A. Livingston, translated by H. D. Kahn. New York: McGraw-Hill.

Murdock, George Peter. 1980. *Theories of Illness: A World Survey*. Pittsburgh: University of Pittsburgh Press.

Nasar, Sylvia. 1992. "The Rich Get Richer, But Never the Same Way Twice." *The New York Times* August 16: E3.

Newsweek. 1984. "Black and White in California." April 16: 38.

Newsweek. 1992. "Perspectives." June 15: 17.

Newsweek. 1993. "A New Era of Segregation. December 27: 44.

Nicholson, Jennifer. 1992. "Closing the creation and evolution gap." *The State* June 14: 1D, 9D.

Oppenheimer, Andres. 1993. "Many Latin American leaders follow advice of fortunetellers." *The State* June 27: 5D.

Paget, Marianne A. 1990. "Performing the Text." *Journal of Contemporary Ethnography* 19 (April): 136-155.

Passel, Jeffrey S. 1991. "What Census Adjustment Would Mean." *Population Today* 19 (June): 6-8.

Pollard, Sidney. 1965. *The Genesis of Modern Management: A Study of the Industrial Revolution in Great Britain*. Cambridge, MA: Harvard University Press.

Pollner, Melvin. 1987. *Mundane Reason: Reality in Everyday and Sociological Discourse*. Cambridge: Cambridge University Press.

Population Reference Bureau, Inc. 1992. *1992 World Population Data Sheet*. Washington, DC.

Powers, William T. 1973. *Behavior: The Control of Perception*. Chicago: Aldine.

Reiman, Jeffrey. 1990. *The Rich Get Richer and the Poor Get Prison: Ideology, Class, and Criminal Justice*. 3rd edition. New York: Macmillan.

Robertson, Richard J. and William T. Powers (editors). 1990. *Introduction to Modern Psychology: The Control-Theory View*. Gravel Switch, KY: The Control Systems Group, Inc.

Robey, Bryant. 1989. "Two Hundred Years and Counting: The 1990 Census." *Population Bulletin* 44 (April): 3-38.

Rothschild, Joyce and Raymond Russell. 1986. "Alternatives To Bureaucracy: Democratic Participation in the Economy." Pp. 307-328 in *Annual Review of Sociology*, volume 12, edited by R. H. Turner and J. F. Short, Jr. Palo Alto, CA: Annual Reviews, Inc.

Rothschild-Whitt, Joyce. 1979. "The Collectivist Organization: An Alternative to Rational-Bureaucratic Models." *American Sociological Review* 44 (August): 509-527.

Sakamoto, Bob. 1990. "Eavesdropping on locker room talk: A glossary for football fans." *The State* September 13: 5-D.

Saluter, Arlene. 1989. "Singleness in America." Pp. 1-12 in *Studies in Marriage and the Family*, U.S. Bureau of the Census, Current Population Reports, Series P-23, No. 162, Washington, DC.

Samuelson, Robert J. 1992. "The Value of College." *Newsweek* (August 31): 75.

Sarason, Seymour B. and John Doris. 1979. *Educational Handicap, Public Policy, and Social History: A Broadened Perspective on Mental Retardation*. New York: Free Press.

Schegloff, Emanuel A. 1968. "Sequencing in Conversational Openings." *American Anthropologist* 70 (December): 1075-1095.

Schegloff, Emanuel A. and Harvey Sacks. 1973. "Opening Up Closings." *Semiotica* 8 (4): 289-327.

Shapiro, Andrew L. 1992. "We're Number One! (Really?)" *The Nation* 254 (April 27): 552.

Shepelak, Norma J. 1987. "The Role of Self-Explanations and Self- Evaluations in Legitimating Inequality." *American Sociological Review* 52 (August): 495-503.

Sherif, Muzafer and Carolyn W. Sherif. 1956. *An Outline of Social Psychology*. Revised edition. New York: Harper and Brothers.

Sherif, Muzafer and Carolyn W. Sherif. 1966. *Groups in Harmony and Tension: An Integration of Studies on Intergroup Relations*. New York: Octagon Books.

Shorter, Edward. 1975. *The Making of the Modern Family*. New York: Basic Books.

Sivard, Ruth Leger. 1989. *World Military and Social Expenditures*. 13th edition. Washington, DC: World Priorities.

Sivard, Ruth Leger. 1991. *World Military and Social Expenditures*. 14th edition. Washington, DC: World Priorities.

Skolnick, Arlene. 1991. *Embattled Paradise: The American Family in an Age of Uncertainty*. New York: Basic Books.

Snow, David A. and Leon Anderson. 1987. "Identity Work among the Homeless: The Verbal Construction and Avowal of Personal Identities." *American Journal of Sociology* 92 (May): 1336-1371.

Sonenstein, Freya L., Joseph H. Pleck, and Leighton C. Ku. 1991. "Levels of Sexual Activity Among Adolescent Males in the United States." *Family Planning Perspectives* 23 (July/August): 162-167.

Sowell, Thomas. 1987. *A Conflict of Visions*. New York: Morrow.

Sowell, Thomas. 1990. *Preferential Policies: An International Perspective*. New York: William Morrow.

Spector, Malcolm and John I. Kitsuse. 1987. *Constructing Social Problems*. New York: Aldine De Gruyter.

Stark, Rodney. 1992. *Sociology*. 4th edition. Belmont, CA: Wadsworth.

The State. 1993. "Hawaii considers gay marriage." May 7: 3A.

The State. 1993. "N.J. court allows lesbian to adopt partner's daughter." August 11: 3A.

Stedman, Lawrence C. and Marshall S. Smith. 1985. "'Weak Arguments, Poor Data, Simplistic Recommendations': Putting the Reports Under the Microscope." Pp. 83-105 in *The Great School Debate: Which Way for American Education?*, edited by B. Gross and R. Gross. New York: Simon and Schuster.

Steffensmeier, Darrell J. and Robert M. Terry. 1973. "Deviance and Respectability: An Observational Study of Reactions to Shoplifting. *Social Forces* 51 (June): 417-426.

Stevenson, Harold W. and James W. Stigler. 1992. *The Learning Gap: Why Our Schools Are Failing and What We Can Learn from Japanese and Chinese Education.* New York: Summit.

Stewart, Robert L. forthcoming. *Living And Acting Together.*

Stewart, Robert L. and Larry T. Reynolds. 1985. "The Biologizing of the Individual and the Naturalization of the Social." *Humanity and Society* 9 (May): 159-167.

Stone, Deborah A. 1984. *The Disabled State.* Philadelphia: Temple University Press.

Strang, David and James N. Baron. 1990. "Categorical Imperatives: The Structure of Job Titles in California State Agencies." *American Sociological Review* 55 (August): 479-495.

Straus, Murray A. and Richard J. Gelles. 1986. "Societal Change and Change in Family Violence from 1975 to 1985 as Revealed by Two National Surveys." *Journal of Marriage and the Family* 48 (August): 465-479.

Straus, Murray A. and Richard J. Gelles. 1988. "How Violent Are American Families? Estimates from the National Family Violence Resurvey and Other Studies." Pp. 14-35 in *Family Abuse and Its Consequences: New Directions in Research*, edited by G. Hotaling, D. Finkelhor, J. Kirkpatrick, and M. Straus. Newbury Park, CA: Sage.

Takaki, Ronald. 1993. *A Different Mirror: A History of Multicultural America.* Boston: Little, Brown.

Taylor, Steven J. 1987. "Observing Abuse: Professional Ethics and Personal Morality in Field Research." *Qualitative Sociology* 10 (Fall): 288-302.

Thompson, E.P. 1963. *The Making of the English Working Class.* New York: Pantheon.

Thompson, E.P. 1991. *Customs in Common.* New York: The New Press.

Troyer, Ronald J. and Gerald E. Markle. 1983. *Cigarettes: The Battle over Smoking.* New Brunswick, NJ: Rutgers University Press.

Turner, Ralph H. 1976. "The Real Self: From Institution to Impulse." *American Journal of Sociology* 81 (March): 989-1016.

Tyson, Remer. 1983. "Changing Color: South Africa's Peculiar Little Relief Valve." *The State* July 17: 1B, 13B.

U.S. Bureau of the Census. 1975. *Historical Statistics of the United States, Colonial Times to 1970, Bicentennial Edition, Part 1.* Washington, D.C.

U.S. Bureau of the Census. 1989. *Statistical Abstract of the United States: 1989*. (109th edition) Washington, DC.

U.S. Bureau of the Census. 1991. *Statistical Abstract of the United States: 1991*. (111th edition) Washington, DC.

U.S. Bureau of the Census. 1992. *Statistical Abstract of the United States: 1992*. (112th edition) Washington, DC.

U.S. Department of Education, National Center for Education Statistics. 1991. *Digest of Education Statistics 1991*. Washington, DC.

U.S. Department of Education, National Center for Education Statistics. 1993. *Digest of Education Statistics 1993*. Washington, DC.

Wardhaugh, Ronald. 1985. *How Conversation Works*. Oxford: Basil Blackwell.

The Washington Post National Weekly Edition. 1992. "Sex Tests for Athletes." February 24-March 1: 26.

Weber, Max. 1968. *Economy and Society*, edited by G. Roth and C. Wittich. New York: Bedminster Press.

Weinberg, Martin S. 1965. "Sexual Modesty, Social Meanings, and the Nudist Camp." *Social Problems* 12 (Winter): 311-318.

Whalen Jack, Don H. Zimmerman and Marilyn R. Whalen. 1988. "When Words Fail: A Single Case Analysis." *Social Problems* 35 (October): 335-362.

Whyte, William Foote. 1991. *Social Theory For Action: How Individuals and Organizations Learn To Change*. Newbury Park, CA: Sage.

Wilson, Jean D. "Sex Testing in International Athletics: A Small Step Forward." *The Journal of the American Medical Association* 267 (February): 853.

Wilson, James Q. 1989. *Bureaucracy; What Government Agencies Do and Why They Do It*. New York: Basic Books.

Wilson, James Q. and Richard J. Herrnstein. 1985. *Crime and Human Nature*. New York: Simon and Schuster.

Wilson, William J. 1987. *The Truly Disadvantaged: The Inner City, the Underclass, and Public Policy*. Chicago: University of Chicago Press.

Wolfe, Alan. 1989. *Whose Keeper? Social Science and Moral Obligation*. Berkeley: University of California Press.

Wood, George H. 1992. *Schools That Work: America's Most Innovative Public Education Programs*. New York: Dutton.

Zimring, Franklin E. and Gordon Hawkins, 1992. *The Search for Rational Drug Control*. Cambridge: Cambridge University Press.

Zinn, Howard. 1980. *A People's History of the United States*. New York: Harper and Row.

Zurcher, Louis A. 1983. *Social Roles: Conformity, Conflict, and Creativity*. Beverly Hills, CA: Sage.

Zwerdling, Daniel. 1980. *Workplace Democracy: A Guide To Workplace Ownership, Participation, and Self-Management Experiments in the United States and Europe*. New York: Harper and Row.

DATE DUE